tic Reckonings

Erotic Reckonings

Mastery and Apprenticeship
in the Work of Poets and Lovers

Thomas Simmons

University of Illinois Press   *Urbana and Chicago*

© 1994 by the Board of Trustees of the University of Illinois
Manufactured in the United States of America
C 5 4 3 2 1

This book is printed on acid-free paper.

Library of Congress Cataloging-in-Publication Data
Simmons, Thomas, 1956–
     Erotic reckonings : mastery and apprenticeship in the work of
poets and lovers / Thomas Simmons.
        p.   cm.
     Includes index.
     ISBN 0-252-02120-7 (cloth : acid-free paper)
     1. American poetry—20th century—History and criticism.
2. Apprentices—United States—History—20th century. 3. Women
poets, American—Relations with men. 4. Poets, American—Relations
with women. 5. Influence (Literary, artistic, etc.) I. Title.
PS323.5.S56   1994
811'.5209353   94-2774
                                                              CIP

For Diane Wood Middlebrook

Contents

Acknowledgments   ix

Introduction   1

1. *A Turmoil of Speech*
   The Mentorship of Ezra Pound   23

2. *I Was Dead and Am Alive Again*
   Hilda Doolittle as Apprentice   52

3. *In Light I Live*
   The Mentorship of Yvor Winters   87

4. *The Earth-Bound*
   Janet Lewis as Apprentice   121

5. *Who Shall Deliver Me from the Body of This Death?*
   The Mentorship of Louise Bogan   157

6. *My Secrets Cry Aloud*
   Theodore Roethke as Apprentice   190

Index   219

Acknowledgments

Professors Leonard Nathan and Susan Schweik of the University of California, Berkeley provided expert counsel when I was at an early stage of this project. Their advice and encouragement made it possible for me to complete the first draft of this book, and I remain greatly in their debt.

Gwen Schwarz, Terrie Lyons, and Mark Sullivan helped me to sound a course through the fog of my own misperceptions and anxieties. Though we did not always agree, John Haule generously shared with me his insights into Jungian psychology and the problem of eros. Timothy Dekin introduced me to the poetry of Theodore Roethke and Edgar Bowers. Jennifer Clarvoe introduced me to the criticism of Rachel Blau DuPlessis, and discussed the work of Pound and H.D. with me at length over tea on long autumn evenings in Berkeley. Eric Chivian of the Massachusetts Institute of Technology helped keep my thinking supple and hopeful when both internal and external forces were trying to rigidify and darken it. Among later readers of the manuscript, Diana Hume George and Robert Dale Parker stand out as exceptionally careful and articulate critics. None of these colleagues and readers, of course, can be held in any way responsible for whatever shortcomings inhabit this book.

At the Massachusetts Institute of Technology, I was privileged to receive an Old Dominion Fellowship in 1990 and a travel and research award from the Office of the Dean of Humanities and Social Science in spring 1992. These grants afforded me much-needed support for research and writing. I also wish to acknowledge the assistance of the Office of the Vice President for Research at the University of Iowa.

Librarians at three major research collections in the United States smoothed the task of research. Marcia Bickoff of the Beinecke Rare Book and Manuscript Library at Yale University located relevant letters from Pound and H.D., photocopied them, and patiently answered my sometimes confused queries. Margaret Kimball of the Department of Special Collections and University Archives at Stanford University placed her considerable knowledge of the Yvor Winters–Janet Lewis collection at my disposal, saving me from false starts and futile searches. Hilary Shore was a faithful and meticulous assistant. Janet Ness of the Manuscripts Section of the University of Washington Library quickly and efficiently located and photocopied correspondence between Louise Bogan and Theodore Roethke.

I was also fortunate to be able to conduct three interviews with Janet Lewis, during which we discussed the course of her life, her work, and her husband's work. Although she is in no way responsible for my interpretations, I am very grateful for her willingness to find a place for me in her demanding schedule. I am also grateful to Brigitte Carnochan of Stanford University for her willingness to arrange an introduction with Janet Lewis, and to share her own well-researched insights into the lives and work of Lewis and Winters. Margaret M. Furbush of Los Altos, California, who is compiling a bibliography of Janet Lewis's work, generously shared her bibliographic research with me.

I would also like to acknowledge the patient and judicious support of the editors and staff of the University of Illinois Press. It was Ann Lowry, senior editor at the Press, who first saw the promise in this manuscript, and I owe her a considerable debt of thanks. Rita Darlene Disroe was an ideal manuscript editor, refining these pages with an essential, unobtrusive grace; the acting marketing manager, Barbara Horne, ably charted the public life of the book. Dal Liddle, of the University of Iowa, was a superb indexer.

In any work of this nature, the labor of seeking permission to reprint poems and letters from individual copyright holders and from publishers can be both demanding and expensive. Reprint fees are often quite high, and university press (and even trade) publishers are increasingly unable or unwilling to defray these costs. I thus feel fortunate to have been able to work with particularly cooperative permissions departments at a number of publishers and libraries, as well as with individual copyright holders. Judith Michelman of Harvard University Press, Daniel Allman of New Directions, Patricia Willis of the Beinecke Rare Book and Manuscript Library, Nancy Basmajian and Holly Panich of Ohio University Press/Swallow Press, Jessica Lind of the University of Washington Press, Carol Christiansen of Doubleday, Erika Seidman of Farrar, Straus & Giroux, Ruth Limmer, Janet Lewis, and Edgar Bowers have listened patiently to my arguments for permissions fee reductions or suspensions and have in some cases responded with exceptional generosity. Because my book depends so heavily on quoted sources, I am especially thankful for their help.

The following copyright holders are gratefully acknowledged for permission to reprint the specified poems and letters:

"Living Together," reprinted from *Living Together* (Boston: David Godine, 1973), by permission of Edgar Bowers.

"Further in summer than the birds," reprinted by permission of the publishers and the trustees of Amherst College from *The Poems of Emily Dickinson,* Thomas H. Johnson, ed., Cambridge, Mass.: The Belknap Press of Harvard University Press, Copyright © 1951, 1955, 1979, 1983 by the President and Fellows of Harvard College.

"Sea Rose" and portions of "Sea Lily," "Phaedra," "Toward the Piraeus," and "The Walls Do Not Fall," reprinted from H.D., *Collected Poems 1912–1944.* Copyright © 1982 by The Estate of Hilda Doolittle. Reprinted by permission of New Directions Publishing Corporation.

Quotation from unpublished H.D. letter by permission of the Yale Collection of American Literature, Beinecke Rare Book and Manuscript Library, Yale University.

"Ballad for Gloom," "Anima Sola," "Plotinus," "Scriptor Ignotus," "Song," and "Francesca," reprinted from Ezra Pound: *Collected Early Poems of Ezra Pound.* Copyright © 1976 by the Ezra Pound Literary Property Trust. Reprinted by Permission of New Directions Publishing Corporation.

Quotations from unpublished letters of Ezra Pound by permission of the Yale Collection of American Literature, Beinecke Rare Book and Manuscript Library, Yale University.

"Dedication for a Book of Criticism," "On Teaching the Young," "The Marriage," from Yvor Winters: *Collected Poems.* Copyright © 1943 by New Directions Publishing Corporation. Reprinted by permission of New Directions Publishing Corporation.

"Death Goes Before Me," "Where My Sight Goes," "Song of the Trees," and portions of "To a Young Writer," from Yvor Winters: *Collected*

Poems of Yvor Winters, with intro. by Donald Davie (Athens, Ohio: Ohio University Press/Swallow Press, 1980), reprinted by permission of Ohio University Press/Swallow Press.

Quotations from Yvor Winters letters to Maurice Lesemann reprinted by permission of Janet Lewis.

"The Wife of Manibozho Sings," "Like Summer Hay," "The Earth-Bound," "No-Winter Country," "The Hangar at Sunnyvale," "For the Father of Sandro Gulotta," "Nightfall among Poplars," "Snail Garden," portions of "The Ancient Ones: Betatakin," "The Indians in the Woods," "The Wonder of the World," from Janet Lewis: *Poems Old and New, 1918–1978* (Athens, Ohio: Ohio University Press/Swallow Press, 1981), by permission of Ohio University Press/Swallow Press.

Final two stanzas of "A Tale" and, in their entirety, "Knowledge," "The Alchemist," "Memory," "Song," "Henceforth, from the Mind," "Putting to Sea," "The Sleeping Fury," "Roman Fountain," and "To My Brother," from Louise Bogan, *The Blue Estuaries.* Copyright © 1968 by Louise Bogan. Reprinted by permission of Farrar, Straus & Giroux, Inc.

Selections from Louise Bogan's letters in manuscript and from *What the Woman Lived: Selected Letters of Louise Bogan, 1920–1970,* ed. Ruth Limmer (New York: Harcourt Brace Jovanovich, 1973), reprinted by permission of Ruth Limmer.

Selections from Theodore Roethke's letters (including poems contained in letters), from *Selected Letters of Theodore Roethke,* ed. Ralph J. Mills, Jr. (Seattle: University of Washington Press, 1968), by permission of the University of Washington Press.

"Epidermal Macabre," copyright © 1932 by Theodore Roethke. "For an Amorous Lady," copyright © 1939 by Theodore Roethke. "To My Sister," "The Premonition," copyright © 1941 by Theodore Roethke. From *The Collected Poems of Theodore Roethke.* Used by permission of Doubleday, a division of Bantam Doubleday Dell Publishing Group, Inc.

In the case of Louise Bogan's letters, there are minor discrepancies of punctuation (and, in one case, a disagreement over the placement of a phrase Bogan wished to insert in a sentence) between Bogan's actual holographs or typescripts and Ruth Limmer's published edition of the letters, *What the Woman Lived.* Limmer understandably explains in her "Notes on Editing" that she felt "no need to call attention . . . to such changes as have been made," describing them as "infrequent and insignificant." When it has been possible, however, I have preferred to quote Bogan's actual text; this explains any difference between Limmer's version and my own. I should add that I am grateful to Ruth Limmer for pointing out my misreading of one of Bogan's typescripts.

I remain indebted to a small number of distinguished teachers who listened carefully to the clues I gave about the person I might become. Among these are Jeanne Geselschap, Warren Wilde, Jan Davis Stein, Claire Pelton, and Janet Mohr, all teachers or former teachers at Los Altos High School. In this small group I also include three professors from Stanford University—Diane Wood Middlebrook, Ronald A. Rebholz, and Kenneth Fields. Without their double reach—to me on the one hand, to the experience of art on the other—I might well have gone adrift long before I began my own work as a writer and teacher.

Finally, I wish to thank my immediate and extended family for their tolerance and support during the long course of this project. Lesley Wright, John Simmons, Cynthia Bourgeault, Janet Wright, Melvin Wright, Marilynn Gottlieb, Heather Gordon, Jennie Kiesling, and Dot Stephens listened patiently to my uncivilized discontents and repeatedly reminded me that a good idea should not be allowed to die on the vine.

Erotic Reckonings

Introduction

> Mutual recognition cannot be achieved through obe-
> dience, through identification with the other's power,
> or through repression. It requires, finally, contact
> with the other. . . . Beyond the sensible ego's bowing
> to reality is the joy in the other's survival and the
> recognition of shared reality. Reality is thus *discov-
> ered,* rather than *imposed;* and authentic selfhood is
> not absorbed from without but discovered within.
>   —Jessica Benjamin, *The Bonds of Love*

Mothers or fathers know that they live on through their children. Although children cannot give them personal immortality, they can continue the lineage of their parents; they can pass along something of the
parents' identity. For a writer, however, the possibility of immortality
can arise in two other ways. The writer's work itself may assert so clearly the aesthetic and intellectual values or antagonisms of a particular
period that it secures for itself a place throughout time: it accomplishes
what Shakespeare promises the ironically unknown lover in his sonnets.
Yet even if the writer's work does not appear destined for this kind of
glory, he has another recourse whose relation to parenthood is even more
apparent. He may become a master, or mentor; he may accept apprentices. Like real children, apprentices may affirm the master's presence
in future generations. They may recall his name in their work, or they
may recall his method in their methods; in some way, they perpetuate
his being.

Behind this will to self-perpetuation, in art as well as in life, one finds
the power of eros. The elemental creative impulse that is eros, the passion to live and to extend one's life through others, underlies the relationship between all parents and their children. Yet this relationship is

neither simple nor obvious. Its permutations are so numerous and varied that, nearly a century after the advent of psychoanalysis as a discipline, we still debate the nature of the erotic function in the parent-child relationship.[1] On the other hand, the connections between parenthood and mentorship may seem at first hand almost too simple: we tend to ascribe certain proprietary rights to the mentor as if, with a parent's benign authority, he or she necessarily assumed control of the apprentice's career. Behind our confusions and assumptions, as well as behind the relationships themselves, eros asserts its chameleon presence. Eros may be sexual desire, yet fundamentally it is more than that: it is, as Jung argued, the *anima* archetype, the will toward that which binds us to one another, strengthens our instinctive knowledge, redeems us from the limits of rational knowledge. Such a complex desire confuses us because, more often than not, it presents itself not simply in sexual terms but in terms of power. Where one person may conceivably function as a dominant influence, eros almost inevitably becomes a proposition about power; the propositions themselves have both overt and subtle manifestations.

Sometimes the proposition about power is a direct, creative assertion—that is, a poem or a book. At other times, the proposition defines itself within a relationship: eros proposes its meaning through the relative strength or weakness of the mentor or the apprentice. The first kind of proposition is always intriguing, because the result is so apparent. A book, like a child, may startle the world with its worth and its secrets. The second kind of proposition, however, is much less often discussed, and perhaps more intriguing, because the result—if there is any "result"—is so ambiguous. When, uncertain about his own identity and his own erotic force, a mentor nevertheless pursues his career and draws apprentices into his fold, what kind of power will he wield over these students? Will his uncertainties lead him into dogmatism, or will they permit him an even greater open-mindedness? Will his anxieties about his own identity lead him to attempt to possess the identities of his students, or will those anxieties make him wary of mastering any self beyond his own?

In this book, I examine in some detail certain kinds of relationships between mentor and apprentice, in which the tension between passionate creation and mortal fear translates itself into specific problems of dominance, submission, and defiance. In the introduction I explore some implications of the central terms, "eros" and "mentor," and conclude by considering the possibility that the role of the mentor is inescapably conflicted, divided between allegiance to a tradition and allegiance to the personhood of the apprentice. Implicit in this consideration are principles of seduction, dominance, and cruelty that potentially threaten the mentor-apprentice relationship. In subsequent chapters I offer studies of three pairs of twentieth-century American poets—Ezra Pound and H.D., Yvor Winters and Janet Lewis, and Louise Bogan and Theodore Roethke. In all three cases, the mentor had to struggle both with his or her own sense of identity, and with his or her pedagogic role. This is no surprise; but what is perhaps surprising is the outcome of the struggle. Given the generally admirable reputation that Pound and Winters carry as mentors, it is surprising how much they themselves suffer from the confines of the role. And while the extent to which the apprentices struggle against the masters is hardly unexpected, the subtlety of the struggle—the extent to which the apprentices internalize the critical weight of the masters—is profoundly striking. This is true even though, in the first two cases, the difference in age and reputation between mentor and apprentice is relatively slight: few critics have been willing, for example, to refer to Lewis as Winters's apprentice or H.D. as Pound's apprentice. Yet the psychology of the mentor-apprentice role is clearly identifiable in these relationships. Without question the artist identified as a mentor takes on the mantle of power, instruction, and direction, even though he may attempt to wield it benignly. This mantle is a serpent: ultimately it constricts both the one who wears it and the one who admires it.

Who is a mentor?[2] Out of the welter of texts that treat mentorship implicitly, I have chosen two as essential bases for the current discussion. The first of these is the *Odyssey,* in which Odysseus's comrade-in-arms Mentor—with the help of Athena—takes charge of Odysseus's son Telemakhos.[3] The appearance of Mentor in the role of mentor in the *Odyssey* is seminal, a cultural starting point. The second text consists of the letters between the twelfth-century cleric and philosopher Peter Abelard and his student and lover Heloise.[4] This text is central because it marks another beginning—the overt equation of mentorship and eroticism in post-classical culture. This equation is important not only in its sexual dimension but also in its implications of dominance and submission. The letters of Abelard and Heloise provide a vivid example of power and suffering between mentor and apprentice. Their combined insights provide a useful yet problematic portrait of the mentor.

Though a minor character overall, Mentor performs an essential duty in the *Odyssey* by encouraging and arranging Telemakhos's voyage in search of his father.[5] This journey, which pays homage to the father as it honors the son, inaugurates one of the great themes of the poem. The *Odyssey* is not simply a quest for home, but a quest for identity and adulthood that evolve from home and family. In nurturing this quest, Mentor also identifies and nurtures the traits that most distinguish Telemakhos: courage in the face of threatening and parasitic suitors, devotion to father and mother, faith in self, trust in the gods. Mentor draws Telemakhos further into his own Ithakan tradition by giving him a chance to prove himself. Telemakhos's potentially reckless boast to find news of his father, which draws jeers and threats from the suitors, nevertheless sounds the Odyssean gong of bravery, and Mentor turns the boast into reality. Mentor finds a ship and crew, and gives this counsel to the young man:

> You'll never be fainthearted or a fool,
> Telemakhos, if you have your father's spirit;
> he finished what he cared to say,
> and what he took in hand he brought to pass.
> The sea routes will yield their distances
> To his true son, Penelope's true son,—
> I doubt another's luck would hold so far.
> The son is rare who measures with his father,
> and one in a thousand is a better man,
> but you will have the sap and wit
> and prudence—for you get that from Odysseus—
> to give you a fair chance of winning through.[6]

Mentor does not teach abstract values, or lecture about the gods, or weigh the possibilities of success. None of these approaches, as valuable as they might be, will enable Telemakhos to go forth as confidently as a well-phrased invocation of the father. Mentor's approach suggests that this invocation also invokes a cultural tradition that cannot be passed along in abstract or philosophical speculations. It must be achieved through living. Telemakhos lives it by seeking the father and testing himself against him. He may then become both himself and the embodiment of a tradition. Mentor's role in the *Odyssey* is to make that specific transition possible for Telemakhos.

But who is Mentor when he speaks these words, assembles the crew, and finds the ship? He is Athena. Athena puts on "Mentor's figure and his tone, / the warm voice in a lucid flight of words."[7] Though Athena, who sprang from Zeus's head, the product of godly will rather than sexual generation, is female, her gender owes nothing to gender. Sexuality is explicit in her being, yet its tradition holds no sway for her. She is Zeus's favorite precisely because she constructs that tradition for herself. What is feminine is what she does. She is a warrior, armored for battle, champion of courageous men; she is also, by turns, male, female, Mentor or "the shipman Dymas' daughter,"[8] using whatever identity and gender will swing events in favor of those she loves.

When, for her own ends, Athena becomes Mentor, she implicitly acknowledges his sway over Telemakhos. She validates his role as a wise counselor. But wise counsel is insufficiently effective here. Within the cloak of the mentor must lie the goddess: the self-defined female acquires the identity of the trusted male, using that male mastery of the patriarchal society to achieve a daring and unexpected end. The course Telemakhos takes is full of risk, but it may also bring him to himself. It will allow him to ride the uneasy currents of patriarchal tradition without subsuming his own presence or power. Mentor alone—the man, the wise counsel Mentor—cannot do this. The archetype of the *anima*, Jung's "spontaneous product of the unconscious" that "possesses all the outstanding characteristics of a feminine being,"[9] works through Mentor, complementing his influence with its vision. Although Jung describes the *anima* as a force that may more strongly attach the man to the mother image, this Athena-*anima* loosens the ties that bind Telemakhos to obedient and somewhat passive sonship at the same time she strengthens his ties to a vigorous future.

To the extent that, as Alain says, "The gods are moments of man,"[10] the projection of Athena into Mentor raises lingering problems of interpretation. It might seem possible to read the bonding of Athena and Mentor as an erotic experience tending toward reciprocity and mutuality. Athena is herself and another, while Mentor cohabitates with Athena to become even more the self he must be. Neither identity is destroyed; both seem enhanced. From this point of view, the archetypal value of Mentor and Athena is that of unequals arriving at a kind of parity. Speaking of the erotic context of this kind of "intersubjective" relationship—that is, a relationship with two subjects rather than a dominant subject and a submissive "object"—Jessica Benjamin writes, "The capacity to enter into states in which distinctness and union are reconciled underlies the most intense experience of adult erotic life." "In erotic union," she adds, "we can experience that form of mutual recognition in which both partners lose themselves in each other without loss of self; they lose self-consciousness without loss of awareness. Thus early experiences of mutual recognition already prefigure the dynamics of erotic life."[11]

Yet, in fact, there is no mutuality between Athena and Mentor. There is no recognition of subject and subject. Athena *assumes* the appearance, the selfhood, of Mentor, but manipulates it for her own ends. From a psychoanalytic point of view—reading the story as a model of Mentor's psyche—it would seem that Mentor's entrenched commitment to his masculine will, and the tradition that sustains and requires it, leaves him unprepared to acknowledge the complementarity of an *anima,* an independent erotic force, within him. When that force emerges in a crisis, as it must, he cannot manage it because he cannot recognize it; it thus overwhelms him. It overwhelms the Homeric singer as well, who sees it as an exterior goddess rather than a divided psyche within Mentor.

But another, more striking interpretation of the inequality between Athena and Mentor is also possible. The projection of Athena's power into a context that emphasizes specific characters—Telemakhos, Mentor, and Odysseus—rather than abstract values gives a peculiar force to divinity. Divinity guides only when it disrupts conventional behavior. This disruption emphasizes personhood at the expense of orderly society; it requires a gamble that the emerging personhood of the character will itself reorder society. Yet with this gamble it works against the values of behavior that a wise counselor such as Mentor might represent. The mentor, in short, is presented originally as an inescapably divided character, and the two roles subvert each other. He and Athena together become a risk-taker, a tempter of fate. He becomes less of what he was, that her beloved might become more.

In this odd conflation lie the seeds both of dual personhood—the mentor as subject, the apprentice as subject—and the opposite: powerful dominance and painful submission. If, for the sake of argument, one envisions Mentor as a single human (rather than mythological) being—an entrenched, traditional male under the vigorous guidance of a risk-taking and nurturing feminine self—then mentorship becomes as much focused on the apprentice as on the tradition. For the mentor it is no longer a matter of wielding power for its own sake, or even for the sake of a cultural authority; it is a matter of balancing cultural authority with the personhood that underlies all authority. As Benjamin observes,[12] it is a matter of bringing forth a newly empowered person from the apprentice, so that whatever cultural values are worth preserving lie in one who knows and trusts the strengths of his own, independent being.

But this is a kind of ideal that, though perhaps implied in the Athena-Mentor bond, is scarcely sustainable—either in that text or in others. More often the quest for traditional power and the quest for the personhood of the apprentice conflict. To explore this conflict it may help to examine a text that demonstrates the process at a critical cultural moment—a moment in which the rational mind self-consciously asserts itself against irrational or superrational powers. One sees this vividly in the narrative and correspondence of Abelard and Heloise.

In some ways this story follows old conventions of pride, lust, and a tragic fall. Abelard suggests as much in his *Historia calamitatum,* his construction of the calamity: "But success always puffs up fools with pride, and worldly security weakens the spirit's resolution and easily destroys it through carnal temptations. I began to think myself the only philosopher in the world, with nothing to fear from anyone, and so I yielded to the lusts of the flesh."[13] Yet the story is not simply a morality tale. It evinces the danger of mentorship—*both* to the mentor and the apprentice—when the potential conflicts of *anima* and *animus* find extreme manifestations. Whether or not it has a physical reality, as it does in this case, eros becomes primarily a matter of sexual power, as the mentor defines his mastery in terms of what he believes to be his uninhibited control over his apprentice. This control is not, however, uninhibited. The master inhibits himself by subjugating himself to the intellectual and religious forces that make him a distinguished master. To the extent that he acquires any consciousness of the *anima,* it is to subsume that erotic principle of reciprocity within the mastery that seems to him a cultural given. Yet his will to extend his intellectual values to another leaves so little room for the personhood of the other that it leaves no room for his own personhood: he becomes the victim of humane values inhumanely used.

Part of this danger inheres in Abelard's role. His story evinces the difference between "teacher" and "mentor." Abelard is not simply a talented cleric, but the foremost rhetorician in France in the twelfth century. His reputation for overcoming his own masters, William and Anselm of Laon, in textual disputation, draws him devoted students. About these students, however, he has little to say. They function largely as a collective barometer of his own success, and whatever they take from his work remains largely unrecorded. The situation with Heloise is vastly different. Clearly he is intended to function as more than a teacher for her. The fact that Fulbert, Heloise's uncle and guardian, consigns her to his particular care suggests Fulbert's wish for a close intellectual kinship that might result, not simply in knowledge, but in an application of wisdom to life. Although Abelard notes dismissively that Fulbert loves money— a flaw of character that enables Abelard to move into Fulbert's house for a fee—it is clear that Fulbert also values Heloise's intellect.[14] Abelard's abuse of Fulbert's good faith does not alter the character of the role he might have been expected to play. He was not merely to instruct or even to dispute, but to impart wisdom, to guide, to be a companion.

Instead he extends his mastery to a new depth. His record of pleasures with Heloise grows in drama and sensuality, until "our desires left no stage of love-making untried, and if love could devise something new, we welcomed it."[15] Given Abelard's enthusiasm, one might think that this relationship led him to cherish the personhood of Heloise, the soulmate whom he had accidentally and lustfully discovered. It would be more accurate, however, to say that Abelard discovers a series of ways of distancing himself from the relationship as it intensifies. Heloise surely enters the relationship under extreme duress; Abelard writes that he "often forced [her] to consent" to sexual relations.[16] He is arrogant and self-congratulatory, an extreme of masculine will. Yet Heloise appears to move from duress to choice—or as much choice as can arise from a relationship that begins with rape—to become Abelard's passionate mistress.

When eventually she becomes pregnant, Abelard insists on marriage; he fears the wrath of Fulbert were the child to be discovered. In this case marriage is a diplomatic solution, as well as a way of attributing to Heloise a precise social confinement she has so far lacked. As wife she would be Abelard's servant and mistress of the household, while as lover she would remain uncomfortably close, an archetypal *anima* deeply rooted in Abelard's unconscious. Heloise passionately resists this marriage, not only because she senses the dangers of domesticity to the supple mind but also because she fears the category of wife. What matters between Abelard and Heloise—what has made them special, glorified them, set them apart from others—is their love and lust. Marriage would remove this specialness, consigning them again to conventional behavior they had rejected. Abelard records Heloise as arguing that "the name of mistress instead of wife would be dearer to her and more honourable for me—only love freely given should keep me for her, not the constriction of a marriage tie."[17]

Yet Abelard prevails; they marry; Fulbert is unappeased. Heloise goes to the convent in Argenteuil, while Abelard remains in Paris. Enraged, thinking that Abelard has kept his own freedom while consigning Heloise to the convent, Fulbert has Abelard castrated.[18] The story avails itself of several interpretations, not the least of which is the moral view Abelard prescribes, but one cannot help being struck by the defeat of the masculine will: it becomes the victim of its own system, a crippled servant to an orthodoxy that condemns its efforts to escape. Abelard attributes his tragedy to the sin of pride, but one might equally argue that some tragedy is inevitable when orthodoxies determine sins: for sin manifests the orthodoxy's hatred of itself, and initiates the cycle of potential destruction. The orthodoxy must purge itself to perpetuate itself; the son must both triumph over the father and become the father. Generations of fathers and sons, both physical and archetypal, make war in an intricate balance of self-loathing. Abelard is the victim of this larger scenario.

Yet, agent as well as victim, he turns from Heloise and her devotion as if they comprised a typology, a type of behavior or experience designed simply to lead to something cathartic or more pure. He evidently loses touch with her for nine years. In 1128, when after six years as abbot of St. Denis Adam Suger removes Heloise, now prioress, and her nuns, Abelard does what he can—arranging to give a hermitage near Troyes to the nuns, enlisting the local bishop to win Pope Innocent II's confirmation of the gift, writing letters of direction to Heloise. Yet he can envision his former lover only as a "sister in Christ rather than my wife."[19]

Perhaps this evolution is inevitable for Abelard; it is not, however, inevitable for Heloise. Where Abelard writes largely formal and reasoned letters to Heloise, arguing for their appropriately punished lust and praising her management of the Paraclete, Heloise writes back passionately reproving letters. He indeed has been a mentor; he has shown her the worth of her own feelings. But he has betrayed his mentorship twice—first by not taking it seriously, by seeing it only as a diverting pleasure; second, by viewing the resulting lust and love simply as a transgression. Both of these attitudes deny the authentic selfhood of Heloise. They make her a vehicle of the divine hand, rather than the passionate woman she knows herself to be.

Punishing himself, Abelard relegates himself to the reflexive refuge of the rational intellect. He ignores or does not see the lessons Heloise learns—lessons about what happens when love strikes, crystallizing the identities of two people and transforming them. It is Abelard whom Heloise loves, Abelard whose person she cherishes and lusts for. His presence, being real and emphatic, outshines the presence of God, and his absence is an almost unimaginable cruelty. "At every stage of my life up to now, as God knows," she writes Abelard, "I have feared to offend you rather than God, and tried to please you more than him."[20] She pleads with him not to withdraw further into the icy authoritarianism of reason and exhortation. Instead she begs for his attention, his honest and unflattering care. "Do not suppose me healthy and so withdraw the grace of your healing. Do not believe I want for nothing and delay helping me in my hour of need. Do not think me strong, lest I fall before you can sustain me. . . . I beg you, be fearful for me always, instead of feeling confidence in me, so that I may always find help in your solicitude."[21]

Abelard cannot give this. Heloise comprehends the reality of her feelings, and far from rejecting them acknowledges them as a source of her grief-laden self. She knows the fact of her identity. Abelard deflects this knowledge with an illusion. He never really loved Heloise, he writes to her; it was Christ who loved her, and it was Christ who saved her from the sin of their relationship. "It was he who truly loved you, not I. My love, which brought us both to sin, should be called lust, not love. I took my fill of my wretched pleasures in you, and this was the sum total of my love. You say I suffered for you, and perhaps that is true, but it was really through you, and even this, unwillingly. . . . But he [Christ] suffered truly for your salvation, on your behalf of his own free will, and by his suffering he cures all sickness and removes all suffering."[22] Heloise, says Abelard, was the medium of fate, the vehicle through which he himself came closer to an understanding of Christ's method. Heloise in this context is primarily an object. There is nothing here to suggest that Abelard acknowledges, or is able to acknowledge, Heloise or the struggle that self-awareness presents for her.

His is a pathetic spectacle, but not an incomprehensible one, given his preoccupation with power and dominance and self. Yet it remains surprising that one who in some ways manifests the epitome of a mentor's strength and influence should fall so far because of that mentorship. The outward erotic fact of Abelard's dominance and Heloise's initial submission parallels Abelard's own interior erotic conflict. If one is trained to dominate, to be the self above all other selves, how can one achieve any reciprocity? How can the desire to perpetuate oneself and one's knowledge involve anyone other than oneself? Yet, because dominion is worthless unless it is recognized, the self must have an object for its subject: It must be revered. The irony of a master with a debt to a particular tradition of knowledge is that knowledge cannot revere a human being; only human beings can show reverence. Thus the self-absorbed master cannot return to his own tradition for respect or admiration.

At the same time, he cannot leave that tradition behind, or he will abandon the source of his mastery. His own training is rich in intellectual power, but it is also a void. It lacks personhood. To extend its power beyond himself, he must seek the personhood of another. Yet he may have no understanding that such personhood exists, or is an order of knowledge in its own right. His own intellectual tradition, which has given him stature in return for loyalty, may also limit his approach to a form of knowledge that does not emphasize the primacy of the self or the ability of the self to master a body of knowledge.

But Abelard's mentorship also carries other implications. Abelard's own learning, his method of disputation, his attempt to recast church doctrine in comparatively rational terms, and his battles with papal authorities, all signify *animus:* they reflect a combative temper, a predatory approach to social power, a somewhat paradoxical emphasis on reason and argument, a deference to—or at least uneasy acknowledgement of—paternal authority. Of itself, this fact carries no necessary ethical dimension, but from a psychological—and particularly a Jungian—perspective it is incomplete. The danger, then, is not simply that a patriarchal mentor will dominate his apprentices, but that the mentor himself will never experience the freedom of thought or movement he believes to be his. He will be subservient when he believes himself free, submissive when he believes himself dominant. He will, in other words, operate largely out of self-delusion. Whatever tragedy he engenders, it will mirror his personal tragedy.

Thus the problem of mentorship is not only a gender issue—not only a problem of sexual power when men are mentors and women are apprentices. It is a problem of men, and women, in relation to a dominant tradition. No tradition necessarily dominates its student, or makes him a tyrant; yet because any intellectual tradition or ideology is only half-knowledge—reinforcing the role of the learner at the expense of a larger world of personhood—it runs the risk of dominance, as it runs the risk of subverting the erotic process by which mentor and apprentice come to validate each other's independence and power. It is true, however, that gender issues strongly affect the way one conceives of one's independence either as a mentor or as an apprentice. These gender issues extend to the larger problems of submission and cruelty that occur when, intentionally or unintentionally, the mentor denies or thwarts the identity of the apprentice. As in the case of Abelard and Heloise, this thwarting tends to set the apprentice adrift in a sea of opposites or typologies—categories of life and behavior that tend to prevent the integration of past and present, reason and instinct, intellectual knowledge and personal knowledge, heterosexuality and homosexuality. The effect of this thwarting is erotic domination: the apprentice's life is divided between apparent opposites, and only an apprentice as powerfully motivated as Heloise can attempt a reunion of these categories.

In her essay "Remapping the Moral Domain: New Images of Self in Relationship," Carol Gilligan opens with a comment on Aeneas:

> In Book 6 of the *Aeneid*, when Aeneas travels to the underworld in search of his father, he is startled to come upon Dido—to discover that, in fact, she is dead. He had not believed the stories that reached him. "I could not believe," he tells her, "that I would hurt you so terribly by going." (Virgil, 6: 463–464, p. 176). Seeing her wound, he weeps, asking: "Was I the cause?" (Virgil, 6: 458, p. 175). Yet explaining that he did not willingly leave her, he describes himself as a man set apart, bound by his responsibility to his destiny. Caught between two images of himself—as implicated and as innocent, as responsible and as tossed about by fate—he exemplifies the dilemma of how to think about the self, how to represent the experience of being at once separated and connected to others through a fabric of human relationship.[23]

What Gilligan has observed in the story of Aeneas and Dido is, fundamentally, a conflict between loyalty to a tradition—a body of knowledge, a sense of fate, a destiny—and loyalty to another person. Gilligan's terms differ slightly from the terms used here, but the principle is largely the same. Gilligan notes the conventional interpretation of Aeneas, which argues that he must follow his destiny because he is conceived in the role of hero—the highly individuated, self-reliant man, appropriately detached from a private life that his public life may achieve its appropriate glory. But Gilligan's analysis focuses on the inevitable crisis for the self that emerges from this kind of individuation and detachment. When the self is primary, as it is in a conventional view of Aeneas, and the world a mirror for the drama of the self, that self loses whatever reciprocity it might have with the world beyond. This observation applies not only to literature but to the history of psychology: "When others are described as objects for self-reflection or as the means to self-discovery and self-recognition," Gilligan writes, "the language of relationships is drained of motion and, thus, becomes lifeless."[24] Gilligan argues that, although human psychology offers abundant evidence of reciprocal relationships and a sense of selfhood based on the mutuality of selves, the *study* of psychology has neglected these relationships in favor of an orthodoxy that emphasizes the separate self as the primary psychic fact. This separate self, whose empirical relationship to itself and its acquired knowledge reflects an Aristotelian tradition, remains a potent metaphor for psychic life in western culture. It is, however, only a metaphor; it is one construct of psychic life. Another construct, which Gilligan sees increasingly in her psychological research on images of the self in male and female subjects, emphasizes the primacy of the self in relation to other selves. Although these constructs do not divide simply along gender lines, Gilligan argues, they tend to predominate in one gender or the other: "The pattern of predominance, although not gender specific, was gender related, suggesting that the gender differences recurrently observed in moral reasoning signify differences in moral orientation, which, in turn, are tied to different ways of imagining self in relationship."[25]

Gilligan's concern with the nature of the moral voice in men and women leads, in one sense, directly into the problem of mentorship: who commands authority, how does he or she conceive of authority, and how does he or she use that authority? "One moral voice," writes Gilligan, "speaks of connection, not hurting, care, and response; and one speaks of equality, reciprocity, justice, and rights."[26] Although in some ways these terms may not seem widely divergent, they divide in specific ways related to the life of the self in society.

> The values of justice and autonomy, presupposed in current theories of human growth and incorporated into definitions of morality and self, imply a view of the individual as separate and of relationships as either hierarchical or contractual, bound by the alternatives of constraint and cooperation. In contrast, the values of care and connection, salient in women's thinking, imply a view of self and other as interdependent and

of relationships as networks created and sustained by attention and response. . . . As in the ambiguous figure which can be perceived alternately as a vase or two faces, there appear to be two ways of perceiving self in relation to others, both grounded in reality, but each imposing on that reality a different organization.[27]

The problem of authority becomes, then, an inescapable problem of a gender-related moral voice. When wielded in terms of a "hierarchical or contractual" relationship, authority necessarily takes a different form than when it is used in a context where the self and the other are "interdependent . . . sustained by attention and response." In their extremes, each moral voice pronounces a different end; Gilligan returns to the *Aeneid* for her illustration, citing the classical scholar Marilyn Skinner. "The compelling poignancy and ultimate futility of Aeneas's and Dido's last meeting arise from the recognition that Aeneas's stoic detachment has lost its heroic quality, 'becoming instead pathetically defensive,' and that Dido's death has come to appear less tragically necessary, seeming a 'wretched, preventable accident' (Skinner, p. 12). Thus the costs of detachment . . . become increasingly clear."[28] The cost of detachment is the price of one kind of destiny: Aeneas's destiny is to be a hero, to carry the values of the *animus* to a new place, to found a new-old society. The problem is that, whenever the relationship itself partakes of a hierarchical order, the relationship becomes a kind of erotic deviance rather than erotic fulfillment: hierarchy limits the reciprocal force of the relationship, diminishing the identities of the dominator and the dominated.

Because this kind of order has an institutionalized weight, it cannot easily be excised: it requires not simply an enormous effort on the part of the mentor, but a different way of looking at the value of the apprentice in relation to the value of a tradition. It requires the ascendancy of the moral voice relating to interconnectedness and personal worth, rather than to abstract principles that lie beyond personhood. It also relies on a mentor who understands, as Jean Baker Miller explains, that the most successful mentor-apprentice relationship is the one that ultimately ends the distinction between mentor and apprentice. "The paramount goal is to end the relationship," Miller writes; "that is, to end the relationship of inequality." Miller suggests that this "inequality" has nothing to do with unequal personhood, but rather with unequal ability: "The 'superior' party," she writes, "presumably has more of some ability or valuable quality, which she/he is supposed to impart to the 'lesser' person." What is preserved in Miller's approach is precisely that sense of two subjects, two human beings who enter a relationship not through submission to foreordained hierarchy but through a desire for mutual benefit. "Although the lesser party often gives much to the superior," Miller adds, "these relationships are *based in service* to the lesser party."[29]

Miller perhaps takes the identity of the lesser party too much for granted; this term itself, even within quotation marks, raises doubts about the subject of the apprentice that must quickly be put to rest. Miller raises other doubts as well when she argues that "the superiors hold all the real power."[30] This is surely untrue. Even an abject apprentice, fully obedient to the master's every wish, holds some power over the master, if only by confirming the master's megalomaniac sense of self-worth. Take away the abject apprentice, and the master suffers, although he may not admit it. The master and the apprentice are in fact both bound by the erotic conditions of the relationship, in which desire—the mentor's desire for power and influence, the apprentice's desire for recognition—translates into dominance or submission, depending on the mentor's tendency to objectify the apprentice and the apprentice's tendency to identify with the mentor's power. There is a strange reciprocity of power even here, but it is not a healthy reciprocity, and it does not imply any liberating experience for the apprentice. It does, however, show that such relationships are not static; the power is not all on one side; and the possibility of genuine reciprocity—of an interdependent relationship in which apprentice and mentor approach each other as equals—is at least dimly implicit. Without some fundamental shift toward a personal interdependence between mentor and apprentice, however, any mentorship may carry some of the cultural burden of hierarchy, dominance, and submission. Any mentorship may carry a form of cultural cruelty that will be destructive to both parties.

The difficulty in making this fundamental shift can be seen in one of the seminal texts on mentorship, Bruce Boston's 1976 study, "The Sorcerer's Apprentice: A Case Study in the Role of the Mentor." Boston, a philosopher of education, examines the mentorship of the Yaqui peyote master Don Juan in Carlos Castaneda's series of books on the subject—*The Teachings of Don Juan, A Separate Reality, Journey to Ixtlan,* and *Tales of Power.*[31] Boston offers nineteen different qualifications for mentor and apprentice; these can be seen to fall into two main groups. The first has to do with tradition: Boston argues that the mentor and his pupil "are both servants of a tradition."[32] The second group has to do with self-realization: the mentor, says Boston, teaches *from* his apprentice's experience, rather than teaching *at* the apprentice; the mentor "trains toward the predilection or 'bent' of the individual student."[33] Boston defends his first point with particular emphasis. "The structure of the tradition [which Don Juan is conveying] is clearly hierarchical," writes Boston. He concludes:

> It is clear from don Juan's instruction to Castaneda that the servant role, as I have called it, is crucial to the instruction itself. . . . This general characteristic of servanthood to a larger realm of knowledge, cause, power, or frame of reference marks the mentor-pupil relationship as a whole. The artist introduces his student to Art, the musician to Music, the lawyer to the Law. . . . By submitting to the disciplines and canons of this larger realm, the pupil is then entitled to exhibit mastery, with the knowledge that arrival is always penultimate. Sorcerers die but "power" continues. Lawyers try cases but the Law perdures. Cubism, animism and abstract expression come and go, but Art remains.[34]

This paragraph codifies a standard response to a mentor-apprentice relationship, emphasizing the abstract value of what is being taught over the interpersonal world of the mentor and apprentice. It implicitly justifies this hierarchy on the grounds of human mortality. Humans die but abstract disciplines remain; therefore mentors must direct the student toward the principles of the discipline, relegating the matter of personal development to a subordinate position.

From what we have seen, however, this standard response places both the mentor and the apprentice in danger: it implicitly teaches the apprentice the value of enslavement even as it claims to teach other values, and so rejects the possibility of dual subjects—mentor as subject and apprentice as subject, confirming the other's worth through a process of reciprocal appreciation. This rejection undercuts Boston's second argument for the importance of the apprentice, relegating the apprentice to a condition of diminished identity. Only freedom from the relationship can end the cruelty of this diminishment. No amount of kindness on the mentor's part will suffice, as the philosopher Philip Hallie suggests: "the opposite of cruelty is not kindness; nor is it Christian love (except if that word is subjected to what Montaigne would call a 'long interpretation,' an interpretation entirely in terms of the victim's point of view). *The opposite of cruelty is freedom.* The victim does not need the ultimately destructive gift of kindness when offered *within the cruel relationship.* He needs freedom from that relationship" (Hallie's italics).[35] Because no values can really make sense if the self-worth of the apprentice remains in doubt, the standard approach to mentorship turns reasonable behavior on its head.

In this introduction, I suggest how mentorship and eroticism—or at least one specific concept of eroticism—happen to combine, and how tensions within the role of the mentor can cause that erotic power to translate itself into a force for unwarranted domination. I am only too aware of the objections some readers will have to the use of "erotic" here, and I am equally aware of the outrage some readers will feel when confronted with the suggestion that a hierarchical tradition of knowledge, loosely related to a patriarchal culture, may itself carry seeds of destruction or decay. I remain concerned as well that this study may be misinterpreted on more political grounds. It may be read as a throwback to a time when sexual liasons between teachers and students were less carefully guarded than they are now coming to be. Nothing could be further from my intention here. I do not address, either directly or by implication, the question of whether teachers and their students should enter into consensual relationships, or what kinds of rules, if any, should govern those relationships. Clearly it is possible for a teacher to abuse his or her authority and influence over a student, and to engage that student in a relationship with sexual allure but no real possibility of intersubjectivity. It may also be possible for a student to initiate a seduction for reasons that have relatively little to do with a relationship between two subjects. When, in such cases, the teacher also has some supervisory responsibility for the student, the problems are real. I believe that these problems are separate, however, from the kind of eroticism I discuss here—the kind that sanctions mentor and apprentice.

It is essential to understand that the creative dislocation that occurs in a healthy mentor-apprentice relationship is fundamentally erotic, even if it is nonsexual. Two new people are created through a confluence of intimate perspectives, talents, and experiences; and the kind of devotion one finds even in a nonsexual mentor-apprentice relationship suggests the erotic force behind this mode of self-creation. At the same time, it seems equally important to recognize dangers that lie within the life of the mentor—dangers that, in a sense, seduce the mentor because they reassure him that his relation to a larger tradition is secure, even if this relation jeopardizes his own humanity. These issues—matters, to me, of life and death—are the ones I address in this work.

Notes

1. Jessica Benjamin provides a detailed summary of research on the child-parent bond in *The Bonds of Love: Psychoanalysis, Feminism, and the Problem of Domination* (New York: Pantheon, 1988, pp. 15–31). With regard to the eroticism of the bond, the question becomes more complex. Freud's Oedipal theory most obviously embodies this eroticism (see, for example, "The Sexual Function" in *An Outline of Psycho-Analysis* [New York: W. W. Norton & Co., 1949], pp. 11–12), although Jung posits a more elaborate relationship between the child's psyche and the mythic world of the unconscious, and argues that the Oedipal complex represents "a false aiteology of neurosis which, in Freud, ossified into a system" (C. G. Jung, "Introduction to Wickes's 'Analyse Der Kinderseele,' *The Development of Personality* [Princeton: Bollingen Series XX/Princeton University Press, 1954], p. 46).

The function of eros in Jungian psychology, especially with regard to children, is a prototype of the intersubjective theory of Benjamin: the psychic conflicts it raises in the child offer the possibility of bringing forth previously repressed psychic strengths through a closer and more reciprocal relationship with the parent, particularly the parent of the opposite sex (see Jung, "Psychic Conflicts in a Child," in *The Development of Personality,* p. 29). The term "intersubjectivity" comes from Jürgen Habermas, "A Theory of Communicative Competence," in *Recent Sociology* no. 2, ed. H. P. Dreitzel (New York: Macmillan, 1970); another essential work in the study of the infant-parent bond is Daniel N. Stern's *The Interpersonal World of the Infant* (New York: Basic Books, 1985). Here, as in Benjamin's work, the emphasis shifts from an eros based on sexuality to an eros of attachment and self-affirmation based on clinical studies of infant behavior. See especially ch. 4, "The Sense of a Core Self: I. Self versus Other" (pp. 69–99) and ch. 5, "The Sense of a Core Self: II. Self with Other" (pp. 100–123).

2. The first international conference on mentorship was held in Vancouver, British Columbia in 1986. At that time the first edition of a comprehensive bibliography on mentorship was also issued. See William A. Gray and Marilynne Miles Gray, "Preface," *Mentoring: A Comprehensive Annotated Bibliography of Important References* (Vancouver, British Columbia: International Association for Mentoring, 1986), p. iii. Interestingly, one could argue that the catalyst for scholarship specifically devoted to mentorship was Carlos Castaneda's early writing of his alleged encounters with the peyote master Don Juan

(*The Teachings of Don Juan*, 1968; *A Separate Reality*, 1971; *Journey to Ixtlan*, 1972; *Tales of Power*, 1974). In the mid seventies the educational theorist Bruce Boston issued his seminal mentorship study, "The Sorcerer's Apprentice: A Case Study in the Role of the Mentor" (Reston, Va.: The Council for Exceptional Children, 1976); the case study was Castaneda and Don Juan. William and Marilynne Gray argue that Boston's paper has "conceptual deficiencies" that "stem from exclusive dependence on incorporating the transpersonal/transcendental views contained in Carlos Castaneda's books on Don Juan" (p. 53). Nevertheless, the paper presented a detailed conceptual framework for mentorship, and thus drew attention to a little-studied arena of human relationships.

Other essential works on domination and subordination, though not framed explicitly in the language of mentorship studies, include Jean Baker Miller's *Toward a New Psychology of Women*, 2d ed. (Boston: Beacon Press, 1986) and Carter Heyward's *Touching Our Strength: The Erotic as Power and the Love of God* (San Francisco: Harper and Row, 1989). Miller's discussion of the "temporary inequality" one finds between student and teacher (or mentor and apprentice) is important in its contrast to "permanent inequality," a systemic subjugation of all or most individuals within a given group. (This subjugation may be based on "race, sex, class, nationality, religion, or other characteristics ascribed at birth" [p. 6].) The psychic content of this "temporary inequality," however, is not always clear, and is one of the subjects of my own book. Carter Heyward's passionate and convincing argument for the spiritual value of two-subject (or "intersubjective") relationships also underlies some of the values I set forth in this book.

Behind all these works, of course, lies the Hegelian dialectic between Master and Slave (see G. W. F. Hegel, *Phenomenology of Spirit*, trans. A. V. Miller [New York: Oxford University Press, 1977]). I have profited from this work, and from Alexandre Kojève's *Introduction to the Reading of Hegel*, trans. J. H. Nichols, ed. A. Bloom (New York: Basic Books, 1969), in which the Master is clearly identified with consciousness "existing *for itself*," while the Slave binds himself "completely to his animal life," and "is merely one with the natural world of things." The erotic anxiety implicit in this distinction—the seemingly unbridgeable distance—is fundamental to my sense of the conflict between mentorship and eros. Although I have chosen to explore this conflict in the language of psychology and literary criticism rather than philosophy, I wish to acknowledge the value of Hegel's work to my own thinking on the subject.

3. Homer, *The Odyssey*, trans. Robert Fitzgerald (New York: Anchor Books, 1963), Books 1 and 3 (pp. 25–46).

4. Peter Abelard, and Heloise, *The Letters of Abelard and Heloise*, trans. with intro. Betty Radice (London: Penguin Books, 1974).

5. Homer, *Odyssey*, pp. 26–27, 30–31.

6. Homer, *Odyssey*, p. 27.

7. Homer, *Odyssey,* p. 27.

8. Homer, *Odyssey,* p. 100.

9. Carl Gustav Jung, "Aion: Phenomenology of the Self," in *The Portable Jung,* ed. Joseph Campbell (New York: Viking Press, 1971), p. 151. Jung's discussion of the complementary archetypes, *animus* and *anima,* appears in *Aion: Researches into the Phenomenology of the Self,* vol. 9, book 2, *The Collected Works of Carl G. Jung,* trans. R. F. C. Hull (Princeton: Bollingen Series/Princeton University Press, 1959).

10. Alain [Emile Chartier], *The Gods,* trans. Richard Pevear (New York: New Directions, 1974), p. 125.

11. Benjamin, p. 29.

12. Benjamin, pp. 40–41.

13. *Abelard and Heloise,* p. 65. A scholarly debate continues on the historical legitimacy of the letters (see Charlotte Charrier, *Heloise dans l'histoire et dans la legende* [Geneva: Slatkine Reprints, 1977], and Peggy Kamuf, "Introduction: Prologue to What Remains," *Fictions of Feminine Desire: Disclosures of Heloise* [Lincoln: University of Nebraska Press, 1982], pp. xi–xix). With regard to the problem of mentorship and eroticism, however, the issue is not strictly historical, but interpretive. One wants to interpret the values that remain constant in a historically influential story. That is what I have tried to do here, without discounting the possibility of historical controversy.

14. *Abelard and Heloise,* p. 67.

15. *Abelard and Heloise,* pp. 67–68.

16. *Abelard and Heloise,* p. 147.

17. *Abelard and Heloise,* p. 74.

18. *Abelard and Heloise,* p. 75.

19. *Abelard and Heloise,* p. 96.

20. *Abelard and Heloise,* p. 134.

21. *Abelard and Heloise,* pp. 134–135.

22. *Abelard and Heloise,* p. 153.

23. Carol Gilligan, "Remapping the Moral Domain: New Images of Self in Relationship," in *Mapping the Moral Domain,* ed. Carol Gilligan et al. (Cambridge, Mass.: Harvard University Graduate School of Education, 1989), p. 3.

24. Gilligan, p. 7.

25. Gilligan, p. 8.

26. Gilligan, p. 8.

27. Gilligan, pp. 8–9.

28. Gilligan, p. 13.

29. Jean Baker Miller, *Toward a New Psychology of Women,* 2d ed. (Boston: Beacon Press, 1986), p. 4.

30. Miller, p. 5.

31. Bruce O. Boston, "The Sorcerer's Apprentice: A Case Study in the Role of the Mentor" (Reston, Va.: The Council for Exceptional Children, 1976).

32. Boston, p. 7.

33. Boston, p. 24.

34. Boston, pp. 8–9.

35. Philip Hallie, *Cruelty,* rev. ed. (Middletown, Conn.: Wesleyan University Press, 1982), p. 159.

1

A Turmoil of Speech
The Mentorship of Ezra Pound

When T. S. Eliot dedicated "The Waste Land" to Ezra Pound in 1922, he added a memorable inscription borrowed from Dante—*il miglior fabbro,*" "the better craftsman." Although Eliot's praise was typically deferential, there is reason to think that Pound deserved this praise. Pound's precise editing of the manuscript showed both his sympathy with Eliot's intentions and his ability to bring those intentions to flower in a poem that, left to Eliot alone, was at once too luxurious and too undirected.[1]

But this was by no means Pound's main act of craftsmanship, even in regard to Eliot. The years 1915 and 1916 were pivotal for Eliot, full of personal daring and larger intimations of misery. Having traveled first to Germany and then (after World War I slowly ground to a start) to England, Eliot was supposed to complete his dissertation in philosophy for his doctorate at Harvard University. While he accomplished this project, he did so with the greatest misgivings (and, in 1915, decided to forgo a dissertation defense and thus the degree itself). Although he "took a piece of fairly technical philosophy for [his] thesis," he wrote to his friend Norbert Wiener in 1914 that philosophy "is chiefly literary criticism and conversation about life."[2] Eliot had in fact already given his allegiance to literature and art, where "philosophy is an unloved guest."[3]

It began to be clear, particularly to his father and mother, that Eliot was by no means certain of completing his doctoral work. Their worried, implicitly disapproving letters must have been a tremendous burden to him, hard evidence that he might fail as a son. Compounding this burden in what seems a desperate attempt at self-assertion—or self-destruction—Eliot married Vivienne Haigh-Wood on June 26, 1915, without his parents' knowledge. Attempting to establish a household, make a living by teaching in a private boys' school in High Wycombe, and take care of a neurasthenic spouse (who seemed as miserable in marriage as Eliot was), Eliot showed signs of strain, even disorientation: his letters to his friends are full of references to his wife's illnesses, and he begins to apologize, as he rarely has before, for his own weariness.

Pound moved into this sick-room atmosphere with the confidence of a prizefighter. Two days after Eliot's marriage, Pound wrote a long letter to Eliot's father in which he explored Eliot's prospects as a self-supporting author and literary figure. The letter can hardly have been much comfort to Henry Ware Eliot, for it flattered Pound as much as Eliot and showed the kind of disdain for logical development that would have worried an orderly American patriarch. Yet it was explicit in its support. "As to T.S.E.'s work," Pound wrote, I think it the most interesting stuff that has appeared since my own first books, five years ago."[4] "T.S.E. is," he added, "(as the *Spectator* said of me some years since) 'that rare thing among modern poets, a scholar'. That means not only an advantage in the initial sprint, it means much more: a chance of being able really to finish 'a long distance race', a chance of having matter and volume enough in one to keep on writing more and more interestingly, with increased precision and development."[5] Pound urged Eliot's father to respect his son's authentic talent and to be patient with the slow currents of literary development. Pound had no intention of conciliating Henry Ware Eliot; rather, he intended to educate him and to defend the rising talent of Henry's son Tom in the process.

Pound also worked behind the scenes to make sure that others noticed Eliot's talent. He badgered Harriet Monroe, founder and editor of *Poetry* magazine, for several months to get Eliot's "The Love Song of J. Alfred Prufrock" into print as quickly as possible, insisting that "it was the best poem I have yet had or seen from an American."[6] In 1916, he helped arrange the publication in *Poetry* of other early poems from Eliot, including "La Figlia che Piange" and "Morning at the Window."[7] When Eliot's first book, *Prufrock and Other Observations,* was published in June 1917, Pound contributed five pounds toward the cost of printing without Eliot's knowledge.[8] Pound often acted as an agent for Eliot, cabling Alfred Knopf in 1919, for example, to determine the status of a manuscript of Eliot's poems and essays.[9] Perhaps most important, when Eliot began to show signs of severe strain from his daily labors at Lloyds Bank, Pound undertook a subscription series among patrons of the arts to amass enough money to enable Eliot to live without the need for other income.[10] Pound's determination that Eliot should escape as much drudgery as possible in order to preserve his genius shows both Pound's own genius for identifying talent and the tremendous energy he invested in talented people. Pound was "the better craftsman," but his craftsmanship was not limited to works of art.

Eliot, of course, was not Pound's only find. James Joyce, the sculptor Gaudier-Brzeska, Robert Frost, Hilda Doolittle (H.D.), and a bit later Basil Bunting, James Laughlin, and the sculptor Henge—all experienced Pound's championing. That we have come to recognize all of these people as significant or major contributors to modern literature and art would seem to confirm Pound's distinction as a mentor. It was true, of course, that Pound had his detractors. As early as 1907, for example, when he was twenty-two and beginning his brief teaching career at Wabash College in Crawfordsville, Indiana, he organized a soirée in which, according to one member, Fred H. Rhodes, he played priest to his acolytes: "Ezra gathered around himself a small group of advanced thinkers in the arts . . . to which a very few privileged disciples were invited. . . . After the preliminary formalities, Pound seated himself on a chair, while his disciples and satellites disposed themselves gracefully, but somewhat uncomfortably, cross-legged on the floor, at the feet of the master."[11] This pattern was not to change significantly over the course of Pound's life. Four years later, having moved to London, Pound had essentially taken over Yeats's Monday soirée: "he dominated the room," as Douglas Goldring recalled, "distributed Yeats's cigarettes and Chianti, and laid down the law about poetry."[12] Pound "was like a drop of oil in a glass of water," said Wyndham Lewis; "the trouble was, I believe, that he had no wish to *mix;* he just wanted to *impress.*"[13] Neither Goldring nor Lewis could be described as an enemy of Pound, and yet both saw clearly Pound's urge to rise above even a small, eminent crowd of contemporary authors. As for Pound, he seemed increasingly convinced that his celebrated autocratic behavior was simply a necessary attribute of his mentorship, his way of getting things done.

The matter here, however, is not as simple as either Pound or his detractors would make it out to be. Pound's successes concealed a particularly important aspect of his mentorship—his discomfort with the people he supported. With literature he felt on sure ground; with people

he felt much less secure. Arguably this had much to do with his difficulty to accept what Jessica Benjamin calls "difference," and to enter
into states in which difference and union are both possible. To accomplish this imaginatively was, for Pound, a high achievement, akin to the
mysteries of Eleusis; to accomplish it with other human beings remained
for him an authentic mystery.

Having devoted himself as subject to the "subject" of a revised tradition of literature and cultural value, Pound found himself embracing
male personae that, though perhaps unusual in their degree of historical obscurity, were in other ways highly conventional. To retell "the tale
of the tribe" was the role of the Homeric singer, a masculine role in
Pound's terms. It is no accident that virtually every entry in *ABC of Reading* comes from a male author; this emphasis on masculine creativity to
some extent subordinated the issue of eros within the issue of a cultural
tradition—the tradition of the male fraternity of poets, whose primary
relationships were with their art and its traditions—and saved Pound
from having to confront the problem inherent in two human subjects.

The nature of the erotic experience for Pound was to lift the single
soul into spiritual communion with all that was beyond its singleness.
Erotic communion was not, for him, a mutually reinforcing encounter
between two human subjects, as Benjamin describes it. Nor was it an
encounter with a fundamentally different yet equal human being. "Experiences of 'being with' are predicated on a continually evolving awareness of difference," she writes. "The externality of the other makes one
feel one is truly being 'fed,' getting nourishment from the outside, rather
than supplying everything for oneself."[14] For Pound, however, difference
was a threat to his own fragile confidence in his mastery, and having an
"other"—a human being who would confirm his own sense of self—
was fraught with danger. What Pound wanted was to transcend his single self, or at least to use it as a medium for a panoply of identities. In
this erotic fantasy of union lay an awesome power. In it lay, as well, the
seeds of his difficulty with mentorship.

Pound's ambition to redeem himself from the tyranny of history by
recovering the eternal moment of the hero is well known. In a 1927
letter to his father, Pound outlined the "subject and response and counter
subject" of his "fugue," the *Cantos:*

> A.A. Live man goes down into world of Dead
> C.B. The "repeat in history"

B.C. The "magic moment" or moment of metamorphosis, bust thru
from quotidien into "divine or permanent world." Gods, etc.[15]

It would be a mistake to think of these ideas as relatively late arrivals in
Pound's life, for they represent the evolution of a long fascination with
spiritual immanence in the world of mortal bodies. This immanence,
which allows the perceptive human creature briefly to escape his or her
mortality, requires what Kevin Oderman has called "the erotic medium."
A kind of spiritualized sexuality, in which union with spiritual mysteries breeds liberating insight, is the object of Pound's quest. This spiritualized sexuality also inhabits Pound's early poetry and prose.[16] "For
Pound," Oderman writes, "sexuality stood at the threshold of the *mysterium,* though he saw clearly enough that for many it was a source only
of dissipation."[17]

The possibility of "dissipation"—both sexual and intellectual—was
profoundly disturbing to Pound. It meant the opposite of his "repeat in
history"; it meant a life of waste and confusion rather than ecstatic revelation. What was necessary, then, was to develop a mastery, not simply
of sexuality—not simply of the body's physical drives—but of eros, the
combined physical and psychic force of human generation and redemption. To be a medium for eros would be to absolve oneself of the worst
excesses of physical indulgence, and more importantly to attain some
kind of power. As Oderman notes, to be a "servant of Amor" was, for
Pound, to experience an essential education, through which the lover
"feels his immortality upon him. . . . The education is not so much a
matter of refining one's sensibilities, though that too is indicated, as it
is an education in the experience of visionary realities, and the accent
falls on experience rather than knowledge."[18]

One might expect that a soul in quest of immortality through eros
would devote itself to an intimate study of the erotic life, seeking a subject (or series of subjects) to correspond to its own understanding of
itself as subject. Benjamin's observation about the intensity of erotic life,
"in which distinctness and union are reconciled,"[19] suggests that one
approach to erotic spirituality is precisely to recognize the worth of one's
own soul through honoring the worth of another's. In this model of an
erotic relationship, the accent clearly falls on experience rather than
knowledge.

Yet, despite Oderman's assertion, the accent in Pound's case falls on
knowledge rather than experience. It is true that, in his writings, Pound

warns the reader of "the mysteries self-defended, the mysteries that *can not* be revealed. Fools can only profane them. The dull can neither penetrate the secretum nor divulge it to others."[20] The implication here is that, whether or not Pound has perceived the secret, he has at least understood the route to that secret—a route that must remain closed to the uninitiated. Yet the force of this rhetoric, like the force of so much of Pound's prose, is to establish a public pose or persona for the author—a persona that may or may not have much to do with the reality of his life. In fact, Pound's early writings suggest that he has some difficulty with the idea of erotic spirituality through the medium of two equal subjects.

His vision of history, for example, emphasizes the importance of submission. In *The Spirit of Romance* he argues that the study of history is a process of submitting to the influence of great men and great works, after which one may perhaps become great oneself after a fashion—"an omniscient historian. . . . The history of an art is the history of masterwork, not of failures, or mediocrity. The omniscient historian would display the masterpieces, their causes and their inter-relation. The study of literature is hero-worship. It is a refinement or, if you will, a perversion of that primitive religion."[21] What emerges from this homage to greatness is the necessity of control—control of oneself or the image of oneself, control of one's art, control of one's sexuality. This concern with control extends clearly to the early poetry, where Pound seeks to master, not simply a variety of voices, but a variety of historical or literary identities—Plotinus, Paolo da Rimini, Cino da Pistoia, and many others—as if to extend his own limited mortal self through them. While it might be argued that the early poetry is essentially experimental, a kind of finger exercise for the epic that lay ahead, the experiments cut too close to the character of Pound's life to be merely an exercise. The chameleon Pound, whom one discovers in 1908 or 1909 or 1911 in various verbal guises, is not less disguised in his letters, for example, to T. S. Eliot (or Eliot's father), or to James Joyce, or to Harriet Monroe, or to any of a number of literary editors and reviewers a bit later in his career. The personae he creates in these letters vary greatly, yet they always demonstrate an unusually simple tone and authority. One finds not so much a subject writing to another subject as a young master experimenting with his powers on those around him.

This contrasts in an interesting way with Pound's letters to Dorothy Shakespear, with whom he began to correspond in 1909 and whom he married in 1914. Pound's biographer, Humphrey Carpenter, writes that "Dorothy had originally been intended by [Pound] for the role of disciple rather than confidante or lover";[22] and it is true, in the later letters, that Pound addresses her in the insistent, didactic tone he invoked to lecture so many of his purported inferiors. Yet the earlier letters reveal a somewhat different Pound—an ambitious young man bent on making an impression, a man who has difficulty forming attachments and who prizes adulation, and yet a man as well who admits to stupidity and confusion, indulges in romantic metaphysical speculation, and writes with embarrassingly earnest bravado to Dorothy's father when he questions Pound's worthiness as a suitor. It would be naive to identify this person as the Pound-without-persona; yet it is clear that, when Pound draws back slightly from his quest for the *mysterium,* he is a different young man—a lesser man, in some ways, less vigorous and definite, but also less calculating and self-conscious. His self-portrait in his letters to Dorothy Shakespear reveals a man who, amid confusion and self-doubt, is closer to the source of eros than the other Pound—the persona-ridden creature who expects to master himself and others.

Perhaps because Dorothy never showed the kind of literary talent that drove Pound to mastery—she wrote to him at one point, "I have read nothing & am about to read nothing. . . . How therefore should I have an idea as to what you are to write?"[23]—she did not incite in him the need for a constant and elaborate pose. Beyond this, she represented a world of social distinction that Pound, despite his later deprecations of the idiocies of the bourgeoisie, found seductive. His appeals to Henry Hope Shakespear, Dorothy's father, revealed a suprising, if erratic, concern for financial and personal probity. He showered Henry with bankbooks containing small sums, a letter from the publisher Macmillan regarding future contracts, and a shadowy guarantee of two hundred pounds a year (most likely a result of his friend Margaret Cravens's patronage[24]). Later, when Henry continued to voice doubts, Pound offered a detailed and formally optimistic view of his financial affairs.[25]

The Pound in letters to Dorothy Shakespear and her family is by turns aggressive and tender, confident and full of longing. Responding to Dorothy's teasing about a minor confusion in an earlier letter, Pound writes, "You are very lovely & I am very stupid. One of which facts I have mentioned before, & the other is self evident."[26] Though the matter here is small, the tone differs greatly from Pound's later manifesto-like correspondence. A bit earlier, discussing the progress of his 1911 book *Canzoni,*

Pound comments on the small-mindedness of critics who believe poems can be written by formula, then compliments Dorothy on her own philosophizing.[27] A year later, following Margaret Cravens's suicide, he writes with pain and irony of his encounter with Margaret's aunt, Drusilla Cravens: "I jawed with Margaret's aunt up till about 2 A.M. last night and am this day exhausted, after the manner of a rag's limpness. There is to be no funeral here, and what M. [Margaret] wrote of so blithely, in one of her last notes, as 'The remains' will be conveyed to the U.S.A. As M. is by now a small, fat, brown god sitting in a huge water-lily, splashing over the edge, the performance will probably amuse her."[28]

"Said image may sound ridiculous," Pound added, "but it is a great comfort to one, and is so unanswerably true that I don't dare mention it to anyone else." The conjunction of holiness and the absurd seems companionable to this Ezra Pound, though it dissolves within a decade. There is, more important, a sense of reciprocity with the dead here—a metaphorical communion, in which imagining the afterlife necessarily subverts the need for human mastery. The dead know all and are happy; power descends upon the human being who can reconcile himself to this. Pound suggests here—and, interestingly, in the Pisan cantos many years later, after much evil has befallen him—that he understands this principle. But the labor of mastery that Pound undertakes at about this time increasingly obscures any revelation that Craven's death might have brought.

It is not, of course, as if Pound in these years were simply an innocent abroad, searching for identity and immortality. By the time he met Dorothy he had already completed the first stage of his ambiguous *pas de deux* with Hilda Doolittle, and his aggressive renaming of her as "H.D., Imagiste" came in 1912,[29] during the middle of his cool courtship of Dorothy. It is equally true, as Carpenter suggests, that Pound's relationship with Dorothy was essentially a postadolescent spiritual exercise in which "the ultimate aim is poesia."[30] When eros began to edge toward sexuality, Pound drew back, at least in those early years. Yet in drawing back, in converting sexual instinct into spiritual mystery, he probed another order of power; he became a kind of medium, not unlike the Provençal troubadours he admired at that time.

This mediumistic intrigue is fully present, though not dominant, in Pound's letters to Margaret Cravens from 1910, when Pound was twenty-five, to her death in 1912. Pound first met Cravens, an American pianist who hoped to help support worthy artists with her family fortune, in Paris in 1911. It may be that Pound's posed, courtier-like correspondence stemmed from a particular uncertainty about Cravens's motives; her willingness to supply him with an income so that he could continue as a poet was almost too good to be true. Yet his interest in Cravens (he was alleged to have spent an unseemly amount of time in her Paris apartment[31]), and his genuine grief upon her death, suggest that his pose was not for the sake of social propriety. The more sensible motive had to do with the value of the pose itself. Identifying himself as the troubadour, and Cravens as the beneficent lady, Pound helped to liberate them both from their provincial American backgrounds and placed them in a European tradition that dignified their ambitions.

It is entirely true, of course, that as Pound's friendship with Cravens grew his letters acquired a more personal, idiosyncratic tone. Pound periodically chastised her for her poor handwriting, and for those metaphysical speculations of hers which seemed to him to leave too much room for interpretation. At one point, in 1911, Pound asked her to keep an eye on an acquaintance, Julia Wells: "If a very little lady with no more brains than Mrs. Sill & about the same refinement should land in Paris," he wrote, "could you look after her a little until she gets settled."[32] Since Louise Morgan Sill, the first female editor of *Harper's Magazine,* was also a close friend of Cravens's, Pound's comment could hardly be taken in the mode of the "trobar clus." Elsewhere, Pound described the state of Dorothy Shakespear's health and reassured Cravens about the worth of Abdu'l Baha's teaching: "They have *done* instead of talking," he wrote, "and a persian movement for religious unity that claims the feminine soul equal to the male, & puts Christ above Buddha, to the horror of the Theosophists, is worth while."[33]

Yet, despite Pound's interest in the equality of feminine and masculine souls, his earthly relationship with Cravens maintained a dual hierarchy. He arrayed her in the identity of spiritual (as well as monetary) benefactor, an identity that she accepted, and in so doing she appeared to gain a certain power over him. It was, however, a power that Pound himself conferred—a kind of theatrical submission that nevertheless suggested he was managing the relationship. In his first letter he described her as "part of some larger beneficence that I have no right to interfere with."[34] "No right to interfere"—this from Ezra Pound! A few days later, he exhorted her not to sell a bond to help support him. "There's no earthly reason," he wrote, "why, even if you are preserving my nervous system, no reason why you should slam down a lump sum."[35] Pound's concern had a trace of alarm—one hears a man who cannot quite fathom the ardency of his benefactor—yet he was quick to make amends: "Pardon me," he wrote three sentences later, "for making suggestions to my ruling Providence."

The idea that Margaret Cravens might be in some way "ruling" echoes Pound's favorite Provençal tradition of the time, and although Pound modified that tradition with the flavor of his own life, he never fully departed from it. As the lady she deserved whatever praise and wisdom he could provide; and, though this wisdom might periodically include gentle admonitions (as when he instructed her to refer to him as a "poet or artist" rather than an "author"[36]), it should remain true to the prospect that one might ultimately find that "divine or permanent world." In 1910, on a visit back to Pennsylvania, he speculated on the metaphysics of spiritual strength: "I wonder," he wrote, "how many lives one lives out between birth and death. . . . there has come a curious renewal of that kind of energy that I had before the first *battaglia*."[37] Pound's choice of militaristic terminology to describe his early years of poverty and uncertainty, and his emphasis on mystery—the "curious renewal," with its implicit invocation of a power beyond the self—suggests in part his earnest desire to convey a regenerative experience; but, more emphatically, it identifies itself with a courtly language, and makes Pound the courtier. Pound adopted this tone particularly in his periodic letters of gratitude. In the summer of 1910, he addressed her as the "fountain of my salvation," and later bid his good-bye with a quotation from Horace—"Maecenas, O et praesidium" ("Maecenas, my protection, guardian").[38] Later that year, as he prepared an edition of Guido Cavalcanti's poems for possible publication, he wrote to Cravens, "If I dont dedicate my edition of Guido to you—to whom shall it be dedicated. The ancient custom of dedicating ones opuses to ones patrons—saints & otherwise should not unduly be flouted."[39]

It is possible to read these comments with a slight edge of irony; it is also true that Pound occasionally found himself annoyed with Cravens's insistence on regular correspondence.[40] Yet to resist the face value of these letters is to attribute too much weight to the ironic, mocking side of Pound. Omar Pound and Robert Spoo argue in their edition of the letters of Pound and Cravens that "cruelty and disregard on his part are not to be found in any reliable record of the relationship."[41] Certainly, despite his occasional outbursts of frustration, Pound treated Cravens to a regular diet of admiration, engaging gossip, and gratitude. Pound also empowered himself with these letters; in becoming the master artist who would also serve his patron, he placed the patron in a rather limited role. She could support him financially, but could not direct his art; she could confirm his worth, but could not presume his love, although some of her friends felt she had reason to presume (Hilda Doolittle, for example, thought they might be "kissing"[42]).

In striking the pose of the contemporary troubadour, Pound protected himself from sexuality through eros: his "erotic medium," his transforming spiritual mystery, also kept him at arm's length from a woman who might have sought a different kind of relationship—a relationship between two subjects who mutually reinforced each other's work. Indeed, by the time of her suicide in 1912, Cravens had come to see herself as a failure; she had no "personhood" to speak of. "Her final notes," Omar Pound and Robert Spoo write, "and the testimony of her friends suggest that the predominant motive [for suicide] was an overwhelming sense of personal worthlessness and a feeling that life had become a series of insurmountable obstacles. She was surrounded by doers, accomplishers, 'fame-seekers,' while she herself was accomplishing nothing, or so she felt."[43] There is some reason to think that she, like Hilda Doolittle before her, looked forward to the possibility of marriage with Pound; the rumors circulating in 1912 that Dorothy Shakespear, neither artist nor patron, would be the chosen bride left her even less room for hope. What she had with Pound was not, truly, a relationship, but a theatrical performance with him, of course, as the director. Yet this seems not to have occurred to her until the last days of her life.

For Pound, the art of survival was not simply a matter of literary talent and gross bravado, but a much more private matter of converting the body to spiritual use. That kind of conversion, however, might well imply an equivalence between historical or fictional characters and real people in real bodies; where one could be mastered for the sake of literary or spiritual insight, the other might be mastered as well. In exploring this kind of mastery, Pound made himself a potential danger to those who befriended him or who sought his apparent expertise. Yet the danger was not all external; it also inhabited his own writing. Although his early prose and poetry assume a variety of identities and themes, the subsuming issue is the difficulty of defining one's self in a mortal world where eros may be both creator and destroyer.

"All art begins in the physical discontent (or torture) of loneliness and partiality," writes Pound in his 1908 San Trovaso notebook, adding that man's longing for an end to partialness gives him a powerful creative impetus—enough to nurture "the ancient myths of the origin of demi-gods."[44] Art is a Jacob's ladder to the gods. But human beings, and not gods, control the movement on this ladder—or rather, they give the angels volition. Out of great need, human beings create the gods, and these grateful but imperious creatures return the favor by dispersing clues to the nature of life beyond the single self. Gods and men are necessarily at odds, but great men will always confront the divine longings they have made. In this confrontation they will redeem themselves. In his first book, the 1908 *A Lume Spento,* Pound includes a number of poems that explore this notion of man's relation to the divine. Like much of the book, "Ballad for Gloom" echoes the language—or at least the conjectured style—of the knight at court; but the image of direct combat with God (as opposed to his "green knight," for example), defies the medieval convention of humility before the Lord and the reward of humility, absolution. Man fights and wins, Pound says:

> Who loseth to God as man to man
> 　　Shall win at the turn of the game.
> I have drawn my blade where the lightnings meet
> 　　But the ending is the same:
> Who loseth to God as the sword blades lose
> 　　Shall win at the end of the game.
>
> For God, our God, is a gallant foe
> 　　that playeth behind the veil
> Whom God deigns not to overthrow
> 　　Hath need of triple mail.[45]

Yes, God overthrows us to save us—that much is conventional in Pound's poem; yet the image of God as a combatant implies a wealth of early modern egoism, a healthy arrogance lying beyond the confines of convention. Man's relations with the divine are uneasy, even perilous; but man must attempt to overstep the confines of mortal convention, or else lose his chance to perceive the consolations of life—the divinely-ordained bonds between human beings of different times and places, apart from the "loneliness and partiality" of ordinary selfhood.

In theory, the self that seeks to escape these limits grows stronger. A demigod itself, it becomes aware of powers unknown to ordinary humans, and virtually seduces itself with its own glory. Pound treats this theme in several poems from the first book, including "Anima Sola" and "Plotinus." "Anima Sola" includes an epigraph from Empedokles that suggests that the speaker is "God, a sphere, round, rejoicing in complete solitude."[46] Yet, as the poem begins, the speaker appears defiant and proud. Defiance and pride are scarcely attributes of God the creator, who has nothing to defy and no reason for pride, since He created the only standard there is; these are rather attributes of a human speaker imagining himself as divine.

> Exquisite loneliness
> Bound of mine own caprice
> I fly on the wings of an unknown chord
>   That ye hear not,
>   Can not discern
> My music is weird and untamed
> Barbarous, wild, extreme,
> I fly on the note that ye hear not
> On the chord that ye can not dream.[47]

Later, Pound moves more explicitly away from the theme of Empedokles. He identifies specifically a "God-man," whose experience of this godliness makes him at once unfit for ordinary human life and free of its victimizing limitations:

> My music is your disharmony
>   Intangible, most mad,
> For the clang of a thousand cymbals
> Where the sphinx smiles o'er the sand . . .
> I kiss the nameless sign
> And the laws of my inmost being
>   Chant to the nameless shrine.[48]

Finally, Pound asserts the ultimate liberty of the "God-man": he escapes the need to compromise, to acquiesce to others' wishes, or to acknowledge an authority other than himself:

> And lo! I refuse your bidding.
> I will not bow to the expectations that ye have.
> Lo! I am gone as a red flame into the mist,
> My chord is unresolved by your counter-harmonies.[49]

The divine selfhood of Pound's God-man leads to mere joyous caprice in "Anima Sola"; in "Plotinus" it leads to creation, to selves drawn out of the self.

> As one that would draw thru the node of things,
>   Back sweeping to the vortex of the cone,
>   Cloistered about with memories, alone
> In chaos, while the waiting silence sings:
>
> Obliviate of cycles' wanderings
>   I was an atom on creation's throne
>   And knew all nothing my unconquered own.
> God! Should I be the hand upon the strings?!
>
> But I was lonely as a lonely child.
> I cried amid the void and heard no cry,
> And then for utter loneliness, made I
> New thoughts as crescent images of *me*.
> And with them was my essence reconciled
> While fear went forth from mine eternity.[50]

Pound includes a footnote in the manuscript of the poem, recalling Plotinus's teaching that "one could not dwell alone but must ever bring forth souls from himself."[51] The poem is a *tour de force* of egoism, a magnificent statement of the God-man's power to cure the loneliness of the self through the self. This sense of self is perhaps the opposite of ordinary conceptions of human selfhood; for while the ordinary human self is limited in its longevity and creative power, the God-man's self is on the order of a dynamo, constantly regenerating itself and enlarging its own being by continually redefining its multiplicities.

In *A Lume Spento,* Pound seeks ways of referring the self back to an internal source, rather than outward into a world of reciprocal selves. Of the poems that deal directly with this theme, "Scriptor Ignotus" is in some ways the most interesting, because it tips the scale of the God-man more wistfully toward the reality of man. It acknowledges, rather than simply waving away, the hardships of the single, mortal self. At the same time it also brings in the Poundian vision of eros. Love, the greatest obsession, may be both the straightest and most difficult route beyond the dying self: the erotic impulse is not simply to find sexual fulfillment with another, but to embrace, possess, and transform that other self—and one's own self as well. The idea of two subjects does not exist here; instead one finds a dominant self, whose spiritual instinct leads it to an erotic embrace of the submissive other.

Pound includes a note with the "Scriptor Ignotus," identifying the speaker as Bertold Lomax: "Bertold Lomax, English Dante scholar and mystic, died in Ferrara 1723, with his 'great epic,' still a mere shadow, a nebula crossed with some few gleams of wonder light. The lady of the poem an organist of Ferrara, whose memory has come down to us only in Lomax' notes."[52] The speaker of the poem stands in a position of power—power granted by his epic vision, which among other things will confer a Ronsardian immortality on the lady.

> "When I see thee as some poor song-bird
> Battering its wings, against this cage we call Today,
> Then would I speak comfort unto thee,
> From out the heights I dwell in, when
> That great sense of power is upon me
> And I see my greater soul-self bending
> Sibylwise with that great forty-year epic
> That you know of, yet unwrit . . .
>
> Dear, an this dream come true,
> Then shall all men say of thee
> "She 'twas that played him power at life's morn,
> And at the twilight Evensong,
> And God's peace dwelt in the mingled chords
> She drew from out the shadows of the past . . .[53]

The poem has a curiously double sense of power. On the one hand the poet, the epic-visionary, is master; that is, he controls both the words and the saga of the "great forty-year epic . . . yet unwrit," while she seems destined to become a character in that script—a creature to be moved, not the unmoved mover who is the poet. Yet as the poem continues, Pound makes clear that the beloved in this poem is as dear to the speaker as Beatrice to Dante, or as Helen to Ronsard:

> So hath the boon been given, by the poets of old time
> (Dante to Beatrice,—an I profane not—)
> Yet with my lesser power shall I not strive
>   To give it thee? . . .
>
> If so it be His will, with whom
> Are all things and through whom

> Are all things good,
> Will I make for thee and for the beauty of thy music
> A new thing
> As hath not heretofore been writ.
>   Take then my promise![54]

The balance of power shifts; in the courtly tradition the beloved becomes the one whose favor must be sought, and the poet who seeks to embrace her self—to make her a part of his own liberation, his epic—finds a wall he may not by his own will scale. He may promise her immortality, but he cannot guarantee that she will accept it; he can re-create his self, but he cannot finally re-create her self as well.

The tension implicit in this balance of power is profoundly unsettling, though it arises only slightly in this poem. It is the two-edged sword of Pound's eccentric vision of eros: the urge to expand one's own self through the love of another is also a potentially self-destructive urge, depending on the depth of the other's commitment. Eros is an affront to mastery, yet mastery cannot be attained without eros. Thus the troubadour in any century must walk a fine line, balancing his own hymns of devotion with the authentic separateness of the self to whom they are addressed. For Pound, this need for balance places a check on the Plotinian ambition of self-creation: one cannot, as it turns out, create *all* selves, and those beyond one's own power imply one's own limits, one's own less than successful move toward the God-man. *A Lume Spento* reflects an important duality—Pound's fascination with modes of escape from the single self, and his wary recognition that eros may restrict as well as permit these escapes. On the one hand it includes poems like "Plotinus"; on the other hand it includes a number of poems, cloaked in the ritual of the "trobar clus," in which Pound masters not the voice of the beloved, but the voice of the hopeful or defeated lover. The most famous of these is "Cino," but others—such as "Song" or "Na Audiart"—also reveal this double-edged mastery.

Throughout his early poems, Pound struggles with the problem of erotic mastery. In "Na Audiart," he adapts the tale of Bertran de Born and My Lady Maent of Montaignac, in which the spurned troubadour attempts to create the lady's equal by "borrowing" the attributes of other ladies and assembling them in a poem. This act of assembling an ideal lady—with its characteristic twist of shaming the Lady Audiart by forcing her to envision her aged and unlovely body—is particularly striking, given Pound's apparent will to mastery. Nothing would seem to demonstrate erotic mastery more than a man-created woman, and yet this act of mastery confirms a profound weakness: the man cannot in fact master the real self of the real woman, the woman he cannot have. In "Donzella Beata," Pound seems to reject mastery for a kind of equality: He invites a maid to boldness rather than to "tearful, fearful longing."[55] Yet this boldness by no means necessarily implies equality; Pound wishes her to use her boldness to make the first move—to come to him—rather than to await his overtures. In "Ballad Rosalind," the Lady Rosalind returns from a ten-year captivity to find that her father does not, cannot, recognize her: In his isolation he has decided that she is gone, and his decision imprisons him in an interior reality that the outside world can no longer penetrate. In the brief "Song," Pound again retreats to the world of the self, in which eros is all interior:

> Love thou thy dream
> All base love scorning,
> Love thou the wind
> And here take warning
> That dreams alone can truly be,
> For 'tis in dream I come to thee.[56]

As haunting a spell as one might wish to cast over one's beloved, the poem nevertheless admits defeat—"dreams alone can truly be"—because whatever route exists from self to self is inherently unstable and unreliable.

This simultaneous erotic anxiety and will to master appears not only in *A Lume Spento*, but in the 1908 *A Quinzaine for Yule*, the 1909 *Personae*, the 1911 *Canzoni*, and the 1912 *Ripostes*. In such poems as "To La Contessa Bianzafior (Cent. XIV)" and "Partenza di Venezia" in *A Quinzaine for This Yule*, or "Piere Vidal Old" and "Laudantes Decem Pulchritudinis Johannae Templi" from *Exultations*, or "Canzon: The Yearly Slain" from *Canzoni*, Pound repossesses and masters old voices, making them his own; yet the underlying theme of isolation, sexual anxiety, and abandonment is too clear to be a matter of happenstance or poetic exercise. This theme remains even when Pound begins a major shift of voice and method in the 1912 *Ripostes*.

To be sure, *Ripostes* has its share of the "stilted language" Pound later ridiculed. But there is also a greater critical self-consciousness about that language, and one great effort to achieve a new voice. In "Phasellus Ille," Pound gives a docent's tour of a museum piece—a *papier-mâché* editor. "Its mind was made up in 'the seventies,'" writes Pound, "Nor hath it ever since changed that concoction."[57] In this poem one finds the archaic expressions and contractions that limit Pound's own earlier poems, but here they are associated with decay. Even before Ford Madox Ford's celebrated criticism of Pound's diction, Pound himself begins to appreciate the limits of the old style. Though in *Ripostes* Pound continues his efforts to master old voices, the most powerful of these voices is no longer the troubadour's elegant or witty lament, but rather the anonymous Anglo-Saxon's recollection of adventures. Pound's rendition of "The Seafarer" appears in this book; and in such poems as Δώρια or "The Picture" one hears Pound struggling for a plainer diction, less dependent on the rhetorical flourishes left over from the Pre-Raphaelites. His greatest success in achieving this new plainness is undoubtedly "Portrait d'une Femme"; yet even in this harbinger of a new poet, one finds the old theme ascendant. The poet is fascinated with the lady, yet all his mastery is directed toward the poem itself. The lady will not be mastered. In the poem Pound becomes a kind of voyeur, yet in the end he himself must resort to a subterfuge to master the lady in language: he must disarm the woman, dismissing her and at the same time acknowledging her unattainable identity.

The Pound one meets in *Ripostes* is scarcely a heartbeat away from the Pound one thinks of as the architect of modernist poetry, the founder of Imagism and Vorticism, and the influential champion of a dozen young, talented poets. Yet in *Ripostes* one still finds Pound perplexed with the soft wall of eros, which both invites him to abandon the partiality of the single self and challenges him with the knowledge that living selves, selves outside one's own imagination, cannot be mastered in the same way as the selves of Bertrand de Born or François Villon. Again and again Pound takes as his themes the love songs of the troubadours, which either elevate women to a form of immortal art or lower their ungrateful selves almost to the grave; yet given his early prose writings, his purpose seems largely to master the voices of these dead masters, to live through them as an artist rather than merely to imitate their themes. As Pound's work proceeds, however, and his voices change, it becomes clear that these erotic themes are indeed his own preoccupations, and that as he has enlarged his identity by mastering the voices of others he has also arrived at the central, inescapable problem of eros. To love oneself is, like Plotinus, to re-create the self continually; but if one loves another, do one's intellectual acts of recreation lose their potency? Can the mastery of an art be extended to the mastery of another self? Or is the gap between art and the exterior self unbridgeable? An ordinary person might acknowledge that the mastery of an art has little in common with the nature of an erotic bond between two people, but for Pound that answer appears to have been insufficient. The danger of this confusion is most obvious in his relationship with his most devoted friend, would-be lover, and apprentice.

For H.D., Pound was the master enthraller, the father-lover whose lure was both a passionate comfort and an emblem of mortality.[58] For Pound, H.D. was the evidence of a profound uncertainty underlying his masterful persona. In H.D. he saw both the possibilities of an escape from the single self, and an enduring feud between these supposedly unified selves. To master the identity of the river-merchant's wife or of the secret admirer of Francesca was one thing;[59] to master the identity of H.D. was another, for even in the act of assisting in the birth of that identity Pound found himself up against the intractable conditions of social reality—"marriage" and "custody," as H.D. suggests in 1957.[60]

To give oneself over to eros was to assert the possibility of self-transformation; Piere Vidal, who "ran mad, as a wolf, because of his love for Loba of Penautier," represented but one variety of the chameleon self.[61] To give oneself over to marriage, however, was to place this questing self in tandem with another, under the socially ordained yoke of "custody"—one self took care of the other, one relied on the other, and at some level interdependence and a nurturing of difference were essential virtues. Pound, whose later affair with Olga Rudge helped divide his life, as Humphrey Carpenter writes, into "sealed compartments,"[62] had great difficulty in reconciling himself to these constraints. Nor could he abandon the one woman—H.D.—who seemed to him to embody both an archaic eros and a talent in need of mastery. His behavior toward H.D. between 1905 and 1908 is painfully complex: he draws close to her, he flatters her, he revises her work, he entices her, he becomes engaged to her, he breaks the engagement and leaves for Venice, he comes back to haunt her as the Cheshire cat of mentors. In conventional terms he masters only the role of the unreliable young man with poor prospects. In reality, his flight is much more intriguing. It does not simply suggest that he is unready for the erotic constraints of marriage, represented in the socially honorable guise of "commitment"; it suggests as well that he is unable to extend his will to master other selves to the one self that really matters, the living self a breath away from his own. The fact that he is unable to do this does not, however, suggest to him that his will to master is faulty, or that there is a fundamental difference between fictional and actual mastery. Pound's will to master remains intact; what ensues in his personal life is bitterness and confusion.

Because H.D.'s father burned most of the early letters between H.D. and Pound,[63] it is difficult to establish in detail the fluctuating pattern of their relationship. Yet the essence is clear, not only from H.D.'s memoir *End to Torment* but also from the surviving letters between her and Pound. In these letters, written late in life, as each of them looked back over a formidable and complex past, one finds ample evidence of Pound's will to master and his ambivalence toward it. On February 23, 1957, H.D. apologizes for her laconic letters with what seems a hopelessly gentle reproof: "There is much to say," she writes, "but you always seem to turn on me, at a moment of *rapprochement*."[64] Sandwiching this observation between praise of Pound's *Women of Trachis* and a question about his access to a new kind of phonograph, H.D. suggests that what she says is scarcely shocking: On the contrary, it is as familiar as books or records, as familiar as their past. Pound's response four days later comes in the same vein. "I dunno wot yu mean 'turn ON'/" he writes on February 27. "OBviously I believe certain things or I wdn't be here/ and seeing danger where some people pick up snakes etc/"[65] Pound frames his response with a comment about the new television on his ward at St. Elizabeths, and with a criticism of his approach to the letter—"I shd/ , of course, have started this on plain sheet of paper and enclosed printed matter/"

Though Pound rejects H.D.'s criticism, his comment includes a taunting sarcasm that encircles them both. Twisting H.D.'s words into a sexual innuendo, he plays for a moment the role of the bitter and rejected suitor. On at least three occasions he tried to "turn on" H.D., and on three occasions something intervened—either the clock, or H.D.'s father, or giggling spectators at a party.[66] These exterior interruptions mimicked an interior interruption, at least on Pound's part (and perhaps on H.D.'s as well), in the early years. Between 1905 and 1907 Pound turned to her, and turned from her. In 1912 he turned back to her again, this time more visibly as a mentor, but with the old erotic confusion intact: reincarnating her as "H.D., Imagiste," he added this identity to one of her poems "in London, in the Museum tea room, at the bottom of a typed sheet, now slashed with his creative pencil, 'Cut this out, shorten this line.'"[67] As Pound began to exert himself forcefully over H.D., his exertions had a furtively tragic component: he hung back, controlling and yet unable truly to act. He could not manage the kind of erotic mastery he managed over historical characters, and—more painfully— he could not permit himself some actual conjunction with this woman, this other self or subject.

It may have been that H.D. did her part to increase the confusion. Her lightly-fictionalized memoir *HERmione* explores the life of a young woman who feels both liberated and trapped by her image of Ezra Pound and what he represents as a suitor. Then, too, her increasing awareness of her bisexuality added a conscious mythic dimension to her life, a quest that fell beyond the comforts of conventional behavior. Yet when H.D. planned to accompany her soulmate Frances Gregg on her honeymoon with Louis Wilkinson in 1912, it was Pound who stepped in to forbid the arrangement. Part brother, part thwarted lover, he headed off H.D. before she reached Victoria Station:

> I found Ezra waiting for me on the pavement outside the house, off Oxford Circus, where I had a room. His appearance was again unexpected, unpredictable. He began, "I as your nearest male relation . . . ," and hailed a taxi. He pushed me in. He banged with his stick, pounding (*Pounding*), as I have said. "You are not going with them." I had seen them the day before at their hotel, off Victoria Station. It was all arranged. . . . "There is a vague chance that the Egg," (he called her), "may be happy. You will spoil everything." Awkwardly, at Victoria Station, I explained to a married Frances, with a long tulle travelling veil, that I wasn't coming. I had changed my mind. Awkwardly, the husband handed me back the cheque that I had made out for my ticket. Glowering and savage, Ezra waited till the train pulled out.[68]

Though confused and ambitious, Pound was as yet neither reckless nor given to harm-doing. His attention directed itself, in others' lives, to moments when love might lead to catastrophe. But it is important to see how he acts by negation rather than affirmation. He affirms nothing about H.D.'s erotic need; he affirms nothing about the comfort she finds in Gregg's sexuality or in her mutually sustaining relationship with Gregg. Pound cannot know that Gregg is the precursor of Winifred Ellerman, "Bryher," who in later years will become H.D.'s companion and lover; yet Pound might well see that what H.D. is seeking is something even the world of poetry and art cannot give. She seeks the love of a like-minded companion or, failing that, the master who can turn her into her own soul without turning her into a fiction, an abstraction. Yet Pound does not see this. He cannot be the equal subject, the interdependent other, but neither can he be the master he envisions himself as being. He holds back, never quite resolving the scenes that, with the best of intentions, he sets in motion.

Repeatedly—in 1907, 1912, 1919, and even in later years—Pound may have had the opportunity to fulfill his erotic fantasy of something beyond the single self. H.D. describes herself as a willing participant in this experiment, and her later sadness at his withdrawal is the sadness of one who knows her suitor's masks too well.

> We were curled up together in an armchair when my father found us. I was "gone." I wasn't there. I disentangled myself. I stood up; Ezra stood beside me. It seems we must have swayed, trembling. But I don't think we did. "Mr. Pound, I don't say there was anything wrong...." Mr. Pound, it was all wrong. You turn into a Satyr, a Lynx, and the girl in your arms (Dryad, you called her), for all her fragile, not yet lost virginity, is *Maenad, bassarid*....
>
>   Mr. Pound, with your magic, your "strange spells of old deity," why didn't you complete the metamorphosis?[69]

It may also be true that H.D. herself, in asking Pound to "complete the metamorphosis," adopts a role of subservience that can only further mislead a young man intrigued with mastery. Whether or not H.D.'s longing is free from implied self-deprecation, however, her need for metamorphosis—and Pound's—suffers beneath their confusion. Certainly Pound repeatedly gives evidence of the conflict between erotic contact and mastery. When H.D. gives birth to her daughter, Perdita, in 1919, Pound is present during the lying-in. H.D. recalls the occasion in a mock-dialogue with analyst Erich Heydt, as she tries to understand Pound's conflicting messages: "'And he came to you in the Nursing Home, you said, and wanted you to have his child—.' 'Well, wanted the child that I was about to have to be his, to have been his, "My only real criticism is that this is not my child."'"[70]

It is, of course, possible that H.D. misrecalls Pound's language on this occasion, but if she is accurate the word *criticism* speaks vividly here: At a liminal moment in H.D.'s life, Pound responds to her as a work of art, not as a person. She is the imaginative identity he ought to have mastered; perhaps, in his own mind, he did master her; and yet this child, this clear new life, is not of his making. Richard Aldington married her, slept with her, fought with her, made love to her; Cecil Gray made love to her, fathering Perdita. Pound cannot accept the finality of this physical creation. For this to have happened without his sexual involvement is somehow wrong, unartistic. He confesses to H.D. that he wanted to father their child, but the confession is full of a kind of coercive longing rather than direct passion. Many years pass before H.D. escapes the spell of this longing: in fact, one of the structural principles of the 1957 *End to Torment* is her evolving vision of "the Child" she and Pound should have created, which she identifies simply as *"eros."*[71]

For H.D., eros is the psychosexual guarantor of life, which brings together discrete identities without merging them. Ultimately, though not in her early years, H.D. saw the apparent human master as a witting or unwitting servant to his deeper self. Pound, on the other hand, saw this "Child" eros as a problem precisely because it lay beyond his control. Fundamentally it manifested itself as physical, as "loneliness and partiality,"[72] which propelled him toward his quest for an escape from the single self. Yet H.D. recognized an eternal truth, and an essential individual tragedy, which Pound could not escape. She suffers, but he suffers as well, though he may be the agent of both forms of pain.

Pound's incarceration in St. Elizabeths Hospital between 1945 and 1958 remains a political and psychological controversy, but in one sense it was strikingly consistent with the rest of his life: Pound the man, the physical being, was immobilized. It was, of course, possible for his acquaintances and admirers to visit him, but these visits were on the order of intellectual pilgrimages, for Pound could only exert his presence over those who chose him first. They could choose him; he could not choose them or could choose them only by negation, by refusing to see them. In one sense, then, Pound's incarceration represents the underlying flaw in his will to master—the flaw of physique, of fleshy, human independence. The soul *is* isolate, yet for some the body is a gift: that isolation itself defines the limits and necessities of life, as it did for H.D. For Pound, however, the body ultimately becomes a kind of curse, even though—when intellectualized, when admired in the Praxitelean mold—it assumes a divine character.

Bodies are stubborn temples: they house souls in private splendor, along with secrets no exterior master can fully fathom. Pound, as late as 1959, still resists this reality. It can be no accident that his letters read like cantos, for the form offers him some protection from an apparent reality he cannot reconstruct. This reality consists largely in the alleged intransigence of his friends; unlike the imagined identities in the *Cantos,* the real people do not extend Pound's own identity. They seem simply to drag it down. In a letter to H.D. dated May 10, probably 1949, Pound complains of William Carlos Williams's "TOTAL lack of any sense of humor" and implies that Williams has misunderstood Pound's essential mission;[73] in an undated letter, probably from 1958, he expands the theme: "P.S. as most of the male eng/ and am writers of our generation either live at level of farm animals, guitar yodlers, or with total pusillanimity avoid all vital subjects, I happen to wonder in passing whether from and in Zurich you have ever heard of, let alone read, any author worth attention."[74] Pound's doubt even about H.D., who may— as far as he knows—hear of great works without bothering to read them, suggests the extent of his alienation from his old companion. Yet the alienation grows wider than this. On June 26, probably 1959, Pound writes H.D. from Rapallo:

> My friends are such chaRRRming people, but inefficient as coons at a clam bake.
>> and NO coherence among 'em.
> AND none of them ever contradicts a damn lie issued by the crablice and Dexter White, Og. Reid gang.
>> the supposition being that I can answer ALL the damn swine and cimini . . .[75]

Pound's friends do not cohere, either among themselves or with him; as far as Pound can tell, they have spun off into their own vortices, and will not come to his defense. In a letter from September 8, 1959, Pound again sounds this theme:

> Not since Brigit [Patmore], Richard [Aldington], the four of us, has there been any harmony around me.
> their irritations with each other used to amuse me,
>> never seeming to have
> any very serious root. . . .
>> What, damn it, do you think is the reason why my friends don't get on *with each other.?*[76]

Given Pound's response to H.D., it would make sense to conjecture that Pound's friends do not get along to his satisfaction because they have tired of competing both for his praise and abuse. Or more than this: they have grown into themselves, beyond Pound's vision for them, and found in Pound a friend who could not follow. Pound, whom H.D.

has said turns on her at the moment of rapprochement, gives ample evidence of this in his later letters. In a letter dated May 31, probably 1954, Pound offers his blunt reading of both the failings of western culture and of H.D.; yet the conclusion is an odd combination of insult and tease, as if Pound trusted neither one nor the other:

> I cant blow everybodies' noses for 'em.
> Have felt yr/ vile Freud all bunk/ but the silly Xristers
> bury all their good authors/ . . .
> And yu hv/ prob lost yr/ latin (if yu ever had much)
> by hellenism . . .
> You got into the wrong pig stye , ma chère. But not too late to climb
> out.[77]

Behind Pound's grumbling is a sense of hopelessness: Freud is bunk, the Christians bury their good authors, and H.D. herself has forsaken Roman insights for "the wrong pig stye" of Hellenism. Yet the presumption here is striking even for Pound, considering that he admits in a letter that probably dates from the fall of 1959 that "In fact I dont know much of what has gone on in your head for the past 40 years."[78] His attitude in the 1954 letter is scarcely an exception. On April 11, 1957, for example, he resurrects the old charge, though in more muted language:

> Very sorry to hear you have had a set back.
> [Norman Holmes] Pearson writes that a EPizl might divert
> you , but wotter'ell am I to write ,
>   you never seem to git
> aboard anything
> that interests me. IF I send you name of book worth
> reading
> , I have no idea you wd/ bother to get it , et cetty
> ROAR.[79]

Although Pound's tone here is playful, gentle, his implication is clear: H.D. is an unreliable correspondent, an unfaithful reader, a poet of limited intellect. Pound suggests that he has left her behind; ironically, the situation may be the other way around. Pound's impression of H.D. contrasts sharply with the content of H.D.'s actual letters, which frequently refer not only to her own work but to Pound's; she mentions his new *Cantos* and translations of his work into German, she tries to send him newspaper clippings about his work when she can find them, she tells him about articles of his that she has read. Clearly she is far from the unreliable and unappreciative friend Pound implies, even though she suffers from Pound's own fickleness and faltering.

For Pound does falter as a mentor—not because he is not a brilliant poet, but because he cannot carry his mode of operation, his will to master, from the world of the imagination to the world of the living body. In the *Cantos* he is master—even, ironically, of his own downfall in the *Pisan Cantos,* although the pathos of those poems foreshadows his own admission that he cannot lift the "great ball of crystal"[80] he has created. Nevertheless he has spun himself into an astonishing array of identities, and his "tale of the tribe" has much of the myth of the eternal return in it. In the world, however, he confronts loneliness and partiality; he is arrogant, aggressive, disappointed, bitter. At some level he himself recognizes this failure. When H.D. writes to tell him about her memoir of their relationship, which at Norman Holmes Pearson's suggestion she has entitled *End to Torment,* Pound responds pathetically, "Torment title excellent, but optimistic."[81] He has not ceased to torment her, or himself.

Whether H.D. ever confronts Pound with this question is unclear, although it is clear that, at one point, H.D. finally spurned him. In his letter of September 8, 1959, which focuses in general on his alienation from his friends, Pound recalls this rejection: "You also said," he writes to H.D., "not if you were the last man."[82] As we will see in the next chapter, Pound's closest apprentice—or rather, the apprentice who most clearly seemed to invite his effort to escape the confines of the single self—finally breaks away from his spell, though she remains faithful to his memory. Her story is one of triumph. It may be that, from an artistic standpoint, Pound's story is one of triumph as well: the *Cantos* are, to use a phrase that Richard Wilbur coined to describe Hart Crane's *The Bridge,* "a magnificent botch of a poem."[83] Yet if the *Cantos* reflect Pound's will to master current and historical identities beyond himself, Pound's own life reflects a wider defeat. The mentorship he brought to those imagined identities, as he marshalled them and organized them and explored them ideogrammatically, could not survive the stubborn humanity of the real world.

Notes

1. T. S. Eliot, *The Waste Land: A Facsimile and Transcript of the Original Drafts Including the Annotations of Ezra Pound,* ed. Valerie Eliot (New York: Harcourt, Brace and World, 1971).

2. T. S. Eliot, *The Letters of T. S. Eliot,* vol. 1, 1898–1922, ed. Valerie Eliot (New York: Harcourt, Brace Jovanovich, 1988), p. 81.

3. Eliot, *Letters,* p. 81.

4. Eliot, *Letters,* p. 100.

5. Eliot, *Letters,* p. 101.

6. Eliot, *Letters,* p. 106n.

7. Eliot, *Letters,* p. 153n.

8. Eliot, *Letters,* p. 179n.

9. Eliot, *Letters,* pp. 266, 296n.

10. Eliot, *Letters,* p. 385; see also Ezra Pound, *Selected Letters, 1907–1941,* ed. D. D. Paige (New York: New Directions, 1950), pp. 172–73.

11. Humphrey Carpenter, *A Serious Character: The Life of Ezra Pound* (New York: Delta Books, 1988), p. 79.

12. Carpenter, p. 171.

13. Peter Ackroyd, *Ezra Pound* (New York: Thames and Hudson, 1987), p. 24.

14. Jessica Benjamin, *The Bonds of Love: Psychoanalysis, Feminism, and the Problem of Domination* (New York: Pantheon, 1988), p. 47.

15. Pound, *Selected Letters,* p. 210.

16. Kevin Oderman, *Ezra Pound and the Erotic Medium* (Durham, N.C.: Duke University Press, 1986).

17. Oderman, p. 7.

18. Oderman, p. 14.

19. Benjamin, *The Bonds of Love,* p. 29.

20. Ezra Pound, *Guide to Kulchur* (New York: New Directions, 1952), pp. 144–45.

21. Ezra Pound, *The Spirit of Romance* (New York: New Directions, 1968), unnumbered preface.

22. Carpenter, p. 238.

23. Omar Pound and A. Walton Litz, eds., *Ezra Pound and Dorothy Shakespear; Their Letters, 1909–1914* (New York: New Directions, 1984), p. 56.

24. Omar Pound and Robert Spoo, eds., *Ezra Pound and Margaret Cravens: A Tragic Friendship, 1910–1912* (Durham, N.C.: Duke University Press, 1988), p. 6.

25. Pound and Litz, p. 87.

26. Pound and Litz, p. 55.

27. Pound and Litz, p. 38.

28. Pound and Litz, p. 118.

29. There are different shades of opinion on the importance of Pound's naming of "H.D., Imagiste." "H.D. began her official career as a writer with a crisis of naming," Rachel Blau DuPlessis observes, referring to the British Museum story (*H.D.: The Career of That Struggle* [Bloomington: Indiana University Press, 1986], p. 6), but DuPlessis also notes that H.D. later used various pseud-

onyms, and that "over her whole career, she conceived of some of her work as not-H.D." Humphrey Carpenter accepts Richard Aldington's assertion that neither he nor H.D. was "very keen on the label" (Carpenter, p. 187). "Perhaps Ezra thought Doolittle too ridiculous a name for a poet, though Shaw's *Pygmalion,* which ever afterwards made it seem a little absurd, did not receive its first performance until the next year, 1913." At the same time, Carpenter suggests that H.D. may have seen the name as an expedience, a concession to Pound. "It was only through [Pound]," Carpenter quotes Aldington as saying, that we could get our poems into . . . *Poetry*" (Carpenter, p. 187).

30. Pound and Litz, p. 21.
31. Pound and Spoo, p. 93.
32. Carpenter, p. 155.
33. Pound and Spoo, pp. 85, 95.
34. Pound and Spoo, p. 11.
35. Pound and Spoo, p. 17.
36. Pound and Spoo, p. 26.
37. Pound and Spoo, p. 41.
38. Pound and Spoo, pp. 49–50.
39. Pound and Spoo, pp. 54–55.
40. Pound and Spoo, p. 52.
41. Pound and Spoo, p. 113.
42. Pound and Spoo, p. 112.
43. Pound and Spoo, p. 114.
44. Quoted in Louis L. Martz, "Introduction," *Collected Early Poems of Ezra Pound* (New York: New Directions, 1976), p. xiv.
45. Pound, *Early Poems,* p. 39.
46. Pound, *Early Poems,* p. 19.
47. Pound, *Early Poems,* pp. 19–20.
48. Pound, *Early Poems,* p. 20.
49. Pound, *Early Poems,* p. 21.
50. Pound, *Early Poems,* p. 36.
51. See Pound's note to this poem in *Early Poems,* p. 296.
52. Pound, *Early Poems,* p. 26.
53. Pound, *Early Poems,* pp. 24–25.
54. Pound, *Early Poems,* pp. 24–25.
55. Pound, *Early Poems,* pp. 26–27.
56. Pound, *Early Poems,* p. 46.
57. Pound, *Early Poems,* p. 186.
58. H.D. identifies Pound as a passionate (though ultimately chaste) lover in *End to Torment,* ed. Norman Holmes Pearson and Michael King (New York: New Directions, 1979), pp. 12, 17, 54–55; she identifies him with her father on p. 48.

59. Ezra Pound, "The River-merchant's Wife: A Letter," *Selected Poems of Ezra Pound* (New York: New Directions, 1957), p. 52; "Francesca," *Collected Early Poems of Ezra Pound,* p. 121.

60. H.D., *End to Torment,* p. 47.

61. Ezra Pound, "Piere Vidal Old," *Collected Early Poems,* pp. 109–11.

62. Carpenter, P. 474.

63. H.D., *End to Torment,* p. 38.

64. Letter from H.D. to Ezra Pound, Feb. 23, 1957, in the collection of the Center for the Study of Ezra Pound and His Contemporaries, the Beinecke Library, Yale University.

65. Letter from Ezra Pound to H.D., Feb. 27, 1957, the Beinecke Library.

66. See H.D., *End to Torment,* pp. 12, 17, 54–55.

67. H.D., *End to Torment,* p. 40.

68. H.D., *End to Torment,* pp. 8–9.

69. H.D., *End to Torment,* p. 17.

70. H.D., *End to Torment,* p. 30.

71. H.D., *End to Torment,* pp. 51–52.

72. Quoted in Martz, "Introduction," *Collected Early Poems.*

73. Letter from Ezra Pound to H.D., May 10, 1949, the Beinecke Library.

74. Letter from Ezra Pound to H.D., Jan. 5, 1958, the Beinecke Library.

75. Letter from Ezra Pound to H.D., June 26, 1959, the Beinecke Library.

76. Letter from Ezra Pound to H.D., Sept. 8, 1959, the Beinecke Library.

77. Letter from Ezra Pound to H.D., May 31, 1954, the Beinecke Library.

78. Undated letter (probably 1959; opening salutation "Dear H.D.") from Ezra Pound to H.D., the Beinecke Library.

79. Letter from Ezra Pound to H.D., Apr. 11, 1957, the Beinecke Library.

80. Ezra Pound, "Canto CXVI," *The Cantos of Ezra Pound* (New York: New Directions, 1972), p. 795.

81. Undated letter from Ezra Pound to H.D. (opening salutation is "Dearest H"), probably written between 1957 and 1959, the Beinecke Library.

82. Letter from Ezra Pound to H.D., May 31, 1954.

83. Richard Wilbur, *Responses: Prose Pieces, 1953–1976* (New York: Harcourt Brace Jovanovich, 1976), p. 126.

2

I Was Dead and Am Alive Again
Hilda Doolittle as Apprentice

The importance of the public persona and the concealed private life is something one tends to equate with modernist writers. Though this is not entirely true—Yeats's autobiography and Williams's autobiography dignify the exception—it is true enough to raise curiosity. T. S. Eliot had a morbid fear of biographers, and Pound avoided private revelations until relatively late in his life. "I have no inclination to start dying before it is necessary," Pound wrote in 1927 to a correspondent who urged him to begin his literary autobiography.[1] One might argue that Pound permitted disclosures about his private life—the publication of his selected letters in 1950 and his correspondence with James Joyce in 1967[2]—only when his public persona had crumbled. In the wake of its demise one would have to seek redemption in one's private as well as one's public past, and Pound saw this as an inescapable process. Moreover, his willingness to give access to his so-called private world—a world that included many now-celebrated authors—could be seen as a way of re-creating a vivid public persona, in which Pound became once again—as Horace Gregory said—"the minister without portfolio of the arts."[3]

In any case, that public persona counted most; the private realm was secondary. This was true as well for Yvor Winters, who along with his wife Janet Lewis burned virtually all of their essential correspondence in the 1930s. In Eliot's and Winters's cases, particularly, one sees the dread of personal interpretation, the fear of gossip; what matters is the art. When a reader's interest is turned from the art to the person, the reader loses sight of what mattered most to the artist; the reader becomes a socially sanctioned voyeur. This, at least, is the dominant modernist view. But the other side, the unexplored implication, is equally clear: the artist's personal life informs and directs his work, and may well involve issues of eros and power that affect the words on the page. These issues become particularly important in the life and work of Hilda Doolittle, whom Pound named H.D.

Of all the modernist writers, H.D. did the most to make her life her subject. "She herself is the writing," she says of Helen, her own persona, in her last volume of poetry, *Helen in Egypt*.[4] Although one might argue that any writer's work, no matter how furtive, is a form of autobiography, H.D. drew enormous strength from that thinly veiled autobiographical mode: she exorcised the demons of selfhood in her writing. Two of her novels—*HERmione*, written in 1927, and *Bid Me to Live*, written in 1939—precisely explore the upheavals of her early life, incorporating the central players—Ezra Pound, Frances Josepha Gregg, Richard Aldington, D. H. Lawrence, Cecil Gray—with little more than changes of name. In *Nights*, written when H.D. was in Switzerland in the 1930s, the narrator explores the suicide of a bisexual woman, a fiction that nevertheless left H.D. room to explore the two traits Sigmund Freud told her she had to hide—"one that you were a girl, the other that you were a boy."[5] In *The Gift*, she records her experiences in London in the blitz—the apparent nadir of barbarity, where nevertheless some psychic redemption from the past came to her aid. And in her two most celebrated autobiographical works—*Tribute to Freud*, written in 1933 and 1944, and the 1958 *End to Torment*—she records her experiences with Freud and with her first fiancé, Ezra Pound.

Given this unusual emphasis on autobiography, it may seem curious that, until the 1944 collection *Trilogy*, H.D.'s poetry is profoundly unautobiographical. This statement, perhaps, is peculiar, since one can of course read essential details of H.D.'s experience from the poems. Yet more than any other modern poet, H.D. sets her poetry in a cultural context that constrains its energy and subject matter in specific ways. This is the culture of classical Greece, directing the motion of her poems until the outset of World War II. As H.D. writes in a 1934 letter to her companion Bryher (Winifred Ellerman),

> My work is creative and reconstructive, war or no war, and if I can get across the Greek spirit at its highest I am helping the world, and the future. It is the highest spiritual neutrality. . . .
>
> The Greek will hold me to my centre, now whether here or in London.[6]

Early critics of H.D.'s work concentrated on her debt to the imagist movement and particularly to Pound's 1913 manifesto "A Few Don'ts." She found herself too regularly defending herself against the charge that she never escaped that early influence. Yet a much more intriguing problem lies in H.D.'s choice of classical Greece as an intellectual and spiritual refuge. Why, when her prose writings show her keen personal wrestlings with sexuality, submission, and spiritual liberty, do her poems disguise these same wrestlings, or set them in a context that seems to defy the personhood of H.D.?

The answer, or at least one answer, has a great deal to do with Pound and with the appeal of the public persona in a paternal culture. In H.D.'s early poetry, one finds a voice seeking refuge in a kind of expanded imagism—a will to the truth of the moment that, though always changing, always endures. That refuge, to some degree, mitigates the force of the sexually hierarchical world against which H.D. must define her identity. And yet these poems pay homage to that world as well. They adopt its fundamental, classical mythologies, its heroes, its "great works." Later, in the mid twenties, as H.D. moves toward the denied voice—the voice of the woman in ancient Greece—she maintains her poetic explorations within the confines of that classical mythology. Beyond the poetry, she expands her exploration of spiritual mysteries to include occult traditions that emphasize the power of both women and men; she begins to fracture the orthodoxies, as Susan Stanford Friedman explains: "The orthodox traditions created a masculine imagery of God and used this ideology to justify taboos against women in the priesthood and to rationalize cultural beliefs in male superiority. The heterodox mystical traditions, on the other hand, legitimized the place of women as symbol in the divine pantheon."[7]

Yet these heterodox traditions reveal themselves only belatedly in H.D.'s poetry. In the later poems H.D. begins to reconstruct mythologies and adapt characters—Helen foremost among them—in ways that signal her slow withdrawing of consent from the paternal world she had long fought. At the end she no longer fights; she re-creates her life. For many earlier years, however, she labored under what Rachel Blau Duplessis has called "romantic thralldom." Unequal to the paradigmatic male model of achievement, she too often worshipped it, and in doing so left little room for her own emerging identity.[8] In examining her early work, and her own paradigms of enthrallment, one can see the matrix for the failure of reciprocal or, as Jessica Benjamin says, intersubjective relationships: a gender-based sense of subjugation haunts this poet. At the same time, one can see the distinctive role of H.D.'s poetry as a mediator between unresolvable paradoxes. Life, which appears in such ugly splendor in her novels and memoirs, is compressed into the meditative distance of art *via* poetry. The poetry is at once a departure from the conflicts of life and a full admission of their authority, the ultimate revelation of concealment. Through her poetry—which defines her as an artist until the publication of her prose works late in her life—H.D. anchors herself in the world of the public persona. This concealing persona also suggests again the fundamental conflict between the authority of a tradition and the authority of personhood. Where knowing knowledge is raised above knowing self and other, some kind of subjugation of the self becomes inevitable.

Like "eros" and "mentorship," "romantic thralldom" is a potentially ambiguous term. DuPlessis, however, defines it succinctly: "Romantic thralldom is an all-encompassing, totally defining love between apparent unequals. The lover has the power of conferring self-worth and purpose upon the loved one. Such love is possessive, and while those enthralled feel it completes and even transforms them, dependency rules. The eroticism of romantic love, born of this unequal relationship, may depend for its satisfaction upon dominance and submission."[9]

By whom is H.D. first possessed? A Freudian would point to the father, and would not, on the whole, be wrong. An austere man, professor of astronomy and mathematics at Lehigh University and then at the University of Pennsylvania, Charles Doolittle lived in a somewhat abstracted and unexamined world of patriarchy. His dominating presence in the family derived not so much from a will to dominate as from the combined cultural authority of his career, his reputation, and his supporting actress—Helen Wolle, his second wife and H.D.'s mother. William Carlos Williams, who often visited the family in their Upper Darby house near Philadelphia in 1905 and 1906, recalled that H.D.'s mother "led a harrassed life and showed it: with her hair drawn tightly back like all capable women. . . . When they were at dinner and Mrs. Doolittle noticed that the Professor wished to speak, she would quickly announce: Your father is about to speak! Silence immediately ensued. Then in a slow and deep voice, and with his eyes fixed on nothing, as Ezra Pound said, just above, nothing nearer than the moon, he said what he had to say. It was a disheartening process."[10] One pleased the professor by demonstrating a talent in his own field, as his son Eric did; Eric, who in 1909 had a part of the family home to himself as an assistant at the university, excelled in mathematics. H.D. was not a scientist; she failed at her father's work. "Conic sections would whirl forever round her for she had grappled with the biological definition, transferred to mathematics, found the whole thing untenable. She had found the theorum untenable until she came to conic sections and then Dr. Barton-Furness had failed her, failed her . . . they had all failed her. Science . . . failed her . . . and she was good for nothing."[11] Here, as transformed into the autobiographical fiction of *HERmione,* the double-edged word-play is clear. Hermione's mathematics professor fails her by giving her a failing grade, but also fails her by not permitting himself a context in which to respond to her own humanity. She is an "F" to him, nothing more. In this sense, H.D. felt betrayed by the wider realm of her education and family: from them she regularly received "F"'s, though she did not know why.

She was devoted to her father with an uncomprehending anger. She bore a physical resemblance to him, "with her long feet and hands, her luminous probing eyes."[12] She found him unreachable and yet could not reject him; in analysis with Freud in 1933, she recalled repeatedly that she was her father's favorite child.[13] In her 1943 volume *The Gift* she re-invokes him with an appraising insight whose awe the years had tempered:

> There are all these things on the table and Ida is still here and it will get late. The clock will strike. Papa will want his late-evening supper, maybe he wants it now. "I'm going out again," said Papa, as if he knew what I was thinking, but he looked round the table, as if he came from another world, another country. . . . He goes out to look at the stars. . . .
> We would have asked him more, but it's better not to have things like that explained; Papa does not explain them. . . .
> We would not want to change our father for anyone else . . . but that is what you can do.[14]

In hindsight, H.D. observes pointedly that one can change one's father—one can shift patriarchal allegiances. From a psychological point of view this makes sense. Moving beyond the narrow social world that the father defines, one nevertheless carries one's unresolved feelings toward that august authority. One simply transfers them to other men. But there is another force at work here as well. It is not only the unreachable person of the father whom H.D. reveres and fears; it is that which makes him unreachable, that body and tradition of knowledge that defines him as an intellectual male. Professor Doolittle's way of knowing, not simply his abstracted manner, makes him desirable and dangerous. He knows the world through numbers, scientific observations, and precedents; he knows the world through the intellectual domain that typically has been reserved for men. It is, H.D. believes, an initiating knowledge, and through it one gains access to mysteries— mysteries that are better not explained to children like H.D. who, in any case, have been told they are not "gifted."[15]

When H.D. shifts allegiance from her biological father to other fathers, she is not simply seeking alternatives for an extended Oedipal crisis. She is seeking, rather, a mode of knowledge that, because it also acquires social power, must be superior to her mode of knowledge. Knowledge of abstractions, hierarchies, and orders necessarily supercedes knowledge of people and their reciprocities, which is what H.D. knows in *HERmione.* H.D. falls to romantic thralldom not simply out of sexual desire, or out of a desire to gain the unreachable father, but out of a will to gain access to powerful knowledge. She must know what will give her power, what will liberate her from being "ungifted" and "good for nothing." Yet this desired form of knowing, an archetypal *animus,* denies her own necessary knowledge and places her in the untenable position of dichotomized or divided selfhood. The one mode of knowledge—abstract, hierarchical, and conferring power—opposes her sexuality and places her at the mercy of men who demean her. The other mode of knowing, the reciprocity that affirms each knower's identity, leads her toward the lesbianism that assuages but does not heal the dichotomy of knowledge. One sees this pain vividly in *HERmione* and *Bid Me to Live;* one sees it tangentially in the work that is supposed to be H.D.'s greatest achievement—the achievement by which she is to be remembered—her poetry. The poetry most clearly demonstrates H.D.'s thralldom because it evolves out of her submission to an authority beyond herself. The novels record a different H.D. because, in essence, they *were* written by a different H.D. To understand this difference, however, it is essential to take up the matter of thralldom and its bearing on the question of originality in the early poems.

———

The question of whether a work of art, or a human being, is "original" ascribes a particular virtue to originality. The original creation is something that has never existed before, a testament to the endlessly regenerative power of eros, a possible argument for a kind of immortality. And yet, of course, the word itself is a pun, for what it asks for is a rootedness in origins—origins that psychoanalysis would surely attribute, not to something invented out of whole cloth, but to something archetypal and shared. This may be more true for Jungian than for Freudian analysis, yet the power of the unconscious to manifest itself through cultural symbols is crucial to both forms of psychoanalysis. What matters is not fame or brilliance; what matters is the character of one's vision of archetypes or other symbolic representations of reality. Contravening for a time the "flagrant inauthenticity"[16] of ordinary life, this vision allows one to record an experience in congruence with whatever elemental intuitions share the heart and mind.

Yet this question of archetypes is also a question of knowledge. The experience of an archetype may be private and incontrovertible, but the concept of the archetype—the approach to knowing that it represents—raises again the issue of dominance and submission. The principle of a mystery, of an undiscovered but potentially liberating mode of knowledge, is not restricted to gender. Both sexes need release from the ignorance and miseries of the unexamined life. Yet the way one structures one's approach to this mystery will affect both the content of the mystery and the independence of the knower. To pursue some version of primary experience by tracking back through the annals of culture—by exploring, for example, the modes of rationality and irrationality in ancient Greece, as H.D. did—is to grant those annals a shaping force in one's thinking: one knows oneself primarily in relation to that body of knowledge. This is not an insignificant "originality," a return to origins, but it raises essential questions: are these "origins" germane to this particular knower? Or are they, in some way, culturally sanctioned or defined so that the knower is always subordinate to the known, the tradition?

In both her prose and her poetry, H.D. suggests that thralldom to knowledge is tantamount to erotic submission. Yet the prose finds its voice in an originality that resides within the contemporary experience of the author—not within an external body of knowledge. This is possible in part because H.D. tended to reserve her prose as a private means of self-exploration. *HERmione* and *End to Torment* were not published during H.D.'s lifetime; *Bid Me to Live* appeared only in her last year of life; *Nights* was published pseudononymously; *Tribute to Freud* was not published until 1956, when H.D. was 70. By implication, then, H.D.'s prose was not a means by which she defined herself to an audience; it was not a public performance.

Her poetry is a very different story. It was her poetry that linked her to Pound—who first told her her poems were "rotten"[17] and then reincarnated her as "H.D., Imagiste"; it was her poetry that made her public reputation as an artist, thereby giving her a certain creative credibility among a small group of savants. And it is her poetry that most strongly registers a debt to a mode of knowledge and a tradition, a tradition in which she is often cautioned not to go too far. She acquires the cultural vigor of ancient Greece as a means of rescuing herself from an American identitylessness. Yet, as a woman, she finds resistance to her choice of rescuers. In *Bid Me to Live,* she records a comment from D. H. Lawrence, known as "Frederico" in the novel, about her version of Orpheus and Eurydice: "How can you know what Orpheus feels?" Lawrence asks. "It's your part to be woman, the woman vibration, Eurydice should be enough."[18]

This exchange is, in a sense, the perfect problem for the classical mode of knowing. It assures that H.D. will never quite be successful and guarantees what she learned so long ago from her family and what she rediscovers in analysis with Freud: she is a failure because she is female. In this return to her self-proclaimed "origins," she progressively loses her originality, because she must conceal herself behind the potent mask of erotic submission: the modes of speech she appropriates for her poetry belong to men. Much later, beyond even the seemingly constructive thralldom of Freudian analysis, H.D. invents a method of working back through her experience that enables her to align the private voice with the public persona. In a sense she invents her own body of knowledge, becoming— as Susan Stanford Friedman has argued—her own analyst, a father and mother figure to her own self.[19] At this point the public mask of failure begins to disintegrate. One can see the high cost of enthrallment to that public mask simply by looking at the early poems.

One of the central weaknesses of the early poems is also, at least initially, one of their distinguishing strengths: the haunted voice, alternately wounded and defiant, adapts the imagist mode to define itself as a style. Thus, in the 1916 "Sea Rose," for example, one finds virtue ascribed to that which is "despised and rejected of men." The old biblical theme is reincarnated in an image of a rose by another name.

> Rose, harsh rose,
> marred and with stint of petals,
> meagre flower, thin,
> sparse of leaf,

more precious
than a wet rose
single on a stem—
you are caught in the drift.

Stunted, with small leaf,
you are flung on the sand,
you are lifted
in the crisp sand
that drives the wind.

Can the spice-rose
drip such acrid fragrance
hardened in a leaf?[20]

In this poem one sees the flaw behind arguments for H.D.'s debt to imagism. Like many of H.D.'s poems, this one is not so much about image as about value. It does incorporate significant, allusive images, so that it might be seen to fulfill Pound's dictum of "an intellectual and emotional complex in an instant of time."[21] Yet the most important shift is not visual. This occurs between the first and second stanza, where the sea rose—after enduring the expected criticism—becomes suddenly "precious." What is fundamental here is not the image of the sea rose, or even its juxtaposition with some striking counter-image, but the metaphorical value of the rose. In drawing on this metaphorical value, H.D. might be seen to invoke an ancient strength in her poetry, even as she grounds it in the compressed language of imagism. In this sense one might argue that her poetry surpasses the narrow confines of imagism, managing a fusion of perception and interpretation.

Yet this reading is unsatisfactory, paying too little heed to the enormous weight of value running throughout the poem. H.D. lavishes a sympathy on this rose out of all proportion to the subject itself, out of all proportion to imagist expectations. This is a poem about the very human experience of being different, being embattled, and being admired. But where do we locate these highly charged observations? In the sea rose? How can the rose bear this attribution of human feeling? It cannot; we are not talking about a sea rose. But, in a sense, we are also not really talking about anything, because the poem defies its real subject with its imagistic subject. The poem has love and outrage, but we are not really sure where the outrage is directed and who has received the love. There is more than a trace of irony in referring to this as an "imagist" poem, for it is the image—the device thrown up in front of reality—that conceals the real power of the poem. Pound's movement was meant to strip reality bare, not disguise it; yet in this consummate imagist performance, a work of public approbation, H.D. has skillfully concealed her human subject.

One finds a similar situation in many of H.D.'s other early poems, among them "Sea Lily" and "Sheltered Garden."[22] The first stanza of "Sea Lily" might well serve as a metaphorical synopsis of H.D.'s early life:

> Reed,
> slashed and torn
> but doubly rich—
> such great heads as yours
> drift upon temple-steps,
> but you are shattered
> in the wind.

Granted a biographical license, one could point out the strange duality of physical violence and sanctity: the "great heads . . . drift," "slashed and torn," "upon temple-steps." The locus of creativity and feeling, the real home of the soul, is mutilated in this poem—a bloody paradigm for the psychic mutilation H.D. felt as an adolescent—yet the head still finds its refuge among the rich mysteries of the temple. Though this refuge is partial—the wind "shatters" the creature—it cannot be defeated:

> Yet though the whole wind
> slash at your bark,
> you are lifted up,
> aye—though it hiss
> to cover you with froth.

One might argue that this last stanza wills a sanctity to the mutilated head. The exigencies of life cannot finally pull it, pull H.D., down.

Yet, again, this reading is unsatisfactory. For one thing, it is careless. It permits, for example, the same head to be "slashed and torn," to "drift"—in what condition?—"upon temple steps," and then to be "shattered." Few objects that can be slashed and torn can also be shattered. While it is certainly possible to slash a human head, it is not, strictly speaking, possible to tear or shatter it: skin may be torn, but torn skin still implies, though horrifically, a relatively intact skull, not one broken cleanly into many pieces—shattered. The cleanness of that word, in fact, would make it a grotesque parody of destruction when applied to a human body. Thus, held to its vocabulary, the poem cannot be about human creatures. It may be about what it claims to be about, sea lilies in a classical setting, although even with this subject the problems of vocabulary remain.

The violence of the poem's diction, however, and the assignations of value—the "doubly rich" heads, and the implication of virtue inherent in their final lifting up—draw this poem away from the stated subject. Where, then, is the authentic subject? Where is the experience to ground the exceptional yet almost off-hand words of assault and mutilation? Where is the human context for the refuge from what is arguably a fantasy of violation in the last stanza, where the storm may "cover you with froth"? The subject of the poem may well be this powerful, shadowy claim of human violence, but tamed and purified in the context of the sea lily it becomes merely tantalizing. It yields a horror that the imagist subject mutes almost as quickly as a startled waking mutes a nightmare.

Even in the early poems where the experience of the speaker is the primary subject—in "The Gift," for instance, or "Sheltered Garden," or "Acon"—the circumstances of a powerful emotional experience remain wrapped in mystery, concealed through the allusive compression of imagism. One finds in "The Gift" a portentious night that the "you" and "I" spend together, but one also finds traces of a quasi-Eleusinian mystery—"initiates," "that other life," "the moment of ritual."[23] The poem provides no context for its feeling, but neither does it reject it; instead, it begins to clothe the feeling in the ambiguous language of popular classicism, so that trigger-words for ancient mythologies become further deflections of authentic experience. This happens in "Acon" and, perhaps most memorably, in "Hermes of the Ways," where H.D. anchors in classical mythology a Dante-esque desire for communion with the messenger of the gods.

"Hermes of the Ways" was the poem Ezra Pound found so rich with promise in September 1912. In *End to Torment*, H.D. recalls the encounter: "'But Dryad,' (in the [British] Museum tea room), 'this is poetry.' He slashed with a pencil. 'Cut this out, shorten this line. "Hermes of the Ways" is a good title. I'll send this to Harriet Monroe of *Poetry*.' . . . And he scrawled 'H.D. Imagiste' at the bottom of the page."[24]

For H.D., this moment of creation as a poet comes in the context of "first love," whose significance "cannot be over-estimated."[25] Even though five years have passed since Pound broke his engagement with H.D., even though the setting is now London rather than Wyncote or Philadelphia, H.D. still finds a lure and a power in the Poundian mystique. Writing about the experience forty-six years later, H.D. envisions the source of the power in a collision of opposites—"Angel-Daemon" or the "mariage du ciel et de la terre."[26] Yet even here H.D. makes a curious assessment of her early career—her resurrection at Pound's hands and the life beyond: "But in the end, intellectual and physical perfection, the laurel wreath of the acclaimed achievement must be tempered, balanced, re-lived, re-focused or even sustained by the unpredictable, the inchoate, challenged by a myth, a legend."[27] It may be that one could ascribe "intellectual and physical perfection" to the most spare and controlled of H.D.'s early poems, like "Hermes of the Ways"; but the most striking characteristic of the poems as a whole is their imperfection, their imbalance of image and feeling. They are not failures, exactly, but they are not H.D.'s voice. They are a constant compromise between the appropriate, modern, mannered poetic persona, and H.D.'s own authentic sense of personal and cultural entrapment. In that compromise, they acquire a weight of unanchored feeling that moves toward a stereotype of "feminine" poetry. Ultimately, then, H.D.'s early poems are noteworthy as much for their spiritual conventionality as for their contemporary style. They sound a note of longing and alarm that seems "right" for a female poet. Yet they neither identify the source of this longing or alarm, nor indict the society that helps to engender these feelings.

The use of masks in literature is so common that to criticize it in this instance may seem merely a way of inventing a problem. The process of William Butler Yeats's career can be viewed as a succession of masks, as Richard Ellmann has explained, and Ezra Pound's *Personae* affects the same sense of possibility. Later, as we shall see, the first poems of Louise Bogan rely heavily on the kind of mask associated with the creation of literary types. Yet typology, the representation of reality in terms of conventional or traditional figures, is always a risk because it exalts the convention above the experience of the author. It grants tradition a potentially unwarranted role in defining the voice of the new speaker. James Breslin writes, "Traditional forms, because they are imagined as dissociated from and imposed upon contemporary experience, may kill as they protect, and they may not even protect very effectively."[28] Although Breslin is concerned here with matters of poetic form, his point applies equally to matters of theme. Any received mythology may usefully shape a poet's experience, but it may also constrain that experience by subsuming the poet's voice in its own range of knowledge. One sees this recurring problem in H.D.'s *Hymen,* published in 1921, as well as in the 1924 *Heliodora* and the 1931 *Red Roses for Bronze.*

To be sure, *Hymen* represents a thematic advance for H.D. The passionate voice, by definition fragmentary and acontextual in *Sea Garden,* now speaks through a coherent mythology that gives a certain context to the speaker. In *Hymen* one finds meditations on specific mythological figures—Thetis, Leda, Hippolyta—but, perhaps more important, assumptions of the mythological voice. H.D. experiments with the identity of Hippolytus and Phaedra. In "Phaedra," she attributes a profound confusion to the wife of Theseus, whose unrequited love for Theseus's son Hippolytus ultimately drives her to accuse him falsely of rape, and to kill herself. What is striking about H.D.'s version is the contrast between a native magic or faith, in which Phaedra has placed her trust, and a new magic of unrelenting fate that threatens to overwhelm the reality of her world:

> Think, O my soul—
> what power has struck you blind—
> is there no desert-root, no forest-berry
> pine-pitch or knot of fir
> known that can help the soul
> caught in a force, a power,
> passionless, not its own?
>
> *So I scatter, so implore*
> *Gods of Crete, summoned before*
> *with slighter craft;*
> *ah, hear my prayer:*
> *Grant to my soul*
> *the body that it wore,*
> *trained to your thought,*
> * that kept and held your power,*
> *as the petal of black poppy,*
> *the opiate of the flower.*
>
> *For art undreamt in Crete,*
> *strange art and dire,*
> *in counter-charm prevents my charm*
> *limits my power:*
> *pine-cone I heap,*
> *grant answer to my prayer.*[29]

H.D. defines the force against Phaedra as "passionless,"that is, fully intent on its end, beyond human supplication, as befits Aphrodite, who propells Phaedra toward her doom. Yet the profound irony here is that passion, not passionlessness, leads to doom. "Phaedra" is a poem of enthrallment. The voice of the poem begs the lesser gods of Crete to come to its aid, to "grant" a "body" that is "trained to your thought." The spare, hard feeling in this poem is electrifying: the suppliant calls on a god whom, we know, will not save her, and the end is foretold:

> The poppy that my heart was,
> formed to bind all mortals,
> made to strike and gather hearts
> like flame upon an altar,
> fades and shrinks, a red leaf
> drenched and torn in the cold rain.[30]

It cannot be said, as one says of the earlier poems, that "Phaedra" suffers from an incongruence of feeling and subject. Surely the demise of Phaedra deserves the keen pronouncements of pain and confusion that inform H.D.'s poem. Yet even with a seemingly appropriate subject, H.D.'s poem appears self-defeating, because the subject itself is entirely conventional—and H.D.'s treatment of the voice is equally conventional. While she eschews Edwardian formalism, H.D. nevertheless adheres strictly to the formality of the myth: we know what tortures and confusions will occur in her poem, precisely because these tortures and confusions are contained in the received myth of Theseus, Hippolyta, Phaedra, and Hippolytus. There is no suprise here—no hint that a contemporary human being has revised a mythology and thus regained his or her life. In this sense "Phaedra" contrasts distinctly with, for example, Pound's "Francesca," in which the voice of the poet draws its vigor from a revised mythology:

> You came in out of the night
> And there were flowers in your hands,
> Now you will come out of a confusion of people,
> Out of a turmoil of speech about you.
>
> I who have seen you amid the primal things
> Was angry when they spoke your name
> In ordinary places.
> I would that the cool waves might flow over my mind,
> And that the world should dry as a dead leaf,

Or as a dandelion seed-pod and be swept away,
So that I might find you again,
Alone.[31]

Rather than fulfilling expectations, this poem challenges them immediately with the problem of the narrator: is this Paolo, or is it Pound himself as an imagined, potent voyeur? Either answer challenges the received mythology. If it is Paolo, he is not the suffering, doomed lover of the *Inferno,* but rather an independent and outraged man, confident in his judgment of Francesca's virtue. The character of defiance in the poem, and the speaker's decision to honor Francesca despite all judgment to the contrary, channels the mythic energy in a new way: against the tradition of divine judgment Pound postulates a counter-authority, the erotic righteousness of the created, which challenges the authority of the myth. As we have seen, this maneuver shows Pound's own ambivalence toward eros and authority, yet even in this way it represents a new, unpredictable molding of myth: the myth serves the interpreter. In H.D.'s poems, by contrast, the interpreter serves the myth.

This remains true even as the received myth clearly becomes inadequate to H.D.'s voice. In *Heliodora,* H.D. moves closer to a private declaration of strength and pain, yet the context has come to seem unhelpfully artificial. "Toward the Piraeus,"[32] for example, is a poem of explanation to a dangerous lover: why has the speaker rejected him? She will tell all, but only in the context of the "Greek" who can "slay with [his] eyes." The italicized prologue of the poem, a supplication to the quasi-divine Greek, frames the poem as a meditation on a classical paradigm.

> *Slay with your eyes, Greek,*
> *men over the face of the earth,*
> *slay with your eyes, the host,*
> *puny, passionless, weak.*
>
> *Break as the ranks of steel*
> *broke when the Persian lost:*
> *craven, we hated them then:*
> *now we would count them Gods*
> *beside these, spawn of the earth.*
>
> *Grant us your mantle, Greek!*
> *grant us but one*
> *to fright (as your eyes) with a sword,*

> *men, craven and weak,*
> *grant us but one to strike*
> *one blow for you, passionate Greek.*

What matters most is the value assigned to the "passionate Greek," who is as far superior to the Xerxes's Persian forces as the Persians are to current men, the "spawn of the earth." These "hosts," a strategic pun, are "puny, passionless, weak," yet they hold the speaker—and her kind—in thrall. She appeals to an archaic strength to redeem her from a suffering that is not so much physical as psychologically degrading.

The types or figures here have a mythic cast. The wrongly conquered suppliant, still defiant and proud, calls upon her tradition to slay the worthless victors whom fate has cruelly placed above her. These types reappear to a certain extent in the poem that follows, but they—and the tone of the prologue—seem wholly at odds with the subsequent voice of the poem. This voice strains toward confidentiality and personal assertion, yet at critical moments turns away from personal experience, concealing it once again in the original mythic motion of the poem. What is most striking here is the conflict between voices—the one theatrical, well-rehearsed, secretive, and the other muted, meditatively frank, and confidential. The result is a poem that resists its own subject, and in doing so reveals more about the subject and the author than the actual words can possibly say.

Nowhere is this conflict more clearly revealed than in the final section of the poem, in which the speaker invokes and praises her experience with something other than chastity, which she does not name. The refusal to name here again suggests an uncertainty in the poem that the concealed context does much to exploit. The additional ambivalence toward the self—now subjugated to the male, now separate but lesser, now worthy of praise—encapsulates the confusion by which the poem operates.

> It was not chastity that made me cold nor fear,
> only I knew that you, like myself, were sick
> of the puny race that crawls and quibbles and lisps
> of love and love and lovers and love's deceit.
>
> It was not chastity that made me wild, but fear
> that my weapon, tempered in different heat,
> was over-matched by yours, and your hand
> skilled to yield death-blows, might break

> With the slightest turn—no ill will meant—
> my own lesser, yet still somewhat fine-wrought,
> fiery-tempered, delicate, over-passionate steel.

This conclusion is wrought more in terms of an apology than an *apologia*. The speaker feels compelled to assuage the "you"'s implied confusion or displeasure with an explanation of her coldness. To apologize to the man who might have destroyed her is to follow the classic behavior of the terrorist's victim, and surely an element of terror stalks this poem: one sees its cool obliqueness in these final stanzas, in which eros— too potent or sacred to name—becomes a pair of unmatched weapons, the tools for battle. The speaker acknowledges that the battle is already lost; the "you" might destroy her unintentionally, "no ill-will meant." Thus she withdraws from the field.

But from which field does she withdraw? Is it the field of antique combat, pitting a classical greatness against "the puny race"? If this is so, the greatness is male—at least according to the prologue. Where, then, does the speaker find her place? If the field is contemporary, like Eliot's scenes of seduction and bar gossip in "The Waste Land," then what are the "weapons"? What, indeed, can they be, when the first section of the poem suggests that the woman is permanently enthralled even as she seeks escape? If the weapons are words themselves, how do they defend the identity of one who finds herself returning to illusions of power at the moment she unmasks a private pain?

It is possible, of course, to speculate about answers to these questions. Yet the poem is not forthcoming, because it ultimately retreats from the vigorously personal experience that is its primary subject. Although it is less indebted to classical mythology and mystery than other poems in *Heliodora*, its debt becomes strong at moments of critical interpretation: the classicism becomes both a cloak of intellectual legitimacy and a winding sheet. This classicism itself might well be the "you," except that every classical reference in the poem subverts this interpretation. The classical allusions that dignify the poem also limit its success—especially to one critic, Ezra Pound, who had been registering his disgust with H.D.'s classicism since the early 1920s. In a letter to William Carlos Williams, Pound trivialized H.D.'s investment in classical knowledge, referring to her as "that refined, charming, and utterly narrow minded she-bard."[33] Pound later responded to her 1928 volume *Hedylus* with scathing criticism.[34] While it may be that Pound's criticisms stem in part from his ambivalence toward erotic mastery, it can hardly be disputed that H.D.'s poetry suffers a significant decline between the mid-teens and the early thirties. Drawing on the classical source of her "originality," she contorts her work into mannerisms of diction and suppressions of experience that seem scarcely credible in one of her talent. Yet for a number of years she remains faithful to this patriarchal source of originality, affirming her unsuitability as a recipient of this knowledge: seeking the tradition of the father, she guarantees through her own confusions and suppressions that she will never succeed in this tradition. Indeed, she remains faithful to Pound as well, appropriately earning his disgust even as she follows the path he originally sketched for her. In one sense her decline as a poet signals the flaw in Pound's tradition of knowledge. She indicts his mastery with her failure.

In reality, the drama is more complicated, for H.D. genuinely believed herself to be on a quest for a new knowledge—a knowledge channeled through classical experience—and she found a certain refuge in Greece at a time of acute crisis in her life. In 1919, having narrowly escaped mental disintegration and death, H.D. traveled to the Scilly Islands with her infant daughter Perdita, and Bryher, their rescuer. Pausing on the islands on her way to Greece, she composed a brief volume of reflections, *Notes on Thought and Vision,* which Albert Gelpi describes this way:

> "Notes" is filled with dualisms that seem to split experience at all levels: body and spirit, womb and head, feeling and thought, the unconscious and ego consciousness, female and male, nature and divinity, classical and Christian, Greek and Hebrew, Greek and Egyptian, Sphinx and Centaur, Pan and Helios, Naiads and Athene, thistle and serpent. But the impulse behind "Notes" is to account for those mysterious moments in which the polarities seemed to fall away, or—more accurately—to find their contradictions lifted and subsumed into a gestalt that illuminated the crosspatch of the past and released her to the chances of the future.[35]

"Notes" suggests H.D.'s nascent view that the power of classical knowledge can be adapted or harnessed to support her own mystical experience—an experience that, because it is fundamentally private, exists in the troubling zone beyond traditions of human knowledge. This quest for a context for her mystical experience leads H.D. toward the kind of psychoanalytic exploration of her life that ultimately frees her from subservience to patriarchal influences. In the crucible of World War II, as she writes *The Gift* and *Trilogy*, she reaches back to find the father; in the authenticity of her private search she finds that the father no longer masters her. By the late twenties, however, her poetry—her public medium—seems further from this resolution than ever. The poems evince continual frustration and indebtedness, never coming to terms with the creditor. This does not mean that H.D. is blind to the thralldom under which she labors. On the contrary, only the enthralling medium—the poetry—binds H.D. In her prose—particularly her 1927 autobiographical novel *HERmione*—she reveals a keen insight into her predicament, and a voice that, though not without its flaws, registers her uniqueness.

In *HERmione*, Ezra Pound (as George Lowndes) first returns to Hermione's consciousness via an abstraction, a letter—"Hermione, I'm coming back to Gawd's own god-damn country."[36] Conflating colloquial and profane diction, this abstraction implies a powerful—and an anxious—social presence behind it. The writer of these words can make himself appear comfortable with his own unusual relationship to traditions of knowledge and behavior, even if he is not. He has access to knowledge, and has liberated himself—apparently—from its worst constraints; most of all, he wants Hermione.

She needs an escape from lifeless Pennsylvania; he can provide it. She needs an affirmation of her sexual identity; he can affirm it. She needs to laugh at the idiotic formalities of her constrained life; he is the "harlequin" who can make her laugh.[37] He is almost too perfect an escape, and therefore too powerful. He has everything; why should he have her? In mulling him over, before his arrival, Hermione alternately rues his coming, trivializes his "Punchinello"[38] persona and tastes the Italianate form of his name, Georgio, on her tongue like a fine dessert.[39] She has created for herself a spell of him—one of her making, not his—and she places herself under this spell half-unwillingly, half-desperately. At the same time, she harbors some abysmal confidence in herself, which both preserves her and limits her: "She knew she was not drowned. Where others would drown—lost, suffocated in this element—she knew that she lived. She had no complete right yet to this element, hands struggling to be pulled out. . . . she wanted George to pull her out, she wanted George to push her in, let Her be drowned utterly."[40] Something separate, unique, and eminently worthy exists within H.D., within Hermione, but nothing in the world confirms it: there is no reciprocity. There is only the old morality of having to earn one's worth, of earning the abstract and gender-related "right" to one's own being. Hermione cannot avoid conceiving of her difference in these rigid terms, and thus longs for salvation—either through identification with George, or through identification with the intoxication of thralldom. Either way emperils the nascent self.

But George, as the savior, is a close match to her longing. He creates a language for Hermione's uncertain, unique self, framing it in the conflicting vocabulary of classicism and the common life: "George was the only young man who had ever kissed Her. George was the only person who had called her a 'Greek goddess.' George, to be exact, had said ruminatively on more than one occasion, 'You never manage to look decently like other people. You look like a Greek goddess or a coal scuttle.' George said she looked like a coal scuttle. He also said she looked like a Greek goddess. There was that about George, he wanted to incarnate Her, knew enough to know that this was not Her."[41]

The conflict implicit in the last sentence is the essential conflict for H.D. On the one hand, George sees a Hermione behind the persona she creates to survive in blighting Pennsylvania. On the other hand, George cannot see that other creature without wanting to "incarnate" her, to bring her forth as an extension of his own vision. His method of incarnation is tripartite. He plays to her sense of confinement in Pennsylvania; he queries her about what she does, what meaningful labor she performs; and he makes more or less chaste love to her. In each of these efforts he gains some power over her. Yet he also raises Hermione's suspicions about this power, about her relationship to it. Even as he encircles her with his net of knowledge and desire, she sees an escape in the form of a bisexual companion, Fayne Rabb. This, ultimately, is an escape Lowndes cannot tolerate, and leads to Hermione's breakdown.

How does Hermione desire George? She answers this herself:

> She wanted George as a child wants a doll, whose other dolls are broken. She wanted George as a little girl wants to put her hair up or wear long skirts. She wanted George with some uncorrelated sector of Her Gart, she wanted George to correlate for her, life here, there. . . .
> She wanted George to say, "God, you must give up this sort of putrid megalomania, get out of this place."[42]

Hermione ascribes to George her own desire to be liberated from "putrid megalomania," a combined sense of being better than and inferior to everyone else; she wants him to draw her into her own reality. He wants to do this; he wants to take her away, wants her to marry him, wants to know what she does with herself.[43] He is, as she says, "made";[44] he has constructed himself out of knowledge and desire, and suggests that she can do this as well. But there is something else—the eros that looks like love but means dominance, one will working on the weakness of the other: "Now more than ever she knew they were out of some bad novel. Sound of chiffon ripping and the twist and turn of Hermione under the stalwart thin young torso of George Lowndes. Now more than ever thought made spiral, made concentric circle toward a darkened ceiling. The ceiling came down, down. The ceiling became black, in a moment it would crush down, crushing Her and George Lowndes under a black metallic shutter."[45] In his erotic passion, as in his literary judgments, George manifests a confidence that Hermione cannot feel. This confidence, ironically, extends even to assault, which H.D. correctly sees as crushing them both with its violent impersonality. Yet Hermione has no authority for her feelings. She believes, as she says, that "women are stronger" than men;[46] yet she must "turn and twist out of [George's] iron arms, because if he had held me, I would have been crushed by iron."[47] Women may be stronger, but have no cultural authority for their strength. Their strength cannot easily protect them from the myths of submission. It is useful to compare this to H.D.'s somewhat earlier poem, "To the Piraeus," because the vision is so similar. In *HERmione* George comes very close to breaking—"no ill-will meant"— the "fiery-tempered, delicate, yet over-passionate steel" of H.D. Yet the difference is only too clear: the novel provides an adequate objective correlative, a context for the extraordinary insight, and thus liberates this insight from the shadows of abstraction.

The other irony, of course, is that George's confidence is more a matter of affectation or culturally ordained show than anything else. He does not know what he wants; or rather, he reveals at some level that he wants power. Beyond that his intentions are unreadable, at least in H.D.'s account. He toys with Hermione, assuming their marriage without, apparently, asking and then lamenting its limitations. Hermione is awkward with company, she will have to learn how to smoke socially, she will threaten him with domestic tyranny.[48] He admires her unconventionality yet describes her closest friend, Fayne Rabb, as "shoddy."[49] Hermione has the innate loveliness of "Narcissa,"[50] but her taste in people and in art is unformed and liable to error. George must correct the error.

This error has an erotic as well as a sexual component: George perceives in Rabb both a threat and a source of power, a way of working Hermione's nascent sense of self against itself. "Hermione," he says, "you and [Rabb] should have been burnt as witches."[51] Through the course of the book George more and more becomes a kind of cultural transubstantiator, a quasi-angelic force who takes the raw matter of Hermione's desire and tries to mold it into awareness, gratitude, and pliancy. This mastery has an inhuman quality. Ultimately it is himself that George masters, and he cannot go beyond his vision of what Hermione should be to bring forth the genuine creature. Hermione comes to see that George the heterosexual suitor is also George the curiously-detached and manipulative enforcer of visions, and neither George can bring Hermione to life. This is so despite George's occasional bursts of sympathy: "Then George said that I was merely human," Hermione recalls, "that I wanted love."[52] But Hermione also understands that George lives lives other than his own: "'George is a lie upon a lie. He is a tatter and a ragbag. George, not so many lives back, was—' 'Was?' 'Was some wandering student, his own Provençal sort of thing carried to its logical conclusion. George is lie upon lie upon lie. George interests me because I try out on George the thing that is in me. The thing that is me.'"[53]

In this conversation with Rabb, Hermione presents not so much a view of reincarnation as a view of a man inventing lives, inventing fictions or "lies," and trying them on as an image of reality. To Rabb, Hermione explains her involvement as a kind of diffident play, as if she and George were operating under the same rules. Elsewhere, however, she asserts this is not true. George, she believes, wants her because she is "decorative" and the object of his passion: "He wanted Her," H.D. writes with an acute double entendre, "from about the middle, the glorious flaming middle, the Great Painters (that came under Florence) section."[54] Hermione knows what George cannot see: "There was something stripped of decoration, something of somewhat-painful angles that he would not recognize."[55] And later, after she has been caught in an erotic embrace with Fayne Rabb and spiraled down into a psychosomatic collapse, Hermione reflects on the lure of Rabb and the socially sanctioned counterweight of George: "Outside a force wakened, drew Her out of Her. Call the thing Fayne Rabb. I clung to some sort of branch that wavered in the wind, . . . a sort of precise character, George Lowndes. Wavering by instinct toward George I found George Lowndes inadequate. He would have pulled back quivering antennae."[56] Rabb is the erotic bond without the conventions of power and submission. Rabb cannot ask Hermione to marry her, and although she exerts a theatrical lure for Hermione, she does not master. The reciprocity in the relationship is obvious and occasionally ecstatic. "She had run and shouted at the sight of Fayne," H.D. writes, "had run to far hills, and found foothold on odd continents. Stones were pulsing beneath thin sandal soles and her feet were shod in purple."[57] Rabb is a locus of fulfillment in the novel. Hermione does not fear for the future in her presence, as she does in George's. The mysteries she and Rabb unlock—mysteries of the sexual soul in communion with another—lead Hermione toward the larger mysteries of Eleusis and Helen which, in H.D.'s hands, will slowly become a route toward self-discovery.

And yet, while *HERmione* ends with a small declaration of independence for the protagonist, the result is at best a truce. Hermione has not come to terms with the power and mastery that George represents; she has found a way to escape it but not to respond to it or against it from the strength of her own being. The presence of George, made vigorous in Hermione's criticism of him at the end of the book, rings the refuge of the novel like a small guerrilla army. Hermione recognizes the stakes of the game, and the ease with which lives are thrown away. She will not throw hers away. She will not become only one thing—a "water lily" to George's "red hibiscus."[58] Yet beyond this role-playing lies the profound uncertainty of sexuality and personal authority. If sexuality is, as Hermione is beginning to see, a route back to the most spiritually potent mysteries, it must be a great power; yet that power is bound up in conventions of knowledge and behavior, sublimated in the cultural authority of a "harlequin" like George or in the wise father and adoring mother, the two-thirds of the enervating trinity H.D. later describes to Freud:

> Here in our father's study, we must be quiet. A girl-child, a doll, an aloof and silent father form this triangle, this family romance, this trinity which follows the recognized religious pattern: *Father,* aloof, distant, the provider, the protector—but a little un-get-at-able, a little too far away and giant-like in proportion, a little chilly withal; *Mother,* a virgin, the Virgin, that is, an untouched child, adoring, with faith, building a dream, and the dream is symbolized by the third member of the trinity, the *Child,* the doll in her arms.[59]

Like H.D. herself, Hermione is both the child and the doll—one a creature, one a thing, neither independent nor wrested free of the family and its cultural authority. Even more, H.D. identifies herself here as the "Mother" as well—virginal, fantastic rather than real, and yet all the more devoted to the "Father" for this overwhelming Oedipal reason. When does the erotic impulse to create leave prohibitions and conventions behind, and channel itself through the new creature, the child? This happens when, as Louise Bogan says in "The Sleeping Fury," the constrained self turns to face the torturer, accepting its history of torment as a primary source of knowledge. This is what H.D. accomplishes in *HERmione*—a feat quite unlike what one finds in her poetry. It is a sign of health, both for the woman and the writer, and foreshadows—not an end to torment—but a route through the bronze doors of tradition.

Facing the "torturer," however that figure may manifest itself, is not the work of one creative effort; it is a continual process of psychic reorientation toward one's past. That H.D. begins this process in her prose—at a time when her poetry seems increasingly constrained and dessicated—suggests both the strength of her insight and the confusion entailed by her earlier incarnation as a poet. To call that old identity— and its progenitor, Ezra Pound—into question was to question the basis of her public being. It was to risk a kind of self-annihilation. Yet, following her crises during World War I—her stillborn child in 1915, the death of her brother Gilbert and the failure of her marriage in 1918, her own confrontation with death following influenza and childbirth in 1919—she lived largely within an awareness of the constant danger of annihilation.

By 1933, when she became Freud's analysand, she had already spent considerable psychic energy pondering the irrational power and destruction of war. "I had begun my preliminary research," she wrote, "in order to fortify and equip myself to face war when it came."[60] Yet she hardly had a chance to face the depth of her own feeling; in 1933 Vienna she was already seeing "preliminary signs and symbols of the approaching ordeal."[61] The tremors of yet another international cataclysm drove her to suppress her earlier fears of mindless cruelty and annihilation: "With the death-head swastika chalked on the pavement, leading to the Professor's very door, I must, in all decency, calm as best I could my own personal Phobia, my own personal little Dragon of war-terror, and with whatever power I could summon or command order him off, for the time being at any rate, back to his subterranean cavern."[62]

Yet her "war-terror" would not be suppressed, for it contained both her greatest threat and her greatest hope; it embraced the raw, destructive knowledge that underlay her own tendency toward thralldom to influential powers. Indeed, her terror was so potent because she saw how this knowledge could destroy itself. The cultural traditions which created the world in which she struggled for her own identity could also wipe themselves out in a matter of days or hours. The knowledge of these traditions, which she sought with the vain hope of making herself acceptably powerful to such mentors as Pound and D. H. Lawrence, was itself fatally flawed or wounded. It had, not an eternity for itself, but a harsh limit.

The angels of death flew from this flawed knowledge in London in 1941, when bombs rained down night after night around the Chelsea home of H.D. and Bryher. The noise was horrific; the fear of death, not so much maddening as absurdly banal and exhausting. "I was sick to death of tension and tiredness and distress and distorted values and the high-pitched level and the fortitude, which we had proved beyond doubt that we possessed," H.D. wrote.[63] At times she would long for the ultimate end to the ordeal: "*But it shall not come nigh thee* at this moment was almost a displeasing thought, for sometimes when the mind reaches its high peak of endurance, there is almost the hope—God forgive us—that the bomb that must fall on someone, would fall on me— but it could not—it must not."[64] Then the cycle of insanity would begin anew: "Yes, we were drowning again. We had had almost a hundred air raids in succession in the worst days; that was after the Battle of Britain and we had recovered and now the tide-wave of terror swept over us again. We were drowning again."[65]

In this context of ultimate danger, when the cultural traditions of public life seemed rent beyond repair, H.D. began to write two of her most memorable books—one in prose, the other in poetry. Both the prose work, *The Gift,* and the volume of poetry, *The Walls Do Not Fall* (later to be gathered in *Trilogy*), record profoundly personal responses to the cataclysm. But while the poetry attempts to envision a mythology that resurrects the dying self, the prose attempts an experiment perhaps even more striking. It seeks to place the author in precise relation to the traditions of knowledge that have so long held sway over her. If *HERmione* was an acute analysis of romantic thralldom, *The Gift* would be a search for even deeper roots to that thralldom—and a quest for alternatives.

Although *The Gift* seems at first glance to be simply a memoir of H.D.'s childhood in Bethlehem and Philadelphia, it is actually a study of modes of knowledge. In this study the father exerts a powerful and sometimes lovely presence. He seeks the mysteries of the stars, mysteries too great for his daughter to fathom, and in doing so he makes it possible for his family to live and eat and prosper.[66] Yet he remains largely alien to the child H.D. Awake when the children are asleep, he seems divorced from their world of toys and dreams. When he occasionally re-enters that world, as he does one Christmas season to buy toys for the children before the appointed time, he seems magical and strange to them, like a god.

For H.D. he is the embodiment of knowledge and power, but he is not actually a source of knowledge and power. By and large the women, and the stories and plays they give to their children, are the source. Attending a local stage performance of *Uncle Tom's Cabin*, with her Aunt Belle, H.D. marvels at the physical reality of what had formerly been simply a story in her mind: "Little Eva was really in a book," she recalls, "yet Little Eva was there on the stage and we saw her die, just like in the book."[67] She reads, or has read to her, a collection of Grimm fairy tales until the book was "falling to pieces";[68] she listens as her grandmother, Mamalie, slides toward senility, calling her by another relative's name and revealing fragmentary histories of the Moravian church in Bethlehem.[69] Above all, she sees what the family makes. At Christmas time they enact a ritual of creation, making foods and tree decorations and a whole world in miniature around the tree, an archetypal act of symbolic regeneration: "We were 'making' a field under the tree for the sheep. We were 'making' a forest for the elk, out of small sprays of a broken pine-branch. We ourselves were 'making' the Christmas cakes. As we pressed the tin mold of the lion or the lady into the soft dough, we were like God in the first picture in the Doré Bible who, out of chaos, created Leo or Virgo to shine forever in the heavens."[70] Unimpressed with the fatal knowledge of mortality, entranced with the act of creating something from mere raw matter, the children return to God the favor he bestowed upon them: "God had made a Child, and we children in return now made God; we created Him as He had created us, we created Him as children will, out of odds and ends; like magpies, we built Him a nest of stray bits of silver thread, shredded blue or rose or yellow colored paper; we knew our power."[71]

H.D. is careful to suggest that this sense of empowerment arises large-

ly from the children's confidence in their innate authority; but she also
suggests that they do not experience this confidence apart from the context created through the family traditions of Christmas, in which Mamalie and Papalie, and later Mama, set the events of wonder in motion.
As the years pass, this gift of mystery and creative power carries the
weight of salvation—or at least a different kind of wonder—when the
darkness of death closes in. When Mamalie dies, H.D. tries to summon
her back, fearful not simply of her own ignorance but of her isolation:
"Oh, Mamalie, there is such a lot I want to know; I want to know what
Paxnous' wife looked like, she was a sort of Princess and Oh, there is
Anna von Pahlen, my dear, dear Anna who was Morning Star like the
Princess with the nine brothers in the story that was lost, and she had
lilies too . . . not like the branch of lilies the Madonna has on Easter
cards or Jesus has on Easter cards when He comes out of the tomb, *pas-
se le tombeau*."[72] The child H.D. understands, at least to some extent,
the degree to which her grandmother represents a different tradition, a
tradition of religious mysticism and rebellion. She knows there are secrets, a mystical "Wunden Eiland" or island of wounds in her grandmother's Moravian faith,[73] and spiritual gifts within this tradition that
H.D. does not yet possess. In going back over this time of childhood
power and loss, the adult H.D. grants a new authority to a kind of
knowledge and tradition that she had formerly allowed to fall dormant.
This tradition validates her will to create—to reaffirm the power of God
through her own homage to God's method; it validates her faith in symbols and spiritual insight beyond the rational mind; it validates her love
of people, and her trust in their personhood as an essential human value. As she re-explores the presence of this tradition in her own background, she stumbles upon a crack in that other tradition—the tradition of her invincible father.

"What it was," she begins, "was not appreciable at the moment."[74]
This shaping event, though clearly powerful, was not fully self-explain-
ing; indeed, one ambition implicit in *The Gift* is to come to terms with
an implicit explanation for the minor crisis that H.D. recalls. "What
happened did not take long to happen." The story is a simple one: H.D.
and her brother Gilbert were waiting up one evening for Papa to return
from Philadelphia. Finally they heard a bump "on the front porch by
the steps, as if someone were coming up."[75] It was their father; but something was wrong. He had been injured somehow and, stumbling into
the house, he bled from the side of his face. H.D. ran to him, helping

him to a chair, wondering all the time what change had come over this man. "His hand did not seem to belong to him," she said, "and his arm seemed like the arm of a scarecrow or a rag doll."[76] Was this husk of a man her powerful and mysterious father? "The blood was running down from the side of his face that was by me," she said, "and there was dust on his coat, and the arm that I had pulled at on the porch hung over the chair."[77] Having taken a streetcar home, her father had signaled the conductor to stop but somehow had not noticed that the car was still moving; he simply stepped off into space. Stunned, with a concussion and a broken collarbone, H.D.'s father stared into space, acknowledging no one. H.D. tried to clean his face and wound, but could not wash the blood out of his beard.[78]

Later, when the doctor came to make the diagnosis and H.D. badgered her brother to explain "concussion," she found her mind freely associating her father's accident with her other fears of abandonment at other times. Once she had been sent to live for a time on a farm; she was afraid her mother and father would never return for her. At another time, she overheard her mother saying in jest that she would leave her husband if he shaved his beard. H.D. didn't get the joke; "I would not leave Papa," she said, "if he cut off his beard."[79]

The fear of leaving, of abandonment, of dangerous wounds brings H.D. back to the London of the bombing, but not before she brings herself to a psychic crossroads. Yes, she has been terrified of abandonment all her life; she has fought to link herself to people and places that will not abandon her. If she has suffered abandonment in any case, it is not from lack of effort to find security. Yet in weaving *The Gift* from the fabric of her past, H.D. comes to see that her conscious method of finding security was to place her hopes in the strong family figure of knowledge and power—the father. This thralldom to the father was itself fatally flawed; it could not withstand the mortal reality of the father's life. There was, however, a competing reality whose ultimate value H.D. had largely ignored—the reality of stories and family lore and nonconformist religion. To learn this—and to shift allegiance from the father to the more generous congruence of childhood and mystery— was to recover "the gift": a sense of personal authenticity, a self-worth unconditioned by submissions or deferential masks. That H.D. is able to do this in the context of war and degradation suggests the strength of her private being; it also suggests the degree to which she had sacrificed that private being to a public persona, which could collapse only when the culture around it collapsed. As H.D. explains, "I, the child, was still living, but I was not free, not free to express my understanding of the gift, until long afterwards. I was not, in fact, completely free, until again there was the whistling of evil wings, the falling of poisonous arrows, the deadly signature of a sign of evil magic in the sky."[80]

The freedom H.D. acquires during World War II to cherish the gift of her authentic self anchors itself in the psychoanalytic method of *The Gift*. Yet it spills outward to cover H.D.'s other work as well: it re-invents her public persona, so that her public voice—her poetry—begins to acquire a confidence and context. In *The Walls Do Not Fall*, H.D. takes the reader on a Dantean quest for meaning through the tombs of mythology. Yet the quest, as universal as any in her earlier work, is also highly personal, framed in a potent outrage against the collapse of civilized knowledge and method. The first stanzas of the poem clearly identify the contemporary, war-time context; they also identify the central paradox of the poem, the archetypal process of mystery and resurrection in the midst of human disaster. This paradox is nothing, however, without the sense of moral outrage that accompanies any recognition of disaster. There is no point to a quest unless the questor is truly in need. H.D. paints her outrage, and her need, throughout the early part of the poem:

> Evil was active in the land,
> Good was impoverished and sad;
>
> Ill promised adventure,
> Good was smug and fat;
>
> Dev-ill was after us,
> tricked up like Jehovah;
>
> Good was the tasteless pod,
> stripped from the manna-beans, pulse, lentils:
>
> they were angry when we were so hungry
> for the nourishment, God;
>
> they snatched off our amulets,
> charms are not, they said, grace;
>
> but gods always face two-ways,
> so let us search the old highways
>
> for the true-rune, the right spell,
> recover old values. . . .[81]

Compactly, with a voice at once political and metaphorical, H.D. shapes the moral climate of the time and its consequences for her: this time needs no God, no "old values." It is a Yeatsian time, in which "The best lack all conviction, while the worst / Are full of passionate intensity."[82] True, H.D.'s poem—like Yeats's—proceeds through generalization and synechdoche. The method is, for example, entirely the opposite of an historically specific text like Samuel Johnson's "The Vanity of Human Wishes." But H.D.'s poem is not trying to argue a political theory or state a precise consequence. It is rather asserting what, in the poet's eye, is an authentically corrupt condition—the condition in which the poet must somehow "search the old highways / for the true-rune." The change lies precisely in the fact that H.D. can, in this poem, place herself in a contemporary context and identify the path she must take to find her equivalent of the Grail. Her quest is universal, yet it is *her* quest: she inhabits this poem in a way she does not inhabit her earlier public work.

> In me (the worm) clearly
> is no righteousness, but this—
>
> persistence; I escaped the spider-snare,
> bird-claw, scavenger bird-beak,
>
> clung to the grass-blade,
> the back of a leaf
>
> when storm-wind
> tore it from its stem. . . .[83]

In these stanzas, for example, one hears an echo of the 1916 "Sea Lily," which is shattered in the sea and yet lifted up. The portraits of endurance and fierce danger have some consonance, but the difference is all: in the earlier poem no specific voice speaks the crisis, while in *The Walls Do Not Fall* H.D.'s own crisis-driven voice gives her endurance a context that evinces its high seriousness. This voice has a wonderful flexibility. By turns analytic, incantatory, pedagogical, it manages to contain H.D.'s reflections on the connections between Egyptian and Christian gods ("for it now appears obvious / that *Amen* is our Christos"[84]) and her fears of abandonment:

> Now my right hand,
> now my left hand

clutch your curled fleece;
take me home, take me home,

my voice wails from the ground;
take me home, Father:

pale as the worm in the grass,
yet I am a spark

struck by your hoof from a rock;
Amen, you are so warm,

hide me in your fleece,
crop me up with the new-grass;

let your teeth devour me,
let me be warm in your belly,

the sun-disk,
the re-born Sun.[85]

Here the language is richly layered. The "Father" is the wailing child's human father, but also the sun-god Apollo and the Egyptian Amen. To be left by the human father is to be abandoned; to be devoured by the human father is to abandon oneself, fearing one's own difference. Either way the child's self loses—unless the child reconstructs the father as a myth, a companion-god whose devouring promises not ultimate submission but rebirth. This is one way of perceiving the course of H.D.'s own mythologizing of her life; more importantly, it is the *poem* that makes this method of mythologizing clear. In *The Walls Do Not Fall,* private meditations fuse with the public person to create—for the first time in the poetry—an original, unified voice.

The congruence of the public and the private persona that H.D. achieves in the early 1940s marks the end of one phase in a long struggle to record an authentic experience in an artistic milieu that prized inauthenticity. For surely a central dimension of H.D.'s thralldom involved, not simply Pound or any other influential artist, but a concept of impersonality and static coolness in art that happily annihilated the merely lonely and partial personality. Pound and Eliot had set in motion a vision of art that emanated directly from their own sense of meanness in the face of the cosmos. They had made themselves mythological, and in Pound's case heroic, by cloaking their art in the heroisms of the past. They had, in another sense, used knowledge to supplant the self.

But this H.D. could not do. The traditions of her male counterparts did not speak to her, in part because—while they possessed at least a sense of the minimal self—she lacked even that. Her quest was not for a route away from the single, mortal self, but a route to that self; and, while she denied this quest in her poetry for many years, she pursued it vigorously in her rising body of prose. Ironically, in seeking the authentic experience of her own identity, she came upon a body of ancient knowledge that suggested to her how the self could both be itself and transcend itself; this brought comfort and the "old highways" of the true rune. In reading her poetry from the 1920s and 1930s, however, one cannot but be struck with the nearness of her collapse—as a public artist and as an unknown, private entity. Her ability to heal those wounds may well have lain in her persistence, as she suggests in *The Walls Do Not Fall*. But the healing could not begin until she began to renounce the public persona that shaped her early success. In the darkness of this renunciation she went to the prose sources of her own myth, her own experience. Writing beyond, rather than for, the men who had directed her, she found the unsubmissive path of self-direction.

Notes

1. Ezra Pound, *Selected Letters, 1907–1941*, ed. D. D. Paige (New York: New Directions, 1950, 1971), p. 212.

2. Ezra Pound and James Joyce, *Pound/Joyce: The Letters of Ezra Pound to James Joyce*, ed. with commentary by Forrest Read (New York: New Directions, 1967).

3. Gregory quoted in Pound and Joyce, p. 3.

4. H.D. (Hilda Doolittle), *Helen in Egypt* (New York: New Directions, 1961), p. 22.

5. Freud quoted in Barbara Guest, *Herself Defined: The Poet H.D. and Her World* (New York: Quill, 1984), p. 209.

6. H.D., letter to Bryher (Winifred Ellerman), Nov. 1934, quoted in Guest, p. 219.

7. Susan Stanford Friedman, *Psyche Reborn: The Emergence of H.D.* (Bloomington: Indiana University Press, 1982), p. 179.

8. Rachel Blau DuPlessis, "Romantic Thralldom and 'Subtle Geneologies' in H.D.," *Writing Beyond the Ending: Narrative Strategies of Twentieth-Century Women Writers* (Bloomington: Indiana University Press, 1985), pp. 66–83. Although DuPlessis is more willing than I am to ascribe H.D.'s late work to the impulse of romantic thralldom, her analysis of *Helen in Egypt* brilliantly evokes the shift in H.D.'s thinking.

9. DuPlessis, *Writing Beyond the Ending,* p. 66.

10. Williams quoted in Guest, p. 17.

11. H.D., *HERmione* (New York: New Directions, 1981), pp. 5–6.

12. Guest, p. 14.

13. See Susan Stanford Friedman, "Against Discipleship: Collaboration and Intimacy in the Relationship of H.D. and Freud," *Literature and Psychology,* 33, nos. 3 and 4 (1987): 95, and H.D., *Tribute to Freud* (New York: New Directions, 1974).

14. H.D., *The Gift* (New York: New Directions, 1982), pp. 40, 52, 19.

15. H.D., *The Gift,* p. 11.

16. Lionel Trilling, *Sincerity and Authenticity* (Cambridge, Mass.: Harvard University Press, 1972), p. 154. While the phrase is Trilling's, his context for it is quite different from my own.

17. H.D., *HERmione,* p. 167.

18. H.D., *Bid Me to Live* (Redding Ridge, Conn.: Black Swan Books, 1983), p. 51. Any student of H.D. owes a debt to ground-breaking critics; I have gained insight particularly from the work of Susan Stanford Friedman, Rachel Blau DuPlessis, and—perhaps the most ardent of H.D.'s interpreters—Alicia Ostriker. Ostriker devotes a long first chapter of *Writing Like a Woman* (Ann Arbor: University of Michigan Press, 1983) to H.D., and returns to her work in *Stealing the Language: The Emergence of Women's Poetry in America* (Boston: Beacon, 1986). In *Writing Like a Woman,* Ostriker explores themes of isolation and transformation in H.D.'s early and later work, and observes an implicit link to Blake: "If *Sea Garden* represents Innocence, the postwar poetry represents Experience" (p. 18). The power of H.D. as a "visionary poet" (p. 8) comes through clearly in Ostriker's criticism; yet I find that I cannot share her confidence in the overall achievement of H.D.'s poetry. The difficulties and lapses in the poetry seem to me full of meaning, and those difficulties and lapses are my primary concern here.

19. Susan Stanford Friedman, "The Writing Cure: Transference and Resistance in a Dialogic Analysis," *H.D. Newsletter* 2, no. 2 (Winter 1988): 25–35.

20. H.D., *Collected Poems, 1912–1944,* ed. Louis Martz (New York: New Directions, 1983), p. 5.

21. Ezra Pound, "A Few Don'ts," *The Literary Essays of Ezra Pound* (New York: New Directions, 1968), p. 4.

22. H.D., *Collected Poems,* pp. 14, 19.

23. H.D., *Collected Poems,* pp. 15–18.

24. H.D., *End to Torment* (New York: New Directions, 1979), p. 18. Other readers of H.D.'s life and work have suggested a less liminal interpretation of this moment; see p. 49, note 29 in this book.

25. H.D., *End to Torment,* pp. 18–19.

26. H.D., *End to Torment,* p. 19.

27. H.D., *End to Torment,* p. 19.
28. James E. B. Breslin, *From Modern to Contemporary: American Poetry, 1945–1965* (Chicago: University of Chicago Press, 1984), p. 45.
29. H.D., *Collected Poems,* pp. 135–36.
30. H.D., *Collected Poems,* p. 136.
31. Ezra Pound, *Collected Early Poems of Ezra Pound,* ed. with introduction by Louis L. Martz (New York: New Directions, 1976), p. 112.
32. H.D., *Collected Poems,* pp. 176–77.
33. Pound, *Selected Letters,* p. 157.
34. See Guest, p. 170.
35. Albert Gelpi, "Introduction," H.D., *Notes on Thought and Vision and The Wise Sappho* (San Francisco: City Lights Books, 1982), p. 12.
36. H.D., *HERmione,* p. 28.
37. H.D., *HERmione,* pp. 33, 34.
38. H.D., *HERmione,* p. 43.
39. H.D., *HERmione,* p. 33.
40. H.D., *HERmione,* p. 63.
41. H.D., *HERmione,* p. 64.
42. H.D., *HERmione,* p. 63.
43. H.D., *HERmione,* p. 68.
44. H.D., *HERmione,* p. 69.
45. H.D., *HERmione,* p. 173.
46. H.D., *HERmione,* p. 173.
47. H.D., *HERmione,* p. 173.
48. H.D., *HERmione,* p. 169.
49. H.D., *HERmione,* p. 171.
50. H.D., *HERmione,* p. 170.
51. H.D., *HERmione,* p. 172.
52. H.D., *HERmione,* p. 185.
53. H.D., *HERmione,* p. 178.
54. H.D., *HERmione,* p. 172.
55. H.D., *HERmione,* p. 172.
56. H.D., *HERmione,* p. 216.
57. H.D., *HERmione,* p. 166.
58. H.D., *HERmione,* p. 224.
59. H.D., *Tribute to Freud* (New York: New Directions, 1956), p. 38.
60. H.D., *Tribute to Freud,* p. 93.
61. H.D., *Tribute to Freud,* p. 94.
62. H.D., *Tribute to Freud,* p. 94.
63. H.D., *The Gift,* p. 136.
64. H.D., *The Gift,* p. 137.
65. H.D., *The Gift,* p. 137.

66. H.D., *The Gift*, p. 52.

67. H.D., *The Gift*, pp. 14–15.

68. H.D., *The Gift*, p. 48.

69. H.D., *The Gift*, pp. 89–100.

70. H.D., *The Gift*, p. 31.

71. H.D., *The Gift*, p. 31.

72. H.D., *The Gift*, p. 99.

73. H.D., *The Gift*, p. 85.

74. H.D., *The Gift*, p. 101.

75. H.D., *The Gift*, p. 105.

76. H.D., *The Gift*, p. 106.

77. H.D., *The Gift*, p. 107.

78. H.D., *The Gift*, pp. 107–8.

79. H.D., *The Gift*, p. 127.

80. H.D., *The Gift*, p. 85.

81. H.D., *Collected Poems*, p. 511.

82. William Butler Yeats, "The Second Coming," *Selected Poetry*, ed. A. Norman Jeffares (London: Pan Books, 1974), p. 100.

83. H.D., *Collected Poems*, p. 515.

84. H.D., *Collected Poems*, p. 525.

85. H.D., *Collected Poems*, p. 527.

3

In Light I Live
The Mentorship of Yvor Winters

To the extent that he inhabits the popular literary imagination at all, Yvor Winters holds the place of the austere curmudgeon, the man of principle who would brook no compromise on matters of art or philosophy. Beyond a small circle of admirers, few people know even the essential biographical details—a considerable irony, given the literary drama of Winters's life.

Born in Chicago on October 17, 1900, the son of a stock and grain broker, Yvor Winters came early to two themes that were to inform the rest of his life—the landscape of California and the moral imperatives of literature. As a child Winters traveled regularly to Eagle Rock, outside of Pasadena, California, where his paternal grandmother made her home. According to Brigitte Carnochan, Winters recalled those western excursions as "the happiest years of his childhood." He learned to read at the hands of his maternal grandmother, who taught him at the age of four by "introducing him to the works of the English historian Macaulay."[1]

Well-read and well-attuned to both the rigors and the adventures of literature, Winters enrolled in the University of Chicago in 1917 and soon joined the Poetry Club. It was an auspicious time to be in Chicago: Harriet Monroe's *Poetry*, founded five years earlier, was daring its public with the works of Ezra Pound, H.D., T. S. Eliot, and Robert Frost. Monroe gathered and published the best of contemporary poetry, along with tamer conciliatory verse, only a few miles from the university buildings and private homes in which the Poetry Club had its meetings. Under the direction of Elizabeth Madox Roberts, the club developed into a close-knit circle; Glenway Wescott, the club's president at the time, remarked on the constancy with which the members exchanged their poems and their views on poetry and life. This continued, as Carnochan notes, even when jobs or illnesses called some members away from the university.[2] The act of writing poetry under Roberts's direction was the act of forming relationships, not only with literature, but with like-minded human beings.

Janet Lewis, who had enrolled in the university in 1918, gained admission to the club in the winter of 1919. Lewis and Winters were not to meet for two more years, however, because Winters—having contracted a serious case of tuberculosis—had left the university at the end of the fall term in 1918. Seeking the dry air conducive to recovery, he moved first to his uncle's home in Riverside, California; then, when it seemed that his case might be life-threatening, he traveled to Saint Vincent's Sanatorium in Santa Fe, New Mexico, and later to Sunmount Sanatorium, where he remained until 1921. Here, confronted with death and abject loneliness, Winters nevertheless maintained his correspondence with the Poetry Club and began those modernist experiments in writing that marked his early career.

The years from 1921 to 1927, though framed with love—Winters met Lewis on May 5, 1921, and married her on June 22, 1926—were years of trial for Winters. For the sake of his health, he remained largely in the Southwest, teaching high school in New Mexico and enrolling in 1923 at the University of Colorado at Boulder for an M.A. in Romance Languages with a minor in Latin. Though easy on his health, the climate was not always compatible with his mind, and other complexities intruded. Since Lewis had also contracted tuberculosis, and was unable to leave the sanatorium in New Mexico following their wedding, Winters had to proceed alone to his first teaching job at the University of Idaho. Married but still effectively a bachelor, increasingly isolated emotionally and intellectually, pushing his modernist literary experiments to the limit, he began a descent into what he later saw as a period of near-madness, which he captured in his story "The Brink of Darkness."

Winters needed rescuing, and Stanford came to his rescue. He enrolled in the Ph.D. program in English in 1927; by the second year he was an instructor in the English department, and he remained at Stanford—traveling through the ranks of assistant, associate, and full professor—until his death on January 25, 1968. Though he was not always regarded as an asset (he was told in 1941 by the chairman of the department, A. G. Kennedy, that he and his work were a "disgrace"[3]), his life was marked by an extensive network of correspondence with some of the most distinguished writers of the time, including Allen Tate, Louise Bogan, and Albert Guerard. It was also marked by his increasing devotion to the moral imperatives of literature. One could, he argued, make statements about the value (and values) of life through literature, and these statements could serve as a defense against the essential chaos of life beyond the mind. As Carnochan writes, "His later 'defense of reason' is logically consistent with what he termed 'the madness of my youth.' The exercise of reason was the way he kept himself from slipping into the darkness."[4]

Among the most celebrated examples of what Winters saw as the exercise of reason was his attack on his friend Hart Crane in *Poetry* in 1930. Yet Winters's scathing assault on Crane's great work *The Bridge* was, he felt, consistent with his own emerging body of criticism and formal poetry. Among these critical works were the 1938 *Maule's Curse: Seven Studies in the History of American Obscurantism*, which examined what Winters saw as irrational obscurities in the work of Emerson, Hawthorne, Melville, and others; the 1946 *Edwin Arlington Robinson*; and the central achievement of Winters's middle years—*In Defense of Reason*, published in 1947.

In addition, Winters published his *Poems* in 1940 and his *Collected Poems* twelve years later. These volumes cast aside much of Winters's earlier experimental work, with its debt to the French symbolists and particularly to Rimbaud, and presented an Yvor Winters whose talent resided in a language of acute description and an emotional sensitivity constrained by logical proposition. Not until 1966, the year of his retirement from the Stanford English department, did Winters publish his early, experimental poems. To this volume he contributed an introduction that is not only his fullest statement of the difficulties of his early years, but is also a testament to his will to live at the mind's edge through literature—and to turn back from that edge, by the grace of reason, when what lay beyond grew too frightening.

Winters's lengthy and passionately argued attack on the irrational in American literature in *In Defense of Reason* placed him well outside the mainstream of critics who saw more complex intellectual content in the work of Hawthorne, Emerson, and Melville; his last book, *Forms of Discovery*, which he completed in 1967 while dying of cancer, was perhaps even more outspoken. He repeatedly earned the praise of fellow poets, however, including Robert Lowell, Marianne Moore—who referred to him as a "badger-Diogenes"[5]—and Hayden Carruth, who wrote that Winters's poem "To the Holy Spirit" "has never ceased to astonish, frighten and console me."[6] Yet his larger reputation as a fanatical rationalist seemed ultimately to dilute the effects of this perceptive praise. This is unfortunate, for Winters was a distinguished poet, in no small part because of the personal conflicts that shadowed his poetry and gave it its dark intensity. It seems likely that revisionist critics will accord him a much higher place in the pantheon of modern poets than he now holds.

But Winters also deserves attention precisely because of his strong defense of the *animus* of tradition and reason in his work. He believed in objective truths; "the work of literature," he wrote, "in so far as it is valuable, approximates a real apprehension and communication of a particular kind of objective truth."[7] To study literature was thus to examine the traditions in which literature was formed for signs of a nearness to or a falling away from this truth. In this regard Winters would seem to be an archetypal mentor: strong-willed, well-read, insistent on the need to preserve the texts, insistent on the importance of making those texts come to life in the lives of his students.

When Winters argued, for example, that a poem "is good in so far as it makes a defensible rational statement about a given human experience . . . and at the same time communicates the emotion which ought to be motivated by that rational understanding of that experience,"[8] he was making a statement not only about literature but about a way of responding to the world. The world was not necessarily rational, but human beings could make rational statements about it to one another, and in doing so could convey a quality of emotion that ought to bind them to the meaning of the rational statement. In his approach to literature, Winters seemed to sketch a model of human relationships as well. Humans were bound to each other by reason of Logos, the conceptual principle immanent in human experience. If Winters and his apprentices experienced difficulties in the course of mentorship, it is not because Winters did not follow a time-honored method of shepherding those who came to him for wisdom. The fault perhaps lay as much in the time-honored method as in Winters.

Winters could be generous and warm, demonstrating beyond his critical judgments a passionate love for poetry and teaching. For one young apprentice, Thom Gunn, Winters made the difference of a lifetime. "Yvor

Winters met me at the Southern Pacific railway depot in Palo Alto on a hot, dry afternoon in early September of 1954," Gunn recalls with some hint of surprise. Having a professor as chauffeur was a little unsettling to the new student from Great Britain. "He took me to the room he had obtained for me, where I left my luggage, and then drove me, by way of the Stanford campus, to his home, where I was to have dinner with him, a dinner he would make himself, as he was alone there that day with his young son, Danny."[9] Over the course of the evening the two men, host and guest as much as teacher and student, discussed contemporary poetry. Gunn left with the somewhat predictable feeling that his answers had not quite been adequate, that he "had failed a test or two most signally."[10] Yet Gunn had found Winters to be a generous if formidable presence—an intriguing subject himself, worthy of further study.

Gunn's initial gratitude for hospitality, and feeling of inadequacy, was to change to anger in the classroom. Once Winters began to propound his critical principles—dismissing Yeats, for example, as a man who ultimately could not think—Gunn felt obliged to rise in defiance: "The first course of Winters' I attended, on 'the criticism of poetry,' was an immediate shock to my assumptions, in that he set about the systematic demolishing of my favorite twentieth-century poet, Yeats, in ruthless detail. . . . I was angry at first and fought him bitterly. I adored Yeats and was grateful to a career which had seemed exemplary to me in showing how a spirit of romanticism could survive, self-correcting and self-nourishing, into the twentieth century."[11] As weeks passed, however, Gunn began to find points of convergence between his own attitude toward poetry and Winters's. He found Winters's defense of the Elizabethan poets to be persuasive, and he found Winters's keenness as a reader enormously revealing:

[Winters showed us] a poem by George Herbert, "Church Monuments," which seemed new to me, and which I immediately agreed was as good as Winters might care to claim. . . . I had read through Herbert's poetry more than once, but had never noticed this magnificent poem before. Why not? . . . . Winters' answer, which I found incontrovertible, was that I had missed it because I was looking for something else, the Herbert style. . . . In looking primarily for the typical, I had missed the untypical, which I had to admit was perhaps the best poem of all.[12]

Gunn's time with Winters, then, was at least initially a process of conversion: Winters engaged Gunn with the force of his arguments, the incisiveness of his reading, and his dedication to the art of poetry. "Bit by bit the thoroughness of his arguments and the power of his examples started to win me over to much of his thought," writes Gunn. "The arguments, however, would have been nothing without the fierce love of poetry that lived behind them."[13] What becomes clear in Gunn's story, as in a number of others, is that this love of poetry circles back to a love of the well-defined life—a life asserted against the dangers and temptations of chaos.

Gunn's recollections of Winters suggest that one of the central functions of mentorship is to persuade the apprentice of his own inadequacies. The apprentice must come to realize his need, not only for instruction, but for a kind of instruction that may violate his previously held convictions about his art; this, for example, is Gunn's experience when dealing with Winters's view of Yeats. On the other hand, the talented mentor will also seek to identify the primary concerns of the apprentice, and to show connections between his own instruction and those concerns. Winters does this with N. Scott Momaday, whose sources of inspiration were as much rooted in the geography of the American West as in English or American literature: "Now and then he spoke to me of New Mexico, sensing my homesickness perhaps. . . . I grew up in New Mexico, and [Yvor Winters and Janet Lewis] had lived there; that landscape was very important to them; they had been restored to health in it; they had married in it. On that basis we knew our first loyalties to one another. Oh, yes, we said, the winters in Santa Fe! Yes, the crooked mountain roads and the little Spanish Colonial villages where the old santeros bide their time."[14] Momaday recalls his geographical connection with Winters only after a more conventional tribute to the master: "When, as a student, I asked him a question concerning a poem, I did not dare to doubt that his answer was the final word. His knowledge of and sensitivity to poetry were unimpeachable, so it seemed to us who were his students."[15] It may have been that Momaday, and other students, did not question Winters's judgment—though this does not necessarily speak well either of the students or of the master; it sounds more like the expected tribute from a student. This predictability disappears from Momaday's writing, however, when he discusses Winters's praise of landscape. Winters reached Momaday through the landscape, and provided Momaday with a formalist approach to the poetic values he found rooted in New Mexico.

The evident care Winters extended to some of his apprentices surprisingly does not clarify the mystery of Winters's actual role as a mentor. Since his death in 1968, his approach to poetry has suffered from both implicit and explicit defiance. The context of this defiance is often complex, even suffused with praise, as Scott Momaday's comments suggest. Robert Pinsky, for example, refers to Winters as a "great teacher" in his volume of essays *Poetry and the World;* he also includes, in his long poem "Essay On Psychiatrists," an extended portrait of Winters, in which the great teacher, even as he belittles his students, also declares himself impervious to madness because he has understood how "the logical / Foundations of Western thought decayed and fell apart."[16] Such accolades aside, very few of Winters's students continued to magnify his literary and critical values. Few continued to demonstrate that the life of the poem existed in its rational propositions, and that the death of the poem came in its devotion to the irrational. Kenneth Fields, Winters's most visible apprentice and coeditor of his anthology *Quest for Reality,* shared with Gunn an interest in hallucinogenic experiment; both poets wrote of these experiences in their poetry of the early seventies. This contact with the irrational—as well as other, related experiences of failed love, jealousy, and despair—altered their poetry in ways Winters could hardly have approved. Pinsky moved clearly from the strategies of direct argument to those of implicit argument—or no argument at all—in his 1985 *History of My Heart;* in such poems as "The Figured Wheel" and "The Changes" he relies on unresolvable paradoxes as aids to understanding when reason alone breaks down. Even Edgar Bowers, whose earlier work drew so clearly on Winters's understanding of reason against darkness, began to court the darkness in his 1973 *Living Together.* The title poem of the collection conveys a longing for completion that reason alone cannot bring:

> Of you I have no memory, keep no promise.
> But, as I read, drink, wait, and watch the surf,
> Faithful, almost forgotten, your demand
> Becomes all others, and this loneliness
> The need that is your presence. In the dark,
> Beneath the lamp, attentive, like a sound
> I listen for, you draw near—closer, surer
> Than speech, or sight, or love, or love returned.[17]

The Other is the antagonist and partner, the shadow-lover on whose presence the poet depends for completeness. The mind alone may define the self but cannot define the totality of the human being. For that, Bowers suggests, the poet must move beyond the mind, or atrophy in its static excellence.

This movement beyond the mind, which characterizes the post-Wintersian work of so many of Winters's apprentices, left Winters behind. It was the crucial maneuver he could not achieve. He did not eschew this movement, however, from some academic willfulness. Winters confronted the irrational at an extreme edge early in his life, and this terrifying confrontation gave him both a profound respect for the dangers of madness and a need to derive strength from the long tradition of European rationalism. An existentialist might argue that Winters *chose* to define the mind primarily as a tool of reason, and reason as a coherent system of cause and effect that did not permit "the hypothetical possibility of a hostile supernatural world."[18] With this act of defining, Winters defined himself. He set himself at a slight remove from a potentially malevolent or meaningless world, and armed himself against darkness by embracing the cultural heritage of Aristotle and Aquinas. These tools of reason gave him standards, and a powerful interpretive strength. Along with his ingrained personal generosity, they made him in many ways an attractive mentor. But they also made him a "limit and antagonist," as Timothy Dekin has said in a somewhat different context.[19] At some point an apprentice would either accept the master, or cross him, for the boundary was clear. Yet the boundary, definite as it was, held its attractions.

In 1947 Winters wrote, "I myself am not a Christian and I fear that I lack permanently the capacity to become one";[20] yet for a man returning from the brink of sanity, the classical Christian tradition provided genuine comfort. In his essay on Henry Adams, one of his best performances in prose, Winters argued, "In the universe of Aquinas, which resembles in many important respects that of his great predecessor, Aristotle, we can learn a great deal by the light of natural reason. The universe was created by God, it is true; but it was so created as to pursue its own laws, and those laws, including many which govern the nature of man, can be discovered with reasonable accuracy after careful examination of the data before us."[21] And a little earlier, Winters celebrated the intellectual force of Aquinas: "Aquinas endeavored as far as possible to establish a separation between philosophy and theology; philosophy was guided by natural reason, theology was derived from Revelation. But he believed that philosophical knowledge was possible, and in his pursuit of it, he composed the most complete and lucid critique of previous philosophy that had been made, and the most thorough and defensible moral and philosophical system, in all likelihood, that the world has known."[22] One of the reasons that Winters's "Henry Adams, or The Creation of Confusion" is such an interesting work is that it acknowledges so constantly Winters's own debt to a particular tradition. Yet, while Winters makes great claims for the intellectual merits of this tradition, his own debt to it is by no means simply intellectual. One could argue that Winters owed his life, or at least his sanity, to it, and that this classical Christian tradition itself functioned as a mentor for Winters.

As Winters explains in the introduction to his *Early Poems,* "in the 'twenties I was not in Paris, nor even at Harvard,"[23] but rather in Los Cerillos, Madrid, and Santa Fe, New Mexico, and Moscow, Idaho—mining towns and small population centers where culture more often than not meant that Winters "was able to keep order at the public dances on Friday nights merely by [his] presence until ten o'clock, but after ten, because of the consumption of liquor, [he] needed (and received) the assistance of the marshal."[24] In many ways Winters represented his own cultural center, and in his time of despair in 1926 he turned inward toward that center, that mentor of tradition, which carried him through.

Winters ultimately swore his first allegiance, not to another subject (as he himself was a subject), but to the *animus* of a tradition. This allegiance did not yield a human relationship, although aspects of it were obviously essential to Winters's humanity. Instead, the tradition required what Jean Baker Miller calls "permanent inequality," in which some trait of the individual "ascribed at birth"—about which the individual can do nothing—serves as a justification for subordination.[25] For Winters this ascribed trait was—as it was to some extent for Ezra Pound—the human frailty of loneliness and disorientation. To escape these curses was to place oneself under the dominance of the saving rational tradition; a scholar of the texts within this tradition would himself master some aspect of an otherwise incomprehensible and frightening world, gaining a kind of power over the forces of chaos. He might well be a mentor. Yet he would never be mutually bound to a subject that could recognize and cherish him as a subject. He would always be subservient to the dominant tradition, and his experience of subservience—whether conscious or unconscious—would tend to be perpetuated in his relationships with his apprentices.

Because the tradition was not human, it could never be a subject in the sense in which a "subject" for Benjamin implies a discrete being whose insights and limits help define oneself. Represented by the historical figures of Aristotle and Aquinas, the rational tradition itself was nevertheless faceless, egoless, and eternal. It rescued Winters but arrived without a presence from which mercy might emanate. All it asked was obedience. If Winters would follow the precepts of reason, they would not betray him into darkness. Rebellion, on the other hand, was fatal. In this sense the rational tradition itself became the father, binding Winters even as it rescued him. And yet its only distinct attribute of the father was its coolness, its authority, and its implicit threat of what might happen if its presence were withdrawn.

Emphasizing judgment, duty, discipline, and justice—the Jungian values of the *animus*—the rational tradition framed Winters's later poetry as it framed his approach to mentorship. The bond between Winters and his students essentially evolved from traditional concepts of the mind and immortality: the role of the teacher was to educate by argument. In so doing the teacher passed something of himself on to the next generation. One extended oneself, not simply in the sexual act, or in the quest to distinguish the apprentice's identity from one's own, but in the will to subordinate oneself to reason. The central trait of a successful mentorship, which Miller identifies as the "end [of] the relationship of inequality,"[26] was very difficult in this context, for mentor and apprentice were always to be unequal, and were to accept this hierarchy for the values it implied. Although Winters might be drawn toward friendship with some of his students—as he was with Gunn in 1956— the risk of deviating from this hierarchy shadowed any close contact with disappointment and danger. Such risk shook the foundations of Winters's own apprenticeship, and it damned the fallen one, as Winters's attack on Hart Crane most vividly demonstrates.

On the other hand, a consistently devoted apprentice could appear to reinforce Winters's values while thriving in her own right. This apprentice, Janet Lewis, embarked in 1926 on a marriage with Winters that in virtually every respect seemed blessed. Happiness and accomplishment followed both writers, and the formal, argumentative poems Lewis wrote between 1930 and 1944 showed both a debt to the mentor and a facility that, in some cases, exceeded the mentor's.[27] Lewis also became the proficient manager of the Winters household, nurturing their two children and taking care of a small host of animals. Yet the Lewis apprenticeship confirms the dangers of Winters's debt to the rational tradition: it identifies the unresolved erotic tensions in Winters's own relationship to that tradition. Because the faceless father figure brooks no rebellion, the identity of the apprentice remains incomplete, unfinished. This is Winters's condition: facing madness, he turns back to reason, and in the cool magnificence of that embrace he finds no need to rebel. Yet without the separation this rebellion connotes, he cannot stand apart from his debt to tradition. In this sense Winters becomes the dependent master. He draws others into his circle of dependence, until the tradition that should most encourage independent action becomes a tool of ensnarement and limitation.

In Lewis's case, it is not possible to argue that her poems reflect a kind of erotic oppression; but it is possible to see in them evidence of a mode of thinking and writing that, given Lewis's background, was ultimately too confining. Lewis implicitly chose the nonconfrontational solution to a conflict with her mentor. She gave up writing poems in 1944, and wrote no more poems until a year or so after Winters's death in 1968. When she began again with poetry, she returned to a theme and mode of writing reminiscent of her earliest work, before her years with Winters. She thus separated herself from the anxieties of the rational tradition. It was Winters's tragedy that he could not do the same. Yet Winters was by no means a simple man or a minor tyrant. He was a man on a "quest for reality,"[28] and he saw a route to reality through the kind of poetry in which ideas mattered above all else. His poems reveal no stereotypical rationalism, but rather an attractive and subtle mind wrestling with ultimate concerns.

———

In 1919 Santa Fe was still a frontier town. Around it the desert swelled placidly and rather ominously to the horizon; scrub pine and manzanita took the place of Russell Square or Brattle Street or the Rue de Rivoli. To be a tourist was not to encounter Santa Fe, for Santa Fe was not for tourists; it was for adventurers and entrepreneurs and traders and victims of disease, particularly tuberculosis, who could profit from the dry, quiet surroundings. For Winters, stricken with tuberculosis after a little over a year at the University of Chicago, Santa Fe was a necessary exile. Once there, he might well have had the sense of being rooted in a hothouse of phenomena, a strange world one could not easily escape no matter how far one pushed the borders: in Gallup, 150 miles west, or Pueblo, 190 miles north, or Las Cruces, 230 miles south, or Lubbock, 275 miles east, the phenomena remained exotic. The sky blazed its blue across a tawny landscape; at sunset the colors went wild. Writing to a friend, Maurice Lesemann, on September 28, 1919, Winters noted, "There is a superabundance of jays and sparrow-hawks here and a dearth of events. If one were to write of pale green clouds in a violet sky, people would say that one was drunk or imitating Conrad Aiken, yet I have seen this here at dusk. This is a very amazing country."[29]

Though Winters was occasionally extravagant with his diction, "amazing" in this case is clearly well-chosen. Winters came under the spell of this landscape. It was not necessarily a happy experience. Writing to Lesemann on February 8, 1919, shortly after his arrival at St. Vincent's, Winters comments tellingly on the power of the New Mexico setting as he describes his encounter with the painter Marsden Hartley: "Most of [Hartley's] pieces are landscapes, and they have a sort of sensuous quality—in fact one of them is almost indecent. He is a post-impressionist, of course, and rather tends to symbolize his subjects. The one landscape I speak of—a New Mexico scene—seems to me to possess a sort of ominous physical mysticism, which I maintain is the principal characteristic of this country as opposed to the more ethereal and spiritual beauty of California."[30] The tone here is erudite, with an interesting intellectual distinction between mysticism and spirituality. But there is much more here—terror, certainly, terror of the human body and the body of the earth. Winters has arrived in Santa Fe because his life is in peril; yet all he can do is wait, and watch. In watching, he comes to express at times an understandable loathing for the human body, whose best friend ultimately is death. Death absorbs, denies, descends inexorably, rejects all human aspirations and loves. Intellectualized, sexuality becomes for Winters the precursor of decay, of disease—of the "physical mysticism" that the landscape embodies, negating the importance of the individual human identity as it absorbs that smaller body into itself. Death is the enemy; sex engenders it. Yet Winters cannot fight back. He is barely permitted to move at all, as he explains in a letter to Lesemann on May 25, 1919. The letter opens with Winters's drawing of what, according to Brigitte Carnochan, is a "drowning figure."[31] It is equally possible, however, that the drawing represents the head and arms of a human skeleton extending above a pile of desert stones. The man has been buried alive; he is not yet quite dead. From horrid sockets his eyes still stare, and his hair stands straight up on his shiny head. Underneath the figure

Winters writes, "That's me." He goes on to describe his regimen at St. Vincent's: "Regarding the shadows, though, I have been lying for eight hours out of the diurnal twelve on a sleeping porch, with nothing in sight but a lawn and numerous trees. Being an invalid, and having very little to occupy my time, I have watched said scene, the most remarkable feature of which is its shadows. And I have made poems about the shadows in order to kill time."[32]

Time, the potential killer, can be killed through art. In this context art becomes a distraction from the quivering tragedy of life. This is not high praise for art. Yet the comment does suggest the primary demands on Winters's consciousness in this period. They were not essentially cultural, or historical, or even aesthetic demands; they were simple, direct matters of life and death. Death surrounded Winters at the sanatorium, and it continued to surround him throughout his next four years in the West. Commenting on life in Cerrillos, New Mexico, following his departure from St. Vincent's, Winters describes a casual regard for both life and death: "Accidents, many fatal, were common in the mines, from which union organizers were vigorously excluded and sometimes removed; drunken violence was a daily and nightly occurrence in both [Madrid and Los Cerrillos]; mayhem and murder were discussed with amusement."[33] Given this context, it makes sense that Winters's early poems should be largely concerned with matters of death, fate, and self-discovery on the edge of consciousness. This was Winters's landscape, almost as much a physical landscape as a psychic one.

Yet even as Winters contemplated his isolation and the proximity of death on the high plains of the American West, he was not utterly cut off from the world of poetry he had discovered in Chicago. Before leaving the university he had made friends with Harriet Monroe, who bestowed upon him a complete set of *Poetry* from its inception to 1918, when Winters began subscribing. In Sante Fe, Winters continued to receive *Poetry* as well as *Others, The Little Review,* and, "as occasion permitted . . . a few later and similar magazines."[34] Initiating a correspondence with Marianne Moore in 1921, he received a warm response, and the exchange of letters continued for several years.[35] Equally important, Moore—who was at the time working in the New York Public Library—sent Winters a number of books of contemporary literature and poetry on extended loan.[36] It was Moore who introduced Winters to the work of Henry James: Winters recalls, "I remember reading *The Golden Bowl,* at the age of twenty-one and with no preparation, while I was a teacher in a coal-mining camp."[37] While in Santa Fe, Winters also began studying French, a fortuitous event with major implications: "there was a French priest in Santa Fe who gave me a few, and my first, lessons in French, lessons which set me to work at a frustrating effort to decipher Rimbaud, a poet of whom my friend the priest thoroughly disapproved."[38]

By 1925 Winters was teaching French and Spanish at the University of Idaho in Moscow, having recently earned his B.A. and M.A. in Romance Languages at the University of Colorado, Boulder. His acquaintance with the work of Baudelaire, Rimbaud, Mallarmé, and Corbière was by that time fairly extensive; he had also come to know the early work of Wallace Stevens, William Carlos Williams, and Ezra Pound. Between 1922 and 1925, he contributed several reviews to *Poetry*— among them a review of *The Collected Poems of Edwin Arlington Robinson* in 1922, William Carlos Williams's *Sour Grapes,* in 1922, Elizabeth Madox Roberts's *Under the Tree,* in 1923, and Marianne Moore's *Observations,* in 1925.[39] He also published two books of poems—*The Immobile Wind,* in 1921, and *The Magpie's Shadow,* in 1922. From one point of view, then, it is certainly arguable that Winters had overcome his exile in the American West and had begun to assert his critical and creative presence in the arena of American poetry.

Yet Winters was very much a poet at risk. He knew well the shadowy companionship of death; he knew the desert landscape and its profound indifference to human life. He also knew, or believed he knew, a modern poetic method that would allow him to explore that dangerous psychic territory, that zone between consciousness and nothingness. In formal terms this poetic method invoked the possibilities of free verse: Winters wrote to Maurice Lesemann in 1919 that he had "definitely given up rhymed verse except for short excursions"; he found free verse "more interesting and more challenging." "I truly believe," he said with uncommonly transparent fervor, "that it can be used for practically anything for which one can use rhymed."[40] In fact *The Immobile Wind* includes twelve poems out of nineteen that involve some metrical formality or rhyme; *The Magpie's Shadow* includes no such poems. Beyond these two books—in the full-length *The Bare Hills,* which appeared in 1927— Winters continued to move forcefully away from formal techniques.

If the formal issue for Winters was free verse versus metered verse, the psychic issue was the irrational versus reason. Winters gratefully accepted Rimbaud's invitation to explore the unknown: "Je veux être poëte, et je travaille à me rendre *voyant:* vous ne comprendrez pas de tout, et je ne saurais presque vous expliquer. Il s'agit d'arriver à l'inconnu par le dérèglement de *tous les sens*. Les souffrances sont énormes, mais il faut être fort, être né poëte, et je me suis réconnu poëte."[41] "You won't understand this at all," says Rimbaud to his friend Georges Izambard in a letter Winters apparently knew well, "and I hardly know how to explain it to you." This is the "poëte maudit," and the role fits Winters. One sees it in his bearing, in a 1920 photograph, as he stands outside the sanatorium in his black ten-gallon hat and Old West riding jacket, staring straight ahead through round, black-rimmed glasses.[42] He is the exile, disguised as a native; he is the adventurer. And the adventure is exactly this "dérèglement de tous les sens," this un-ruling or liberation of all the senses from their commonly-perceived limits. Such a liberation would reasonably appeal to a man who understood the commonly perceived limits of sense to mean, simply and precisely, death.

The kinds of psychic risks Winters runs become increasingly clear in his early poems, and culminate in his 1927 short story "The Brink of Darkness." In these works one sees the influence of Rimbaud and the other Symbolists, as well as of Robinson, Dickinson, and Hardy; one also sees Winters wrestling with the unnerving companionship of death. In "Death Goes Before Me," from *The Immobile Wind*, Winters offers a somewhat sentimentalized portrait of himself and death, yet the language draws on both the formal colloquialisms of Robinson and the apparitional strangeness of Rimbaud.

> Death goes before me on his hands and knees,
> And we go down among the bending trees.
>
> Weeping I go, and no man gives me ease—
> I am that strange thing that each strange eye sees.
>
> Eyes of the silence and all life an eye
> Turn in the wind, and always I walk by.
>
> Too still I go, and all things go from me
> As down far autumn beaches a man runs to the sea.
>
> My hands are cold, my lips are thin and dumb.
> Stillness is like the beating of a drum.[43]

The narrator's encounter with death leaves him at last in a kind of trance: his hands are cold, his lips "are thin and dumb." The result of this experiment is not diminishment, however, but a heightened sensibility. The narrator perceives himself more clearly separate from the rest of mankind, more vividly alone, and more at risk of losing all that is human: "Too still I go, and all things go from me." To be aware of that risk is at least to escape distraction, to escape the unexamined life. Yet in his effort to identify a zone of consciousness between the self and death, Winters also risks excessive consciousness: this is what most threatens his connection with the rest of humanity, as he suggests in another poem from *The Immobile Wind,* "Where My Sight Goes":

> Who knows
> Where my sight goes,
> What your sight shows—
> Where the peachtree blows?
>
> The frogs sing
> Of everything,
> And children run
> As leaves swing.
>
> And many women pass
> Dressed in white,
> As thoughts of noon pass
> From sea to sea.
>
> And all these things would take
> My life from me.[44]

To be too aware, to listen too acutely to all the voices of creation, is to hear "the frogs sing / Of everything." One loses one's selfhood, one's humanity, in a cosmic sea of voices and symbols. It is significant that Winters voices this anxiety in a poem whose formal properties and subject recall somewhat a poem by Emily Dickinson—a poem about which Winters wrote, "[it] ought to have been one of the best and is certainly one of the most fascinating, but it is seriously marred."[45] According to N. Scott Momaday, Winters cared greatly for the poem and, as a professor at Stanford, used it regularly in his classes.[46]

> Further in Summer than the Birds
> Pathetic from the Grass
> A minor Nation celebrates
> Its unobtrusive Mass.
>
> No Ordinance be seen
> So gradual the Grace

A pensive Custom it becomes
Enlarging Loneliness.

Antiquest felt at Noon
When August burning low
Arise this spectral Canticle
Repose to typify

Remit as yet no Grace
No Furrow on the Glow
Yet a Druidic Difference
Enhances Nature now [47]

In Dickinson's poem, the division between human consciousness and the world is nearly absolute. Only in a flash of intuition, a "now," may human beings experience some degree of that "Druidic Difference." The tone of the poem is full of longing. Human consciousness can enable us to observe this non-rational or superrational world, but it cannot allow us to enter it; we can merely witness the gradual grace, and the "spectral Canticle," which typifies repose. Winters came to see this poem as another example of the suicidal impulse that he linked with American Romanticism; to desire an escape from the mind is to annihilate one's identity. Yet in his early years, Winters explored this possibility as well as the possibilities of an excessive or too-sensitive consciousness. If "Where My Sight Goes" suggests the dangers of excess, a later poem—"Song of the Trees," from his 1930 volume *The Proof*—follows the Dickinsonian lead:

Belief is blind! Bees scream!
Gongs! Thronged with light!
        And I take
into light, hold light,
in light I live, I
pooled and broken here,
to watch, to wake above you.

        Sun,
no seeming, but savage
simplicity, breaks running
for an aeon, stops, shuddering, here.[48]

This poem marks the fruition of Winters's earlier work. In contrast to many of the earlier poems, it is quite a distinguished performance, with evocative contrasts in diction and a knife-edged balancing of grace and chaos. Like the earlier work, however, it continues to explore the irrational or superrational human experience. It both points toward a powerful meditative moment and attempts to evoke that moment through dramatic juxtapositions of unexpected words. Interestingly (in contrast, for example, to H.D.'s early poems), the identity of narrator and subject is never in doubt. After an initial explosion of human consciousness, the trees become the consoling narrators, offering a refuge from the sun. The fiction of the poem makes it clear that the trees are being seen: they are at once "pooled" and "broken," an apparently oxymoronic perception that makes sense depending on the light; they are one phenomenon but also a perceived duality, divided in the author's mind against themselves and against the light. Nevertheless, the moment in which they are perceived as undivided offers whatever peace resides in the poem.

In a sense the poem answers that Dickinsonian longing for connection. The "minor Nation" responds to human consciousness, comforts it, establishes a kinship. The trees "watch" and "wake" above the slumbering human soul. The poem also draws heavily on techniques of juxtaposition and simultaneity that one associates with such symbolist works (some of which Winters translated and included in his *Collected Poems*) as Mallarmé's "Brise Marine" or "Prose" or "Sainte" or "Soupir," Baudelaire's "L'Invitation au Voyage" or "La Beauté," or Rimbaud's "Marine" or "L'Eternité."

Taken by itself, "Song of the Trees" suggests that Winters had begun to settle into a satisfactory relationship with the irrational. A self at once "pooled and broken" recalls Yeats's lines from "Crazy Jane Talks with the Bishop"—"For nothing can be sole or whole / That has not been rent."[49] Winters had perhaps come to understand the self as a continual process of destruction and rebuilding. Each new unruling of sense, each effort to mediate between the human and natural worlds, each attempt to extend the self by revising the seemingly intractable limits of death and knowledge, yielded a more powerful poetic talent. Yeats's "foul rag-and-bone shop of the heart" was Winters's gold mine as well.

In fact, however, as Winters continued to confront the irrational he more often found, not ecstacy, but the threat of annihilation. The self that might consent to an ecstatic union, as implied in "Song of the Trees," should never lose its power to form aesthetic judgments. It should be at the same time itself and another, capable of reflecting on its own divine embrace. But Winters found more often that the self attempting this extension risked fragmentation, dissolution, and madness—the genuine rag-and-bone shop, the kin of death. In a poem from *The Bare Hills,* "Dark Spring,"[50] Winters considers ironically the whole process of human generation. April is no elegantly cruel month in this poem, but a time when "rats run on the roof" and the earth thaws around the bodies of the dead. This horror extends to sexuality—both the implicit sexuality of the narrator's mother, and the explicit sexuality of his lover. Winters equates the lover directly with death: her hand is "White, as if out of earth." From this horror the mind may offer some escape, though in this relatively early poem that conclusion remains ambiguous: the studying mind disowns its own breath, and although it can retreat from the horror of the incarnation enough to contemplate its fate, it cannot escape the incarnation. The profound frustration here is palpable: coming to spring "page by page," as the narrator does, is a cheat, yet the alternative is not robust life—nor even an ecstatic communion, an encounter with the phallic trees or the regenerative lover—but earthbound mortality, dirt, grime, dreamlessness, a shadow-Christ.

In "Midnight Wind," overtones of sexual frustration and sadomasochism sweep through the language.

> I pressed you
> into place with
> cold hands, paused
> upon the threshold,
> and went down the road.
>
> The wind came
> down the gulley
> buffeting the earth like a
> great rock—
>
>   I
> trembled in the wind
> but found my door
> and climbed the stairway
> as a man
> climbs out of sleep.
>
> And it was not that
> I did not believe in
> God, but that the quiet
> of the room was more
> immediate—

> it was the
> brute passivity
> of rough dark wood
> beneath my bare feet
> where no wind dared
> fan the naked fact.[51]

The opening three lines are particularly ominous: Who is being pressed into place? What is the place, and what is the nature of the submission? Why is the narrator so detached? The object of his attention is identified neither by name nor by sexuality; the narrator's hands are cold, and his pause upon the threshold lends a pathological air to the preceding events. What comforts the narrator, finally, is not God, but a set of evocative mysteries—the "brute passivity" of the wooden floorboards in a room where "no wind dared / fan the naked fact." If this is pantheism, it is highly charged with sadomasochistic overtones. Some force, equal in brute strength to the narrator, chooses passivity or is made passive; the "naked fact," whatever it may be, is at least blessedly private, a kind of liberation. Not even the wind disturbs it, yet the entire scene is disturbed: the narrator cannot say what he means. The sexuality of this poem manifests itself in powerful and contradictory ways, but no resolution is possible; the best the reader can attain is a kind of draw, in which unnamed and possibly corrupt forces balance each other's brutality and passivity.

Winters has often been thought of as a theorist, a man obsessed with poetic form and moral judgment. Yet it is extremely curious that his early years have been so often overlooked, for they reveal him to be much less a theorist than a man living, an experimenter in the high-risk laboratory of the phenomenal world. For Winters to write about the brink of darkness was for him to stand on the brink of darkness; for him to explore the unruling of the senses was for him to trust Rimbaud's directive as best he knew how—to explore the possibility of meaning beyond reason, to demand that his mind exceed itself. The terror of what he found there was no theory for him; his escape was equally real, and perilous.

By November 1933, when he submitted his doctoral dissertation to the English department at Stanford University, he had already come to the fundamental understanding of reason and poetry that was to guide him through *In Defense of Reason* and *Forms of Discovery*. Writing on the moral nature of poetry, Winters adapts symbolist terminology to a new world of rhyme, meter, and argument:

> We may say that a poem in the first place should offer us new perceptions, not only of the exterior universe, but of human experience as well; it should add, in other words, to what we have already seen. This is the elementary function for the reader. The corresponding function for the poet is a sharpening and training of his sensibilities; the very exigencies of the medium as he employs it in the act of perception should force him to the discovery of values which he never would have found without the convening of all the conditions of that particular act, conditions one or more of which will be the necessity of solving some particular difficulty such as the location of a rhyme or the perfection of a cadence without disturbance to the remainder of the poem.[52]

The first part of this statement might well have been written by Rimbaud in a tame moment; the second part is pure Winters. Poetry has a moral function because it forces the author to confront the essential problem of meaning, to make judgments about what he means and does not mean, to discard the unessential and to use the exact word. For Winters this generally means that formal poetry is the most "moral," because formal poetry exerts the greatest demands on the writer's discrimination and judgment. Convention, too, is important, because it gives the poet a context. The poet without convention is adrift in an uncivilized and uncivilizable world. This context is not only cultural but linguistic. We understand and look for a certain appropriate language in poetry, Winters argues, and a poet who understands this can increase the force of his presentation by balancing convention with certain unconventional or unexpected experiments in diction or meter. Tradition, the tradition of intellectual judgment, is essential in any case. Commenting on contemporary poetry in the fifth chapter of his dissertation—a chapter destined to serve as the basis for "Primitivism and Decadence," a significant portion of *In Defense of Reason*—Winters identifies modern experimental poetry as an outgrowth of either primitivism or decadence, depending on the background of the poet. "Both decadent and primitive lack an understanding and correlation of their experience: the primitive accepts his limitations through wisdom or ignorance; the decadent endeavors to conceal them, or, like some primitives, may never discover them; the primitive, however, treats of what he understands and the decadent of more than he understands. For either to achieve major poetry there is necessary an intellectual clarification of some kind."[53]

Hart Crane, Ezra Pound, Allen Tate, and Paul Valéry are examples of decadent poets, according to Winters; William Carlos Williams, Marianne Moore, and Gerard Manley Hopkins are primitives. What defines them is either a tendency to explore "more than [they] understand" or a tendency to narrow their subjects according to their limited understanding. What makes them less than great is their lack of "intellectual clarification," their inability to merge their own talent and historical moment with the Western tradition on which they more or less unconsciously draw.

The primitive and the decadent in modern poetry—or, as Winters would call it, post-Romantic poetry—constitute a potentially serious intellectual menace, because they extend from the theories and examples of the French and English Romanticists. Winters writes in his dissertation,

> The more typically romantic writers . . . seem to me for the most part rather bad; that is, romanticism appears to me as a vitiating tendency, corrupting various talents in various ways and degrees. . . . The important thing is, that the writers whom I have called post-romantic hold in one way or another similar opinions, and their work thus represents a reaction to some aspect of romantic literature. . . . Post-romantic literature is then by definition that literature in which there appears a conscious effort to correct the laxity and shallowness of romantic style and sentiment, without any clear understanding of the defects in romantic thought which gave rise to that style and sentiment.[54]

The kind of analyses Winters provides of the American "obscurantist" tradition—analyses that embrace T. S. Eliot and Ezra Pound as well as Walt Whitman and Ralph Waldo Emerson—reflect this sense of the "defects in romantic thought." This does not mean that Winters came to object to all discussion of the irrational in literature; his guarded praise for Emily Dickinson, and his celebration of Jones Very and Frederick Goddard Tuckerman, all indicate that he understood the irrational as an essential component of human experience. But it was not a component of the rational experience. Insofar as the irrational comprised a moral experience—and that possibility for Winters was distinctly limited—it commanded the mind to reject it. Those who refused this, as Jones Very ultimately did, fell into the trap of self-annihilation. Yet Winters was willing to admire the poems of Very when, adopting the hypothetical point of view of a deity, he argued for the essential tragedy of the human condition.[55] Winters's psychological crisis of 1926 and 1927 did not radically alter him, despite appearances. The Winters who survived "The Brink of Darkness" and cherished Aristotelian and Thomist thought was never far from the Winters who hoped for some enlarged sensibility, some unruling of the senses.

What did alter greatly was, of course, the emphasis Winters placed on reason as a tool to protect oneself against the excesses of mystical seduction. At a more fundamental level, reason also protected him against the "ominous physical mysticism" he first noticed in Marsden Hartley's paintings. This was the mysticism of the body—that agent of ecstacy and death, that matrix of creative power, that sexual form. Though sexually created, the mind is uniquely empowered either to negate the value of that creation or to turn it into metaphor: the Trinity is one such metaphor, the birth of Athena is another, and even the creation of a work of philosophy or art—any intellectual creation—can be seen, if the creator so chooses, as an antierotic act. The mind triumphs over the body's methods by creating something that will outlast the body.

The erotic anxiety in Winters's work is quite distinct. Apparent during his convalescence at the sanatoriums in Santa Fe, when he comments in letters and poems on the misery of the body, this anxiety manifests itself further in Winters's poetry from the late 1920s. It underlies the dissertation, in which Winters identifies himself as having "ethical preferences of an Aristotelian-Christian variety,"[56] and in which he emphasizes the importance of philosophy as a precursor to any serious study of poetry (a point of view, interestingly, almost exactly the opposite of T. S. Eliot's).[57] The virtue of Winters's theory of morality in poetry—a theory he initiates in the dissertation and develops much more fully in *In Defense of Reason*—is that the mind may find within itself the strength to analyze and discriminate what before was undifferentiated experience. For Winters, the critical faculty is essential to art because without it art is simply meaningless. If, on its face, this concept seems a grim condemnation of creative intuition, one should reconsider it in the context of Winters's life. Winters's career is particularly moving because it demonstrates over and over again the efforts of a brilliant man to keep the wolves of unreason at bay. In Winters's hands, what might have been merely a therapeutic process becomes an argument both for a mode of thought and a sense of art. Art and life are as closely linked in Winters's work as they are in that of any great poet, and if nothing else Winters should be remembered for this.

Yet the danger of this emphatic intellectuality should also be clear. To be grounded in life is to be grounded in the matrix of creation, the body as well as the mind; it is "to accept the waking body," as Richard Wilbur has said.[58] Eros commands that reason accept generation and death, and ironically this is not irrational. In accepting these attributes of human existence one comes more fully to embrace the totality of the self. By itself, reason is aberrant; what it generates is not life, but a series of mutations, of propositions divorced from the world. Dickens satirized the arch-rationalist Gradgrind in *Hard Times* because he saw the life-denying quality of this aberrant reason. The world that Gradgrind sees is not a world at all, but a set of chimerical certainties sailing on a sea of figures.[59] At that same extreme level Gradgrind's world is comforting. He has liberated himself from the messy informalities of the flesh.

While Winters's gradual liberation from his own earlier, messy informalities is far more sophisticated than the Dickensian satire, one serious ground of comparison remains—the concept of reason as a kind of faith. Winters's mind alone could not have healed his tubercular body, but his mind could to some extent liberate him from its worst excesses. Beyond that, his mind could attempt to establish its own limits, as well as its own kind of regeneration through an intellectual tradition. *In Defense of Reason* itself confirms this mental process, but so do many of Winters's later poems—"To a Young Writer," written in 1930, or "For the Opening of the William Dinsmore Briggs Room," composed in 1942, or the poems in between—"To My Infant Daughter," "Dedication for a Book of Criticism," "On Teaching the Young," "Socrates," or "Time and the Garden." Interestingly, these poems also concern themselves largely with various kinds of teaching or mentorship. What matters among them is the debt to a particular tradition, a tradition of the mind: this is the tradition that came to Winters's rescue, this is the tradition he himself will pass on.

In "To a Young Writer," for example, Winters counsels his student to acquire such knowledge that feeling will finally come under its dominion:

> Write little; do it well.
> Your knowledge will be such,
> At last, as to dispel
> What moves you overmuch.[60]

By the same token, in "Dedication for a Book of Criticism," Winters acknowledges his debt to a Stanford professor, William Dinsmore Briggs, and to the intellectual tradition that had become Winters's mentor even before his arrival at Stanford:

He who learns may feed on lies:
He who understands is wise.
He who understands the great
Joins them in their own estate:
Grasping what they had to give,
Adds his strength that they may live. . . .

Heir of Linacre and More,
Guardian of Erasmus' store,
Careful knower of the best,
Bacon's scholar, Jonson's guest,
It was in your speaking lip
That I honored scholarship.

In the motions of your thought
I a plan and model sought;
My deficiencies but gauge
My own talents and the age;
What is good from you I took;
Then, in justice, take my book.[61]

In this poem (as in Pound's *Spirit of Romance*), the goal is to join "the great." To be a "knower of the best" is to define oneself at a pinnacle of human experience. The poem implies that any deficiencies in knowledge or execution lie with the apprentice, and that these deficiencies may be judged according to a "plan and model." In a hierarchy of values under which both mentor and apprentice are subsumed, the mentor rises by translating himself into a knower and standing apart. The apprentice, perhaps capable of following, is nevertheless left with such deficiencies as he may possess. Though the gift exchange at the end of the poem might seem to undercut this sense of distance and inequality, the terms of the exchange are curious. The apprentice receives an abstraction—"what is good"—from the mentor, and offers in return a book, a gift both physical and intellectual. Yet this gift cannot be offered or received on its own terms; it succeeds only within the framework of "justice." The poem brilliantly evinces the "hierarchical or contractual" values that Carol Gilligan contrasts to "values of care and connection."[62] The contrast between these value systems is all the more striking because of the longing for connection underlying the poem.

The "plan and model" Winters sought celebrated the certainty of reason—the assurance of all that man can know, the suspicion of mere opinion or feeling. Winters developed this idea in "On Teaching the Young":

The young are quick of speech.
Grown middle-aged, I teach
Corrosion and distrust,
Exacting what I must.

A poem is what stands
When imperceptive hands,
Feeling, have gone astray.
It is what one should say.

Few minds will come to this.
The poet's only bliss
Is in cold certitude—
Laurel, archaic, rude.[63]

The groping, "imperceptive hands," laden with unhappy sexuality, miss
the poem; "cold certitude," not ecstasy, brings bliss. The antagonism
toward eros here is strong, but not as strong as Winters's sense of debt
to the "few minds" who actually comprehend this.

First on the brink of death, then on the brink of madness, Winters
finds reassurance in the rigors of the mind. Although he never disre-
gards the power of the irrational, he finds the mind to be the essential
tool in combatting it. To create is to move away from the body. As "Time
and the Garden" or "To the Holy Spirit" suggest, the body is a road to
hell, to irrelevance, to meaninglessness. Yet this movement away from
the body unbalances the force of Winters's mentorship. It limits his ability to comprehend modes of being that differ significantly from his own,
and it limits his ability to appreciate the poetry that evolves from those
modes of being. It is ironic that Winters, who came so much to fear
human isolation in the 1920s, adopted a sense of pedagogical mission
which in some ways increased his isolation. The tradition of liberal
thought that ought to have freed Winters and his circle to find their
own way instead became, in Winters's hands, a more or less benevolent
dictator.

"[Winters] wanted to be kind, and he didn't quite know how," recalls Philip Levine, in a 1974 interview with Stanley Plumly and Wayne
Dodd.[64]

In the classroom he was a disaster. He read from his essays. He read *In
Defense of Reason* in one course. And the students sat there. He was very
unperceptive on the level of relationships with people, incredibly. He was
obviously a very close, brilliant reader of poetry. Even when you didn't

agree with his evaluation of a poem, it was clear he could read it very carefully. But it was pathetic the way the students suckered him, kissed his ass, and those were the ones he liked. Kids who had some gumption . . . he wanted to like but didn't. They were "Mad. Mad." You know, he overused the word "mad."

Given Levine's portrait, it is easy to imagine the young Winters as the kind of student the older Winters "wanted to like but didn't." In that kind of student Winters saw his own madness, and the continuing threat to his coherent identity. Levine also comments perceptively on the price Winters paid for his mental salvation: "He was a frustrated prizefighter—underneath all that 'right reason'—and he hadn't the vaguest idea how to box. He would show me how he would fight, and I would say to him (I also trained for a couple of years to fight; I was no good . . . I mean, even though I could have beaten Yvor Winters with my head), it was sad to see that under all this mind business was a man with an unhappy body." The "man with an unhappy body" had difficulty making the connection between his intuitive responses—to students' work and to other established poets' writing—and the orthodoxy he had labored so long to define in his criticism and poems. As Thom Gunn recalls, "I even knew his feeling to run completely contrary to his printed statements: he once said to me of Robert Lowell something like, 'Lowell *has* it, you know—for all his faults he is a poet; damn it he can write,' a remark that any reader and most students of Winters will find nothing less than astonishing. It was perhaps a weakness in his method that he would have been able to find no place for it in his published criticism."[65]

Unlike Levine, Gunn asserts his gratitude for his time as Winters's student. Nevertheless, in kind terms, Gunn identifies a crucial Wintersian rigidity:

> I think it was on my return to Stanford from Texas in 1956 that he asked me to call him by his first name, Arthur. I was moved by the gesture, but on thinking about it was a little depressed. As Allen Tate said to me many years later, when I once met him briefly, "Winters made the mistake of judging people by their poetry." I already knew this; and what was more I knew that my poetry would sooner or later disappoint Winters. He would feel affection for me only as long as he could approve of my poetry and my ideas. . . . I felt as if I were a partner in some doomed love affair from a French novel: I could see an end in sight even while we achieved the point of greatest symbolic attachment.[66]

Though Winters the man might have wanted otherwise, Winters the mind judged people through their work, and too often, as Gunn and Levine suggest, the people became the sum of their poetic propositions. Winters would prod his students to retain the training he had given them; this often brought tactful but exasperated responses. Writing to Winters on November 16, 1966, N. Scott Momaday complains with a knife-edged gentleness: "Your second letter (a postscript to your uncontrolled association) has just arrived. I have the sense that you are trying to impale me upon the angle of your vision. . . . If you persist, I shall soon have to invent my authorities."[67] To invent one's authorities was, of course, to defy the orthodoxy; Momaday's warning came to fruition after Winters's death, when he began to draw more clearly, not only on Kiowa spiritual sources, but also on Kiowa rhythms and modes of language in his poetry. It is interesting how staunchly Momaday continues to defend Winters, however. In his introduction to *The Strength of Art*, for example, Momaday affirms, "There were those who suspected tyranny in such an intelligence, who said that he was a dogmatist. They were mistaken. Yvor Winters was not an unreasonable man in any sense. Indeed, he stood in defense of reason the whole of his life."[68]

There is a diplomatic leap between this language and the language of Momaday's letter. Yet Momaday's comment is interesting because it reflects the generally held notion that Winters was a gentleman, a gentle man. His fiery assertions in print sometimes took a milder cast in the world of human beings. This mildness, however, should not be understood to negate the basic qualities of the Wintersian mentorship— authority, intense intellectuality, and an urgent subordination of self to tradition. These qualities differ markedly from those of another mentorship, Louise Bogan's, in which, although mentor and apprentice eventually parted, they suffered no rupture of church and believer: Bogan nurtured Theodore Roethke's open-mindedness, not his tendency to follow. Winters, by contrast, invited his students to follow his vision; if they saw in it a refuge from chaos, as he did, so much the better. As Gunn notes, "For some of his students his formulations provided a refuge, a harmonious world where everything had already been decided in accordance with certain rules. It became a temporary or lifelong asylum for those who might otherwise have fallen into the arms of a church or a political party. The attraction lay in the logical *completeness* with which he had worked out his ideas, and such students became disciples in a literal sense, limiting themselves to another man's world."[69]

For his part, Winters felt obliged to keep his students closely held to formally rendered stanzas and philosophical precision. His badgering of those who strayed was sometimes tactful, sometimes much less so. In his commentary on one of Gunn's poems, "In Santa Maria del Popolo," for example, he writes, "Like many of Gunn's poems, it exists on the narrow line between great writing and skillful journalism. Gunn's poems seem to come just a shade too easily."[70] Gunn understood Winters to use "journalism" as a serious condemnation;[71] the ambiguousness of the word belies the sharpness of the criticism. To others who sought his comments, Winters was less kind. He upbraided S. Foster Damon, the celebrated Blake scholar, for the "carelessness" of his poetic composition in the spring of 1966. This was too much for Damon, who responded with an outraged rejection of Winters's criticisms—"No. NO!"[72]

The paradigm for these relationships—inasmuch as any relationship can serve as a paradigm for others—is surely Winters's relationship with Hart Crane. Critics since Crane's death have focused on what seems to be almost a kind of treachery on Winters's part. From championing Crane's earlier poetry in his critical work, Winters turns on Crane—without informing him before publication—in a major review of Crane's *The Bridge* in *Poetry* magazine. In a 1927 review of Crane's first book, *White Buildings,* Winters refers to Crane as a "genius" and a "contemporary master."[73] Three years later, Winters launches a devastating offensive. Crane, he writes, "is temperamentally unable to understand a very wide range of experience"; in his poems he heads "precisely nowhere, in spite of all the shouting."[74] Yet the flaw Winters detects has more than personal implications: "[The] poems illustrate the danger inherent in Mr. Crane's almost blind faith in his moment-to-moment inspiration, the danger that the author may turn himself into a kind of stylistic automaton, the danger that he may develop a sentimental leniency toward his vices and become wholly their victim, instead of understanding them and eliminating them."[75] "Stylistic automaton," "sentimental leniency," the "victim" of intellectual vices—these become familiar terms in the vocabulary of Wintersian mentorship, attacking not simply a particular person but a way of thinking about literature and life. Indeed, in his review of Crane's *Bridge,* Winters also attacks James Joyce and William Carlos Williams, whose "anti-intellectualism" threatens the power of words to mean anything at all.[76]

What becomes clear from Winters's point of view is that Crane is the source of treachery. He has betrayed himself, and Winters, by succumbing to a romantic tradition that violates the mind's ability to differentiate meaning from nonmeaning. How far Winters's sense of betrayal took him from the norms of friendship can be imagined. Crane was "shocked to the point of outrage," as Thomas Parkinson notes,[77] and the reasons are not hard to see: "[Winters's review] is by no means pleasant reading. Its praise is grudging and very qualified; its tone at times pedantic, at others surly; and the tone overrides any praise. It is no wonder that Crane found it offensive, and with the background of past praise and admiration from Winters, Crane had every reason to be shocked."[78] Crane, who for all his shortcomings trusted his friends, had by this time four years of close correspondence with Winters. They had met once, during Christmas week of 1927;[79] their numerous letters and exchanges of manuscripts had, at least in Crane's mind, sealed a friendship in which Crane felt vindicated in his attempts to further the experimental character of American poetry. Because, unlike the graduate student and professor Winters, Crane had no institutional affiliations to bolster his identity as an artist, he derived enormous strength from Winters's analyses and praises. His letters to Winters from 1926 to 1930 show gratitude and insight, for Winters was a dedicated correspondent—sending Crane photographs of Indian art from the Southwest, offering him a place to stay in the summer, discussing the role of the poet in contemporary society.[80]

What Crane could not understand, however, was that Winters was himself emerging from experiments with the irrational that would lead him to doubt the superrational experiments in Crane's increasingly difficult poetry. Because, for Winters, the truth of his experience acquired a universal validity, no experience of the irrational could dignify itself against the mind's rational discrimination, and no proponent of such experience—no matter how good a friend or how dedicated an apprentice—could merit a hearing. Crane's own shock and outrage may have come in part from his realization that he was not facing a fickle or untrustworthy friend, but a man whose mind had simply turned against Crane's mind. Yet this was perhaps even more terrifying, because where formerly Crane had found a critical confidant and guide, he now found a closed door. The work he thought of as his masterwork was simply wrong, "anti-intellectual." The result, for Winters, was a clarification of his own values; for Crane, a clearer road to suicide. In those bizarrely different responses one finds an extreme example of the collapse of intersubjective experience. Crane ceases to be a subject for Winters—though he remains an object of intense interest, as Winters shows with his 1947 study of Crane in *In Defense of Reason*. Similarly, Crane's reponse to Winters's assault clearly suggests his own sense of abandonment; his suicide, attributable to no one cause, nevertheless has its roots in his sense of the essential untrustworthiness of the world to which he had—from his own point of view—given so much.

Just as a serious reader of *The Bridge* will acknowledge its shortcomings, yet admire and explicate its sophisticated thinking, a serious reader of Winters and Winters's life will lament Winters's own rigidity in merging the wider world of poetic experience with his circumscribed world of self-protective reason. One can understand, perhaps, Winters's emphasis on his own orthodoxy, and his sense of indebtedness to the Western intellectual values that brought him back from the brink of darkness. Yet it is surely tragic that these values led him to define himself at least implicitly as a mentor with a cultural obligation—that is, a mentor who felt obligated to a particular body of knowledge as his text. His conflict with his mentor was as primal as his students' conflict with him, and he never made peace with the idea of rebellion. Those who rebelled against him, who thought more widely or more radically than he did, were beyond the pale, or "mad." Some rebelled and grew—like Levine, or Gunn, or Momaday; others could not, for various reasons, mount a rebellion. One apprentice—Janet Lewis—rebelled finally by falling silent. Yet perhaps the greatest silence descends around Winters himself, for his wide experience suggests that he had far more to say than he allowed himself to say. Behind the orthodoxy lay a different man, whose adopted voice could not reintegrate the fragments of a great soul.

Notes

1. Brigitte Hoy Carnochan, *The Strength of Art: Poets and Poetry in the Lives of Yvor Winters and Janet Lewis,* with introduction by N. Scott Momaday (Stanford: Stanford University Libraries, 1984), p. 11.
2. Carnochan, p. 13.
3. Carnochan, p. 31.
4. Carnochan, p. 22.
5. Marianne Moore, "To Yvor Winters," *Sequoia: Twentieth Anniversary Issue, Poetry 1956–1976,* ed. Michael J. Smith (Stanford: Associated Students of Stanford University, 1976), p. 63.
6. Hayden Carruth, "Forward," *The Voice That Is Great within Us: Ameri-*

can Poetry of the Twentieth Century, ed. Hayden Carruth (New York: Bantam Books, 1970), p. xix.

7. Yvor Winters, *In Defense of Reason* (Chicago: Alan Swallow, 1947), p. 11.

8. Winters, *Defense,* p. 11.

9. Thom Gunn, "On a Drying Hill," *Southern Review* 17, no. 4 (1981), p. 681.

10. Gunn, "On a Drying Hill," p. 683.

11. Gunn, "On a Drying Hill," p. 684.

12. Gunn, "On a Drying Hill," p. 684.

13. Gunn, "On a Drying Hill," p. 685.

14. N. Scott Momaday, "Introduction," in Carnochan, p. 7.

15. Momaday, "Introduction," in Carnochan, p. 7.

16. Robert Pinsky, "Essay on Psychiatrists," *Sadness and Happiness* (Princeton: Princeton University Press, 1975), p. 72.

17. Edgar Bowers, *Living Together* (Boston: David R. Godine, 1973), p. 75.

18. Brigitte Hoy Carnochan, *The Strength of Art,* p. 22.

19. Timothy Dekin, *Occasional Uncles* (Duluth, Minn.: Knife River Chapbook Series, 1975), p. 8.

20. Winters, *Defense,* p. 408.

21. Winters, *Defense,* pp. 375–6.

22. Winters, *Defense,* p. 374.

23. Yvor Winters, *The Early Poems of Yvor Winters, 1920–1928* (Chicago: Alan Swallow, 1966), p. 13.

24. Winters, *Early Poems,* p. 11.

25. Jean Baker Miller, *Toward a New Psychology of Women,* 2d ed. (Boston: Beacon Press, 1986), p. 6.

26. Miller, *New Psychology,* p. 4.

27. Though Lewis was never Winters's student, she accepted him as a mentor at the University of Chicago and after. Interviews with Thomas Simmons, Dec. 10, 1986 and Feb. 24, 1987.

28. Yvor Winters and Kenneth Fields, *Quest for Reality* (Chicago: Alan Swallow, 1967).

29. Yvor Winters, letter to Maurice Lesemann, Sept. 28, 1919, The Maurice Lesemann papers, Special Collections, Stanford University Libraries.

30. Winters to Lesemann, Feb. 8, 1919, The Maurice Lesemann papers, Special Collections, Stanford University Libraries.

31. Carnochan, p. 14.

32. Winters to Lesemann, May 25, 1919, The Maurice Lesemann papers, Special Collections, Stanford University Libraries.

33. Winters, *Early Poems,* p. 11.

34. Winters, *Early Poems,* p. 9.

35. The correspondence between Marianne Moore and Yvor Winters is in the collection of the library of the Rosenbach Museum, Philadelphia.

36. Winters, *Early Poems*, p. 9.

37. Winters, *Early Poems*, p. 9.

38. Winters, *Early Poems*, pp. 9–10.

39. These reviews are collected in *The Uncollected Essays and Reviews of Yvor Winters*, ed. with introduction by Francis Murphy (Chicago: Swallow Press, 1973).

40. Winters to Lesemann, May 25, 1919, The Maurice Lesemann papers, Special Collections, Stanford University Libraries.

41. Arthur Rimbaud, letter to Georges Izambard, May 13, 1871, *Rimbaud*, ed. with introduction and translations by Oliver Bernard (Harmondsworth, England: Penguin, 1962), p. 6. Bernard's translation of the passage follows: "I want to be a poet, and I am working to make myself a *seer:* you won't understand this at all, and I hardly know how to explain it to you. The point is, to arrive at the unknown by the disordering of *all the senses.* The sufferings are enormous, but one has to be strong, to be born a poet, and I have discovered that I *am* a poet."

42. Photograph of Yvor Winters with John Meem, Alice Corbin Henderson, and Lura Conkey at Sunmount Sanatorium, Santa Fe, New Mexico, ca. 1920. Published in Carnochan, p. 16.

43. Winters, *Early Poems*, p. 38.

44. Winters, *Early Poems*, p. 28.

45. Yvor Winters, *Forms of Discovery: Critical and Historical Essays on the Forms of the Short Poem in English* (Chicago: Swallow, 1967), p. 272.

46. Conversation between the author and N. Scott Momaday, October 1977. Winters always believed that Thomas H. Johnson's reading of the first line of the poem—"further in summer than the birds"—was incorrect; he took the liberty of "correcting" the error in the edition of the poem he published in *Quest for Reality*—"Farther in summer than the birds."

47. Emily Dickinson, "Further in summer than the birds" (# 1068), *The Collected Poems of Emily Dickinson*, ed. Thomas H. Johnson (Boston: Little, Brown, 1960), pp. 485–86.

48. Winters, *Early Poems*, p. 135.

49. William Butler Yeats, "Crazy Jane Talks with the Bishop," *W. B. Yeats: Selected Poetry*, ed. A. Norman Jeffares (London: Pan Books, 1974), p. 161.

50. Winters, *Early Poems*, p. 59.

51. Winters, *Early Poems*, p. 82.

52. Yvor Winters, "A Study of the Post-Romantic Reaction in Lyrical Verse and Incidentally in Certain Other Forms" (Ph.D. diss., Stanford University, 1933), p. 13.

53. Winters, "A Study," p. 247.

54. Winters, "A Study," pp. 3–4.

55. See, for example, Winters's discussion of Very in *In Defense of Reason* (pp. 262–66) or Dickinson (pp. 292–93).

56. Winters, "A Study," p. 10.

57. Winters, "A Study," pp. 27–28.

58. Richard Wilbur, "Love Calls Us to the Things of This World," *The Poems of Richard Wilbur* (New York: Harcourt Brace Jovanovich, 1963), p. 65.

59. Charles Dickens, *Hard Times* (Harmondsworth, England: Penguin, 1964), pp. 48–50.

60. Yvor Winters, *The Poetry of Yvor Winters,* ed. with introduction by Donald Davie (Manchester: Carcanet, 1978), p. 135.

61. Winters, *The Poetry of Yvor Winters,* p. 145.

62. Carol Gilligan, "Remapping the Moral Domain: New Images of the Self in Relationship," *Mapping the Moral Domain,* ed. Carol Gilligan et al. (Cambridge: Harvard University Graduate School of Education, 1989), pp. 8–9.

63. Winters, *The Poetry of Yvor Winters,* p. 146.

64. Philip Levine, *Don't Ask* (Ann Arbor: University of Michigan Press, 1981), pp. 39–40.

65. Gunn, "On a Drying Hill," p. 689.

66. Gunn, "On a Drying Hill," p. 692.

67. N. Scott Momaday, letter to Yvor Winters, Nov. 15, 1966, The Yvor Winters and Janet Lewis Papers, Special Collections, Stanford University Libraries.

68. Momaday, "Introduction," in Carnochan, p. 7.

69. Gunn, "On a Drying Hill," p. 690.

70. Winters, *Forms of Discovery,* p. 345.

71. Gunn, "On a Drying Hill," p. 689.

72. S. Foster Damon, letter to Yvor Winters, May 25, 1966, The Yvor Winters and Janet Lewis Papers, Special Collections, Stanford University Libraries.

73. Yvor Winters, "Hart Crane's Poems," *Poetry* 30, no. 1 (1927): 47–51. Collected in *The Uncollected Essays and Reviews of Yvor Winters,* ed. Murphy, p. 47.

74. Yvor Winters, "The Progress of Hart Crane," *Poetry* 36, no. 3 (1930): 153–65. Collected in *The Uncollected Essays and Reviews of Yvor Winters,* ed. Murphy, p. 76.

75. Winters, "The Progress of Hart Crane," in Murphy, p. 81.

76. Winters, "The Progress of Hart Crane," in Murphy, p. 81.

77. Thomas Parkinson, *Hart Crane and Yvor Winters: Their Literary Correspondence* (Berkeley: University of California, 1978), p. 142.

78. Parkinson, p. 145.

79. Parkinson, p. xviii.

80. Parkinson, pp. 86–92, 94, 95.

The Earth-Bound

Janet Lewis as Apprentice

For his wedding poem, Winters took as his subject not only his beloved bride or the haunting western landscape, but also English Renaissance conceits of the mind-body relationship:

> Incarnate for our marriage you appeared,
> Flesh living in the spirit and endeared
> By minor graces and slow sensual change.
> Through every nerve we made our spirits range.
> We fed our minds on every mortal thing:
> The lacy fronds of carrots in the spring,
> Their flesh sweet on the tongue, the salty wine
> From bitter grapes, which gathered through the vine
> The mineral drouth of autumn concentrate,
> Wild spring in dream escaping, the debate
> Of flesh and spirit on those vernal nights,
> Its resolution in naive delights,
> The young kids bleating softly in the rain—
> All this to pass, not to return again.
> And when I found your flesh did not resist,
> It was the living spirit that I kissed,
> It was the spirit's change in which I lay:
> Thus, mind in mind we waited for the day.
> When flesh shall fall away, and, falling, stand
> Wrinkling with shadow over face and hand,
> Still I shall meet you on the verge of dust
> And know you as a faithful vestige must.
> And, in commemoration of our lust,

> May our heirs seal us in a single urn,
> A single spirit never to return.[1]

The language here, and in certain places the mood, is not far from Donne's "The Ecstasy"; "Thus mind to mind we waited for the day" echoes the fourth, fifth, and ninth stanzas of Donne's poem, in which the souls emerge from the body to make their bond. Winters actually extends Donne's hopefulness, for Donne is content to conjecture the existence of someone who had grown "all mind":

> If any, so by love refined,
>   That he soul's language understood,
> And by good love were grown all mind,
>   Within convenient distance stood,
>
> He (though he knew not which soul spake
>   Because both meant, both spake the same)
> Might thence a new concoction take,
>   And part far purer than he came.[2]

This all-mental voyeur would leave "far purer than he came" because he had witnessed a spiritual kinship, a blending of souls; but Winters suggests that, at least for a time, he and his betrothed actually achieved that blending, and that mental state unencumbered by the flesh. At this point, however, Winters's and Donne's poems differ radically. For Donne makes an elaborate argument in favor of eros and its messenger, the body: once the souls have mingled, "our bodies why do we forbear?" Love is a unifying force, not a divisive force, in "The Ecstasy." The feast that love has prepared for the soul extends to the body as well, "else a great prince in prison lies." To be a mind without a body, except in the context of a conceit, would have been revolting to Donne, as the overall argument of the poem implies; it would be to accept half a life, a perversion of creation.

For Winters, however, the virtues of that half-life seemed so significant that they exalted it above the unity of mind and body. Mind endured and prospered; the body decayed and died. Mind passed on a legacy of thought and deed, a history and a context; the body returned to the earth. Thus it makes sense that Winters would want to kiss, not a body, but "a living spirit." It equally makes sense that, although he might echo the clever argument of Donne, he would try to improve upon it pedagogically. There is a powerful double image, near the end of Winters's poem, of death and the edge of death: The flesh "shall fall away," a traditional metaphor for transubstantiation, but here it also grows slack in a darkened pause. This is the dying flesh of old age, still standing, and still offering the vestigal speaker a chance to prove his fidelity. The underlying image of a "memento mori" gives this final living moment its power, yet the essence of this power resides not in the body but in the mind: the mind-body split for Winters remains absolute. Ironically, the sentiment in the poem is at its strongest here. The quality of devotion, even beyond the grave, is profoundly touching. Winters may have been obsessed with the dichotomy of mind and body, but the poem also suggests his tenderness, his loyalty, and the seriousness with which he took the marriage vows. "Till death do us part" is an insufficient promise. The heirs should "seal us in a single urn, / A single spirit never to return." Though the heirs are supposed to commemorate "our lust," Winters knows better. The single spirit will never return because, in a sense, it was never really of the lustful world; the heirs have got it wrong, as humans so often do. Yet it does not matter, for the "faithful vestige" will attend to its own. This is the sweet projection of a mind at once sentimental and fiercely devoted to the spirit.

The tenderness manifested in this poem had a clear corollary in real life, for Winters and Lewis seem to have created a marriage of notable happiness and endurance. Although separated for the first nine months of their married life due to Lewis's persistent tuberculosis, they lived together in Santa Fe in the summer after their wedding, then moved to Stanford, where Winters enrolled as a graduate student in English. First in Palo Alto, then in Los Altos, they established a home that many students and acquaintances came to remember as unassuming and friendly. The guest list included even those who found themselves more often than not at odds with Winters, such as Theodore Roethke and Robert Lowell, and even these recalled the home as a warm place, hospitable to literary life and conversation. This was due in great degree to Lewis's efforts as a homemaker, for the house was largely, though not entirely, her domain. She dealt with its demands, including the demands of two children, from the beginning of her life with Winters until Winters died in 1968. She continues to live in the home she and Winters built for themselves on Portola Avenue in Los Altos.

The degree of compatibility suggested in this marriage appears as well in the poems of Lewis and Winters, at least through the 1930s. The two poets periodically wrote on the same themes, discussing their work with each other. Both Winters and Lewis wrote poems commemorating the demise of the Navy dirigible *Macon* in 1937. Both also wrote poems on the entrapments of time: Lewis quotes from a Winters poem on the subject in her 1927 poem "Time and Music."[3] Of course there were strains in the marriage, both artistic and personal. Winters's decision to help defend David Lamson, the sales manager for the Stanford University Press, when Lamson was (as Winters believed) unjustly accused of murder in 1933, occupied a tremendous amount of his time and placed an even heavier burden on Lewis to manage the family alone. Eighteen years later, when Lewis received a Guggenheim Fellowship for her projected novel *The Ghost of Monsieur Scarron,* Winters objected strenuously. Paris in 1951 was unsafe in his estimation, and in any case he did not wish to be without her for a year, even though she agreed to take along their thirteen-year-old son Daniel (their daughter Joanna was at that time 20 and living on her own). Although Winters finally consented to the trip, he continued to find the separation a strain, and worried in letters to his friends whether he would ever see his wife and son again.[4] Aside from these periods of upheaval, however, the relationship between Yvor Winters and Janet Lewis seemed remarkably peaceful and prosperous.

Winters wrote and published five collections of poems during their time together, not including *The Early Poems of Yvor Winters* or the *Collected Poems.*[5] He also established the critical reputation he was to have with *In Defense of Reason, The Function of Criticism,* and *Forms of Discovery.* For her part, Lewis published three collections of poems during their years together, along with five novels, one collection of stories, and one children's novel.[6] Given this outline of Winters's and Lewis's life, one would think that Winters managed to merge seamlessly his role as a mentor with his role as a husband. One of his best apprentices also became his wife,[7] and a distinguished writer whose legacy would bring him pride. Including several pages on her work in *Forms of Discovery,* he cannot resist noting that she is merely an "occasional poet," whose "weakness" is "domestic sentiment, which sometimes goes all the way to sentimentality." But he adds, "She is a stylist of remarkable native gift and possesses an unusual knowledge of song and ballad stanzas and rhythms; she has as fine an ear for poetic movement as one can easily find in English."[8]

Yet to consider the Winters-Lewis relationship simply as a great personal and artistic success is to overlook a serious peculiarity in the development of Lewis's poetry. Lewis's early poems draw on her experience with the culture and oral history of the Ojibway Indians, which she encountered during her childhood summers on St. Joseph's Island in northern Michigan. Both imagist and experimental in their use of narrative point of view and compressed, allusive language, these early poems also reflect a close familiarity with the irrational—the world of spirits, demons, and tricksters, the world of feeling that modifies and extends thought. Although Lewis also worked with formal verse during her early years, she devoted increasing attention to more experimental writing. Her 1922 *The Indians in the Woods* collected many of her most interesting early poems. By the late 1920s, however, she had largely abandoned free verse and experiments in narrative and diction for formal verse, whose subjects—compared to the early subjects—became in some ways disappointingly minor. On the other hand, these poems clearly demonstrate both Lewis's determination to make something meaningful from her domestic experience, and her uncertainty over the most fruitful approach to that task.

By the early 1940s, Lewis had produced a number of extremely accomplished formal poems. Yet something was absent from them, some fullness of heart or conviction one senses in the early work. Then she fell silent; from 1944 until about a year after Winters's death, she wrote no poems. When, in 1971, she returned to the genre, she took up some of the old themes in old ways, though with some techniques derived from the Winters years and the wisdom accumulated from an additional half-century of life. Had Lewis simply fallen silent as a poet, and pursued her career as a novelist—a career that was largely outside of Winters's domain as a writer—one might reasonably assume that she chose not to continue working in a medium whose values and demands had been so precisely defined by her husband. That Lewis returns to poetry, however, adds a powerful sense of necessity to this picture. Lewis was, and is, a poet, and she nurtures that identity from her early years.

Although no letters between Lewis and Winters remain—the two of them burned the correspondence at Winters's request in what Lewis calls "the great conflagration" of the late 1930s[9]—it is still clear that one central component of her role as a poet implied a potentially vehement rebellion against her mentor. This was her interest in the irrational, and her comfort with it—her sense that one could derive meaning from it, despite the mind's intransigence. For her to pursue that irrational force—especially as it related to a non-Western tradition—was to transgress the values her husband so powerfully espoused. For her to pursue it in his chosen medium of expression, poetry, was even more laden with risk.

At the same time, this artistic tension came into conflict with her genuine devotion to Winters—a devotion that the institution of marriage sanctioned, but neither guaranteed nor even praised except in the most stereotypical and fictional forms. Lewis also makes it very clear that she felt a strong commitment to motherhood. She explains in a 1986 interview the difficulty of balancing her desire to write with her need to attend to a household with two young children.[10] The fact that she also emphasized this in 1980, in an interview with Brigitte Carnochan,[11] indicates not only the weight of this point in her mind but also the pressing obligation she felt to balance a cultural identity—that is, woman as wife and mother—with a personal identity—woman as woman, mother, lover, writer.

In the potentially oppressive context of this cultural identity, and in the erotic context of her marriage to a powerful intellectual who distrusted the function of the irrational in human life, Lewis continued to draw on one powerful source of eros—the mythologized past of the American Indians, whose embrace of revelation as opposed to reason provided her with a vocabulary for a passionate view of life. Although this passion never left Lewis, an important portion of it did go underground for a quarter of a century. Her devotion to Winters, bound up as it was in the demands of marriage, made more than an extended separation unthinkable; yet to continue with a kind of poetry that did not extend from her own erotic sources was equally unthinkable. To understand how Lewis returned as a poet so many years later, however, it is essential to examine her approach to the irrational, and to a concept of the past that preserves eros without consenting to a fearful or terrified view of mortal life. In these contexts one finds the origins of her private life and a set of sustaining values that the conflicts of adulthood could not, finally, eradicate.

———

One way of making a meaningful connection between the events of the past and one's own nascent identity is to mythologize the past—to convert it into a set of stories whose symbolic meaning reinforces one's own instincts about how to proceed in the world. For Lewis, whose summers in northern Michigan influenced her for so many years, mythology was the domain of the Ojibways. Lewis often passed her days or evenings with the family of Mr. and Mrs. Howard Lewis Johnstone, descendants of the original white settler, John Johnston [*sic*], and his Ojibway wife,

Neengay.[12] From them she learned the Ojibway stories, particularly stories of Manibozho, the deity of the possible and the improbable. For Lewis, Manibozho (or Manibush) would become a central figure. She once described him as "the variant principle of life"[13] and depicted him this way at the beginning of her 1932 novel *The Invasion:*

> Manibush ran in the woods, sometimes as a rabbit, sometimes as a young Indian. The sand point at Chegoimegon was the remnant of the great beaver dam which he built generations ago. The wild rice, the short, blunt ears of maize, the fire, curling in narrow tongues about the birch logs in the center of the wigwam floor, were the gift of Manabozho [sic]. Because of him the gull was white, the kingfisher was barred and crested, the woodpecker red-headed, the sap in the maple trees thin, instead of thick as formerly, the helldiver a red-eyed bird with crooked legs, the squirrel little, the bear big and eating only berries unless attacked, the bark of the red willow good to smoke. Because of him, likewise, the Mide lodge was built yearly on the shore of the Bay St. Charles and ceremonies were performed to heal the sick and even, in the old days, to raise the dead, to enjoy again, in some place far off, their earthly bodies. There was nothing in the woods with which he had not tampered, and the stories told of him were of all varieties, ludicrous, obscene, grave, or sacred.[14]

Manibozho is a tamperer. Behind each formative event in life, whether large or small, miserable or thrilling, he works his spell; "without him was not anything made that was made," though he is not the Creator. Yet he is a life-giver, for tampering gives life. He forms the identity of the bear and the red willow bark; he soars, or mucks around in the obscene and sacred ground of the world. He does not neglect bodies or the pleasures they provide. On the contrary, he does what he can to mediate between the living humans and the dead, who are raised "to enjoy again . . . their earthly bodies." This integration of mind and body is the essence of living. "Be ye therefore perfect" does not enter in here, except if one interprets perfection as the will to act: to partake of life we must muck around in it. Otherwise we stand at the edge, mere thinking spectators.

This idea is at the core of Lewis's early and late poetry. In the act of abandoning spectatorship and thrusting ourselves into the world, we embrace mortality; we become victims of time. Lewis certainly knew this risk as well as Winters, if not better. She was confined to a sanatorium for a much longer time than Winters. She remained in New Mexico from the late summer of 1922 until spring of 1927, with only a brief return to Michigan and Chicago in the summer and fall of 1923.[15] By the time she was readmitted to Sunmount sanatorium, around Christmas of 1923, she was seriously ill. Her brush with death seems to have been significantly closer than Winters's. Yet Lewis did not come to see the body as a horror, as an aberration of the perfection of the mind. On the contrary, she viewed her physical being as an essential vehicle of the dance of life she had come to understand in Michigan; it was inevitable, and it was not to be disparaged. Without entering this dance, as Lewis insists in her late poem "Snail Garden," we cannot know what it means to live at all. We cannot have our lives affirmed by the past—we cannot enter into mythologies of ourselves—because we have not accepted death, the key force that separates present from past. In his embrace of the Western intellectual tradition, Winters focused always on its intellectual durability, its power to transcend time. For Lewis this was an understandable practice, but one that misrepresented the nature of human life. Manibozho, who has many lives, escapes death, as he must, because he is both creature and principle. Yet his need for incarnation is the same as ours, and for him to live out of time would be for him to die. He must enter, he must tamper, to live, and Lewis never rejects his requirements.

Lewis presents Manibozho in different ways in her early work, her poems of the 1920s. A master of the imagist idiom, she makes it uniquely her own, drawing on its compression and allusion and ellipsis to frame the life of the trickster and the traces he leaves. In "The Wife of Manibozho Sings," she imbeds a truth within the muffled anguish of a neglected spouse:

> He comes and goes;
> There is no rest
> While he is here
> Or gone.
>
> I cannot say
> That his feet have pressed
> The leaves
> He was standing on.
>
> He comes and goes
> And the maple leaves
> Lie still
> Under the sun.[16]

Beneath the anger of an individual, a wronged human being, lies a more fundamental issue of identity: who am I in relation to this other, this constant transformation? The paradox is fully realized in the final stanza. I am the moment of the maple leaves, the evidence of inescapable change. This paradox itself might seem to justify fury. I am not who I am, or rather I am both myself and another whose being in time changes me. Yet the ending of the poem resolves rather than perpetuates a discord. It works the charm of a revealed secret upon the wife. She who discovers this paradox of identity both keeps her fury and finds her peace. Knowing the dark and light of the secret, she becomes our confidante, our source. Speaking to herself, she tells us what she can, and in raising her voice she finds a kind of liberation.

This sense of circularity, of constant transformation, appears vividly in another early poem, "Like Summer Hay":

> Like summer hay it falls
> Over the marshes, over
> The cranberry flats,
> Places where
>   the wild deer lay.
>
> Now the deer leave tracks
> Down the pine hollow; petals
> Laid two by two, brown
> Against the snow.[17]

The seasons intertwine, implying each other. Snow falls with the light flurrying of summer hay, where the deer took their ease. Foraging in the winter, the deer return the compliment: their tracks are "petals," suggesting another season, along with the brownness of the earth they barely reveal. Each moment, each creature and season, must be distinct, or time has no meaning; each implies the other, or time is fractured.

It seems natural to think of imagism as a technique for Lewis because its effort to present "an intellectual and emotional complex in an instant of time"[18] links up so clearly with her quest for Manibozho. Seize him and he is gone; yet one is still left with "petals on a wet black bough."[19] But it may have been Lewis's good fortune that she never slipped into a school or movement. Like her trickster-spirit, she adopted and discarded different forms for different mythologies, different movements of thought. Tracking the variant principle of life through imagist instants—which expand suddenly like paper lilies in a glass of water—comprises the method and intellectual gift of *The Indians in the Woods*. But the ideas themselves could inhabit other forms; reflection as well as epiphany commands respect in the early work of Lewis. Perhaps the best example of this is "The Earth-Bound," a poem of the mid-1920s. The surface of the poem is entirely conventional, even defiantly so. The voice is emphatically original.

> Still grove and hill and shadowy grot,
> The flesh of our celestial thought,
> Trammel the mind, however bent
> Upon the heavenly argument.
>
> The spring of wisdom ever flows
> Pure shining water as it goes
> Over the rocks and through the grass
> Whither we stoop to hear it pass,
>
> And healing is a tree whose leaves
> Fall round us like the falling sleeves
> Of love, that bending down at night,
> Covers with them a face alight.
>
> Tangled with earth all ways, we move,
> And sleep at last in heaven that is a grove.[20]

Here is no instant revelation, but an argument, though not a heavenly argument. Lewis acknowledges the incarnation, that trammeling fact, at the same time she celebrates its necessity: to see one's place in the world is also to accept mortality, "the spring of wisdom." Yet this spring "ever flows," constant in its transformations. It neither invites us to listen nor turns us away; still it is ever-present. Here, admittedly, the poem verges on sentiment—the "pure shining water" and the "face alight"— yet even here a hard edge of the mind is at work. Wisdom, which in its sentimental form ought to lead us directly to the "heavenly argument"— the argument that we are purely spiritual—leads us to earth instead. Wisdom leads us to acknowledge our condition, trammeled and tangled as we are. This, in turn, leads us back to the realm of Manibozho. Tampering with our lives, we learn the range of our powers. There is a beautiful cherishing of the other, of difference, in this poem. What is different from us is the world, which must be a subject to us—not an object of argumentation—even as the "face alight" is a subject to the parent whose "falling sleeves of love" imply "the joy of the other's survival and the recognition of shared reality," as Benjamin says.[21]

In the quest for a usable past, one can move two ways—toward the mythology of revelation or the mythology of reason.[22] The first is essentially unitary, pointing toward a binding force. This may be a deity or an emptiness, an inner experience or an incarnate presence or both. The possibilities for the mythology of revelation, in fact, are virtually endless. This kind of mythology also incorporates a set of paradoxes—permanence and passing, mortality and immortality, "the still point in the turning world." One of the essential characteristics of this mythology is that contradictory states can coexist. The immortal moment, for example, the moment in which life falls clear and endless before us, is also the passing moment. The revelation is, in fact, the paradox.

The mythology of reason, however, points toward a fragmentary vision of life. There may be a deity or no deity beyond the human; but as a practical matter reason itself becomes a deity or demigod, shoring itself against the ruins of the irrational world outside. In this mythology the past becomes a source of wisdom and of tragedy; it dignifies the human quest for meaning. This clearly is a central quality of Winters's intellectual tradition. But the mythology of reason does not admit transcendence—or rather, acknowledges that the transcendent is not cognitively meaningful, as A. J. Ayer has said[23]—and so limits the variant principle of life. Winters makes this point abundantly clear, for example, in one of his best poems, "To the Holy Spirit." Reason is powerful and mistrustful; its mythology is one of limits. On the other hand, reason is as unthreatening as the irrational is threatening. Its methods and conclusions are accessible and reliable. In the poetry of Yvor Winters after 1930, one sees this effort to preserve what is accessible. Winters fully understands the dangers of the irrational, and his emphasis on reason is never far from the tragedy that reason must always face a dark opponent. Yet the mythology of reason can be made to confirm life in the present, at least in the context of Winters's poems. Reason defines one's identity; it defies chaos.

One sees Lewis working toward this idea too, though the strain is more evident. It is as if the mythology of reason loosens Lewis's grasp on her own mythologies of revelation, leaving her with her talent but no clear direction for it. She seems to drift: from 1930 to 1944 she devotes herself primarily to topics generated from a source outside herself—illnesses and endings, fireside scenes, symphonies. The seeming confinements of these subjects are what lead Theodore Roethke to write, in his 1947 review of her book *The Earth-Bound* in *Poetry:* "It is perhaps enough that lyric poetry be intense and passionate, however narrow in range. Nevertheless, while one is grateful for the candor, the deep tenderness and simplicity of the best of these poems, one keeps wishing that Miss Lewis would break into other areas of experience. The nursery, the quiet study, the garden, the graveyard do not provide enough material for a talent of such high order."[24]

Roethke is more obtuse than he might have been about Lewis's subject matter: "the nursery, the quiet study, the garden, the graveyard" might well offer arresting material to the poet who saw both her own incarceration and her freedom in relation to them (the early poems of Adrienne Rich offer some example of this). Yet, despite his obtuseness, Roethke is also right. Lewis's middle poems do not seem to lead her toward a sustaining identity as a subject in conjunction with other powerful subjects. They are rooted in ambiguous and self-concealing sentiment. Nevertheless, they also harbor an authentic unease, and even at times an anger, which is closer to what one finds in H.D.'s early poetry than Lewis's formal poetic structure might lead one to suspect. Lewis's efforts to overcome this ambiguity by defining her work in relation to her mentor-husband's gave her no peace; she always came up short. Distancing herself in some way from her poems, she produced work at once highly conventional and unexpectedly ominous, as "No-Winter Country" demonstrates:

> Her letters speak of trilliums, white
> Beside the muddy water courses.
> Cold spring, and then hot weather forces
> Them suddenly north; they leave to-night.
>
> And before I have more than thought of them gone,
> There they are to the town returning,
> And every note has a whiff of the burning
> From brown leaves raked to a heap on the lawn.
>
> A child grows tall whom I've never seen—
> Precipitous seasons run pellmell.
> They might be rumors out of a shell,
> For has time gone by where I live serene?
>
> I feel becalmed in an eddy of time,
> Or shut by happiness, a great hill,

>   Into a valley of calm, and still,
>   These letters come from another clime.[25]

Though the final stanza claims happiness as the dominant emotion, the equation of happiness with an impediment—"a great hill"—is portentious, and the poem itself is not a happy one. The poet is becalmed. Like a spectator, she seems to have stepped out of the dance. This is not cause for overt sadness, apparently; the poet is busy and thoughtful. Yet something is still the matter at some level.

The poem uses two metaphors of stasis—one the Edenic weather, without winter, and the other the eddy, which draws the traveler out of the mainstream. Intriguingly, the two metaphors work apart from each other. The poet does not draw the metaphor of the eddy out from the metaphor of seasonal stasis; there is no sense of metaphoric building or weaving here, despite the "time/clime" rhyme in the last stanza. Even within the structure of the poem there is thus a dividedness or ambiguity. Yet the meanings of both metaphors are consistent. There is "no winter," either in the poet's California home or—apparently—in her soul; yet the poem rightly implies in its tone that the soul cannot flourish without its winters. The soul is not Edenic in its climate. It requires its seasons, its periods of luxury and hardness and regeneration, or it begins to dissolve. Beyond this, the poet spins in an eddy of time, and eddies may dwindle to nothing in a crag or cove. This is a dark poem, a poem without the mythology of revelation, except as that revelation exposes a certain kind of spiritual dryness.

On the other hand, on the few occasions when Lewis engages the mythology of reason she is as subtle and brilliant as ever, although the mythology itself seems to limit the scope of her investigation. Her mind arrays the fragments and shores the ruins of human endeavor; the necessary tragedies nevertheless have a kind of glory to them. In "The Hangar at Sunnyvale: 1937," Lewis demonstrates her revised themes. Written to commemorate the U.S.N. dirigible *Macon*'s crash into the Pacific ocean, the poem still invokes the problem of time; but here the counter-issue is human ambition—the efforts of reason and technical skill to overcome the limits of nature.

>   Above the marsh, a hollow monument,
>   Ribbed with aluminum, enormous tent
>   Sheeted with silver, set to face the gale
>   Of the steady wind that filled the clipper sail,

The hangar stands. With doors now buckled close
Against the summer wind, the empty house
Reserves a space shaped to the foundered dream.
The Macon, lost, moves with the ocean stream.

Level the marshes, far and low the hills.
The useless structure, firm on the ample sills,
Rises incredible to state again:
Thus massive was the vessel, built in vain.
For this one purpose the long sides were planned
To lines like those of downward pouring sand,
Time-sifting sand; but Time immobile, stayed,
In substance bound, in these bright walls delayed.

This housed the shape that plunged through stormy air.
Empty cocoon! Yet was the vision fair
That like a firm bright cloud moved from the arch,
Leaving this roof to try a heavenly march;
Impermanent, impractical, designed
To frame a paradox and strongly bind
The weight, the weightless in a living shape
To cruise the sky and round the cloudy Cape.

Less substance than a mathematic dream
Locked in the hollow keel and webbéd beam!
Of the ingenious mind the expensive pride,
The highest hope, the last invention tried!
And now the silver tent alone remains.
Slowly the memory of disaster wanes.
Still in the summer sun the bastions burn
Until the inordinate dream again return.[26]

Toward its primary subject the poem is both critical and admiring. The dirigible is flawed from the start by its impracticality; yet in another way it honors the inventiveness and daring of human reason, which tries to "frame a paradox"—binding heavier-than-air creatures with a lighter-than-air machine "to cruise the sky and round the cloudy Cape." Interestingly, Lewis still finds the idea of paradox engaging; she raises it explicitly, as she does not in her earlier work, although it is at least initially merely a paradox of physics.

But another hint of the earlier work also inheres. Though Time seems primarily to be the enemy in this poem—a sensible position, given reason's fear of the clock—in fact time is also a secular redeemer. The poem ends with the memory of the disaster waning: humankind tends to forget the magnitude of its past errors. This is a morally neutral statement, yet in the context of the poem's conclusion it adopts a positive tone: the hangar gleams in the summer sun, a kind of icon to the lost *Macon,* "until the inordinate dream again return." Time brings back, not only the will to achieve, but also the dream—the desire to achieve something specific. A dream or vision may be seen as a concommitant to reason; through dreams, reason perceives a possible area of exploration and proceeds to explore it. On the other hand, the yearning in the last two lines seems superrational. The dream is somehow out of scale with the rational planning and construction of a dirigible.

What is being dreamed? A paradox? But not a paradox of physics merely. The poem oversteps its own rationality; it celebrates the thrill of an "inordinate dream" beyond the ability of reason to justify it. In this sense it harbors traces of Manibozho, recalling both the early and later poems. But the traces are small. The main effort here is to acknowledge the sometimes tragic ambition of human reason in the face of time. Only because that acknowledgment gets slightly out of hand does the poem seem daring. The only other evidence of Lewis's earlier career in this poem is the fact that reason *creates* a tragedy. The best that the mind can do cannot equal the powers of nature or even equal its own ambition. Reason is a powerful cheat in these stanzas, although on its surface the poem takes care to indict ambition rather than reason.

After "The Hangar in Sunnyvale: 1937," Lewis's *Poems Old and New, 1918–1978* contains a mere seven poems before its sudden leap to 1971. It is as if one is witnessing a voice dying out, or quelling itself. Is this a fiction? When asked about this in two interviews in the late 1980s, Lewis said that, while she might have fiddled with a few poems between 1944 and 1968—she could not recall with certainty—she had kept nothing from that period, and had in fact published all the poems she intended to publish.[27] In those last poems before the silence of 1944, the sense of an ending is keen. No beginning, no mythology of revelation, seems near.

———

Yet this silence, like so much of Lewis's career, defied expectations and even, to some degree, its own apparent premise: it was a silence full of language, of books, of literary success. Perhaps more important, it was full of the sounds of home and family. It was not the kind of silence Tillie Olsen describes, in which the female talent is suffocated under the overwhelming obligations of domestic life.[28] "Of course I had more or less been told that I couldn't have children," Lewis explained to Brigitte Carnochan in 1980, recalling the years following her recovery from tuberculosis.[29] "I wanted them and Arthur (Yvor Winters) wanted them—this became very important. I'm glad I had them. Any amount of time that was spent on them and not spent on writing was much better spent. The writing was a spin-off; it was a by-product of living."[30]

It is true that Lewis's comments, which subordinate artistic achievement to childrearing, would seem to reflect the conflict of loyalty that Olsen documents again and again in *Silences*. From a somewhat different vantage point, that of Gilligan and Benjamin, one could argue that Lewis's primary sense of artistry was bound up in a web of interconnection, of human relationship, to the extent that the relationships themselves became the primary works of art; the books, as Lewis suggests, might indeed be "spin-offs" of this other artistry. Yet these points of view seem too simplistic to accommodate Lewis's career; her work as a mother and a homemaker, however primary that may have been to her, did not prevent her from establishing herself as a novelist.[31] Shortly before she ceased any serious poetic work, in 1941, she published the short novel *The Wife of Martin Guerre* (her first novel, *The Invasion,* had been published nine years earlier). She followed this in 1943 with *Against a Darkening Sky,* in 1947 with *The Trial of Sören Qvist,* and in 1959 with her most complex work of fiction, *The Ghost of Monsieur Scarron.* Lewis would not be a poet, it appeared; but she would not abandon that presence in the literary world which also confirmed her identity.

It might seem harsh, then, or vaguely absurd, to refer to this period in Lewis's life as a period of silence. Yet a whole range of experience—an entire voice—undeniably had been abandoned; it was, moreover, a voice whose genre—poetry—was as essential to Winters as breathing. He was not on shakier ground as a critic of fiction (or of writers of fiction), but fiction as an artistic genre was not part of the inner sanctum of his life. Winters revealed this position on various occasions, most notably at the end of his life in *Forms of Discovery.* Janet Lewis, he wrote, "has devoted most of her work to fiction, in which, if I may be forgiven for saying so, I think that she is one of the relatively small number of distinguished professionals of our time. By comparison, she has been an occasional poet."[32] Winters clearly felt competent to criticize her poetry, but simply acknowledged the novels as the work of a "professional." This was certainly no criticism, but neither was it literary praise, exactly; it was a gesture of high esteem. Winters had made a similar gesture fifteen years earlier when writing to the Japanese American author Hisaye Yamamoto: "A few days ago I sent you copies of two of my wife's novels. . . . I believe her to be one of the few genuinely civilized fictionists of this period."[33] Again, the language conveys esteem—but not literary criticism or praise. For Lewis to claim fiction as her genre was, then, in part to claim a certain distance from the man she most loved; it was to carve out a silence, however slight, between them. Although Winters might consider fiction inferior to poetry (as he explained to Pearl Andelson Sherry in 1923[34]), and might—despite his devotion to his wife—wonder at her transformation into a novelist, he could not quite reach her as he could when she wrote poetry; she had slipped beneath his highest standards of literary endeavor. Thus she was free.

It was a peculiar freedom, outwardly successful yet hemmed in by persistent anxieties about accident and fate: what did it mean to choose one's own life? What did it mean to respond, as a woman, to a world of men? Years later, Lewis would comment on accident and fate by saying, "chance becomes a means, a method, because the intention seems to emerge irrevocably or relentlessly from chance";[35] she had decided that one shapes one's life intentionally in response to chance, and that this intention becomes the essential manifestation of a combined morality and human intuition. In the 1940s and 1950s, however, this answer was not so clear, and it was fraught with potential misery.

The universe of Lewis's early poems—a universe of native intuition, of the "variant principle of life," and later of rational propositions about that variant principle—grows increasingly obscure in the novels. Instead one finds a dark world where circumstances conspire against the unwitting, and those who build a lifetime of love and trust find themselves destroyed in a moment. At first glance, the three major novels of Lewis's career—*The Wife of Martin Guerre, The Trial of Sören Qvist,* and *The Ghost of Monsieur Scarron*—might seem to be elaborate extensions either of Winters's dark short story from 1927, "The Brink of Darkness," or of her own poem "Helen Grown Old." The power of the irrational in Lewis's novels is destructive and diabolical. Whatever freedom Lewis may have acquired to explore this domain of the irrational, it was a domain she had never crossed before, nor was it one in which she had any clear faith in Manibozho. The dark accidents in Lewis's novels leave Manibozho behind, or—at best—magnify his malevolence and danger.

Lewis identified her three major novels as "cases of circumstantial evidence." As she explains in the foreword to the first of these novels, *The Wife of Martin Guerre,* "I first came upon the story of the wife of Martin Guerre in a collection called *Famous Cases of Circumstantial Evidence.* This volume contained, together with an essay, The Theory of Presumptive Proof, by Samuel March Phillips (1780–1862), . . . many historic accounts of the failure of justice because of undue reliance on circumstantial evidence."[36] Although Lewis's primary source for the book ultimately became Estienne Paquier's *Les Recherches de la France,* it was Phillips's casebook that opened to her her major themes of chance, reason, and the irrational. Roughly, the problem underlying these themes is this: an event occurs; circumstantial evidence dictates that it happened in such a way, or that such a person was responsible for it. But how is circumstantial evidence arranged or ordered? By the rational mind. It is the clear-thinking mind, insistent on a logical sequence of cause and effect, which frames circumstantial evidence in such a way that the guilty may go unpunished and the innocent may be sent to their deaths. Despite its best intentions, then, and with the most painstaking and honest effort, the rational mind may yield the most horrifyingly irrational results. In part this results from the presumption of the rational mind, which assumes that—in the absense of essential knowledge—its own powers of logic may prevail. In part this results from a larger failure of other forms of knowledge, including primary human intuitions about character and behavior, which because they are subrational or superrational are discounted as evidence. In one way or another, Lewis's novels are about the failures of the rational mind—and, indeed, the impossibility of a thoroughly rational universe, given the limits of human knowledge and the complexity of the human psyche.

Although, in this sense, the novels might be seen as works of autobiography disguised as fiction, such a view cannot really be sustained. These novels have none of the autobiographical presence of, for example, a figure like H.D. On the contrary, the historical nature of these novels—each of which is set in a specific era and inhabited by characters far removed from the author's own life—attests to Lewis's determination to make these fully works of fiction. It is perhaps doubly striking, then, how much the themes of these novels mirror the anxieties and uncertainties of her own mind. The historical distance itself gives these themes a contemporary power, if only because—in distancing herself from them—Lewis adjusts points of view and matters of plot in slight ways that reveal her own preoccupations as emphatically as a work of autobiography could do.

The Wife of Martin Guerre has frequently been described as a "psychological novel"; indeed, in his 1947 anthology *Anchor in the Sea: An Anthology of Psychological Fiction*, Alan Swallow included *The Wife of Martin Guerre* with the clear implication that the work was a psychological study.[37] To place it in this genre, however, is somewhat misleading, for it is both more and less than a psychological novel. Although much of the tale seems to occur within Bertrande's mind—she is, after all, the one who must first doubt, then believe, then more elaborately doubt the identity of Martin—Lewis does not create a portrait of a mind and soul such as one finds in, for example, Henry James's *The Portrait of a Lady*. The parallels between Bertrande de Rols and Isabel Archer are certainly powerful; yet the fact that Bertrande is not Isabel says much about Lewis's avoidance of what came to be classical psychoanalytic categories in favor of what Jessica Benjamin would call the "intersubjectivity" (or lack of intersubjectivity) of the main characters. Lewis's novelistic world is fundamentally a place of healthy human animals, who thrive—when they thrive—from a combined sensual and psychic wellness that manifests an instinctive wisdom. Lewis emphasizes the relational quality of this wellness—the way each character's loves, desires, and decisions affect the others—in a manner that might seem to foreshadow Benjamin. Yet Lewis's equal emphasis on the private value of that instinctive wellness gives her work a fundamentally moral quality that seems somewhat alien to the world of psychoanalysis. Hers is not an innocent or sentimental world; it is not without death and sadness; but it has a grace and refreshment, a quality of love, which emanates from and is directed toward creation. Human beings, as part of this creation, respond to this promise of health with instinct and passion. Only the power of the mind and its selfish intentions can distance human beings from these norms of creation.

Early in *The Wife of Martin Guerre,* for example, when Martin and Bertrande are espoused at age eleven, Bertrande is suddenly filled with the "great seriousness" of the marriage; "the realization that henceforth her life lay beneath [Martin's] jurisdiction came suddenly and overwhelmingly to the little girl. . . . She was tired and frightened."[38] Beside this very human response, at once rational and full of the instinct of a threatened animal, Lewis places the instinctive consolation of the body: the bed itself, where Bertrande must sleep with her child husband, comforts her. "The warmth of the flock bed began to enclose the small thin body in something like security," Lewis writes, "a feeling almost as good as that of being home again."[39]

The human mind, of course, is the mode of conscious instinct. It is capable of giving comprehensible shape to the kind of morality Lewis envisions within the world. But it is also capable of much more. It is capable of a selfishness beyond the need to survive; it is at least potentially a dominator, a questor after power. In Lewis's novels this quest for power consistently resides in the male characters rather than the female ones. Intuitive, relational morality defines the lives of the women, while the hierarchies of reason and a hunger for power drive most—though not all—of the men. In its selfishness, the mind may give itself over to deeds that violate the intuitive morality of the world; it may find no satisfaction in the mutual sustenance of such morality, and seek winners and losers. Indeed, as Carol Gilligan has noted, it is characteristic of the rational mind to transpose "a hierarchy of power into a hierachy of values."[40] The validity of certain claims of value—the claim of a husband to his wife, for example—supersedes the human relationships in any given case, assuring that someone will "win"—will find himself in conformity with these abstract values—and someone will "lose."

Although the idea of winners and losers has been ascribed to the creaturely world since the advent of Darwinism, it is foreign to Lewis's earlier universe (and even, in certain ways, to the universe of her novels). A creature who dies, for example, does not necessarily "lose," although a creature who dies loveless or cast out from the human community has lost something immeasurably great. What sustains Lewis's vision is the power of human connection, not the power of abstract judgments about that connection. At the same time, these judgments seem to some degree unavoidable. In *The Wife of Martin Guerre,* certainly, they are the basis of the social order in which Bertrande de Rols lives. As Bertrande comes to her crisis, she realizes that reason alone will lead her astray; yet a reasoned intuition, or intuition alone, may not—will not—be believed.

In her heart, Bertrande knows that the man who, having returned from eight years of wandering, calls himself Martin is a deceiver; yet, rationally, she can prove nothing. Her creaturely instinct and her mind are at odds. Caught between its awareness of the deception and its need for proof, her mind begins to crumble. Ultimately, she confides in Martin's uncle, the one man she believes she can trust, and his own secret doubts about "Martin"'s identity lead him to have the imposter arrested. Then, however, the liabilities of reason descend. Virtually everyone believes this man to be Martin; he looks and acts like Martin, and moreover knows virtually everything of Martin's history; it is thus unreasonable—mad—for Bertrande to accuse him of being an imposter. Even the priest, speaking for the reasonable position of the church, tries to convince her that she is committing a great sin by accusing him.

Against this resistance Bertrande falters, but does not withdraw her accusation. When, in the end, she is proven correct—when the real Martin Guerre appears in the courtroom, confirming the imposter's gambit and upbraiding his wife for her "adultery"—she is at once absolved and convicted: absolved of the "irrational" accusation against her "husband," and yet convicted by her true husband of unfaithfulness. Moreover, she must live with the knowledge that the imposter, Arnaud de Tilh, will die. The law wins, but both Bertrande and Arnaud lose: Arnaud loses his life, and Betrande herself slips toward death with the knowledge that, having sought to restore her world to its earlier intuitive consistency, she has found only disorder and early sorrow.

One could explore many morals within this morality tale, but two of the most striking are Bertrande's profound awareness of the imposter, and her conflict with her community once she begins to act on this intuitive knowledge. Equally important is the role of Arnaud, one of the few men in Lewis's novels whose relation to power is ambiguous. On the one hand he is a rogue, capable of a monstrous evil for the sake of a landed estate and a title. On the other hand he is tender and good-hearted, and his love for Bertrande is nowhere greater than at the moment of his death sentence. He acknowledges, as few other of Lewis's male characters do, the superlative value of her intuitive and creaturely morality, though he has violated that morality in a most fundamental way. Caught somewhere between the corruptions of desire and the relational knowledge of intuition, he is a victim of his own temerity. He does not fear an irrational world; on the contrary he creates his own irrational world, shaped not through intuition but through greed and desire, and in so doing renders himself amoral.

Arnaud's opposite—a man who becomes a victim *because* of his fear of an irrational world—is the protagonist of Lewis's next novel, *The Trial of Sören Qvist.* Pastor Sören Qvist, of the seventeenth-century congregation

of Vejlby in Denmark, is well-loved and known for his kindness and forgiveness. His only flaw, not unlike that of Melville's Billy Budd, is his sudden temper: when his anger flares it is a fury, and its fury from time to
time frightens the pastor deeply. Believing that this anger is his own cross
to bear, and laboring before the sight of God to subdue this beast, Sören
Qvist on the whole manages remarkably well. But he is an innocent. He
has not fully reckoned the depths of human evil, and these depths, combined with his own insistence on a rational world, destroy him.

Despite himself, Qvist despises Morten Bruus, a wealthy and venal
character who seeks to marry Sören's daughter Anna. It is Morten who
easily short-circuits Qvist's compassion, sending him into such a rage
that, at one point, he throws Morten bodily out of his house. Like most
bullies, Morten never allows an insult to go unpunished. Thus he hatches
a clever plot to bring the parson to ruin.

Morten intimidates his brother Niels into applying for work in Qvist's
household; and Qvist, ever prone to forgive and to see God's hand in
what appear to be the vagaries of fate, readily employs Niels. Yet Niels
is a terrible bother to him, as Morten cleverly predicted. Niels does little work, or works badly; his indolence forces the other laborers to take
up his burdens, and thus increases their own hardships. Worst of all,
however, is Niels's effect on Qvist. The entire household gradually comes
to fear Qvist's outbursts at Niels; indeed, Qvist fears them himself. "He
knew," Lewis writes, "that although he held his hands behind him when
he talked to Niels, and did not strike him, yet anger rose in his heart;
and he hated the sight of the man as he had never hated that of any
human being."[41] Ultimately, however, when Niels talks back to Qvist,
the parson attacks him in a rage, striking him on the head with a shovel. Niels, genuinely frightened though not badly injured, runs off, and
Qvist prays for forgiveness:

> "Blessed Lord and Master," he prayed in the quiet of the garden, in des-
> perate humility, "deliver me at last from this temptation. Remove this
> man from my ways. Behold, I am not worthy of the trial. Forgive me
> that I thought to set my strength against his strength, who goeth to and
> fro in the earth, and walketh up and down upon it, now even as in the
> days of the patriarchs. I have no strength, unless You give it me."
> Here Anna found him, still upon his knees.[42]

If the universe were actually working according to the pastor's vision
of it—if God had sent Niels as a test of his humility before the power

of evil, and of his greater humility before the power of God—then Qvist might have well been blessed in this instance. But God did not send Niels; Morten did. And Morten intends a much worse fate for the pastor. Stealing the recently buried body of a local suicide from an unmarked grave, forcing Niels to dress the suicide in his own clothes, striking the body on the head with a shovel, Morten evolves his grotesque plan. After making Niels carry the body back to the pastor's house, Morten enters the house in the dead of night to take Qvist's nightcap and dressing gown. Wearing Qvist's clothes, he then buries the body in Qvist's garden; later, he sends Niels out of Denmark, and with the coast clear, accuses Qvist of having murdered his brother Niels.

Qvist knows that he did not commit this murder. But Qvist is also irrationally afraid of his own wrath, the one power in his life that most clearly seems to move beyond the control of his moral intention or his prayer. It appears to him that God, who tries the souls of human beings to find their worth, has escalated his own trial. As he is taken off to jail, formally accused of the murder of Niels Bruus, the pastor simply says, "In solitude and chains I will possess my soul and await what He in His Wisdom shall decree."[43]

To himself, Qvist is a man with a fatal weakness, which God ultimately must remove in whatever way He deems fit. Thus, in the end, Qvist actually comes to believe himself guilty of a crime Lewis makes clear he did not commit. To the reader, Qvist is clearly a man who loses faith in his own instinctive morality. He loses the creaturely sense of *who he is*. This, in *The Trial of Sören Qvist*, is a dreadful loss, perhaps in some ways more dreadful than the loss of faith in God, because it violates the possibility of any true human meaning. Creatures who convict themselves out of fear of what they might have done cut themselves off from the sources of sustenance that underlie Lewis's moral universe. And yet—as Lewis takes pains to point out at the very outset of the novel—what Qvist does is in some way perfectly consistent with a rational view of the world.

There is, as Lewis suggests, a terrible beauty to Qvist's need to die falsely accused in a just universe rather than to save himself and acknowledge the possibility of injustice on a grand scale. Yet, despite Lewis's defense of Qvist and the "great company of men and women" like him, the fate of the parson is an object of disgust. And Lewis knows this— or, rather, makes the reader's disgust more passionate by contrasting Qvist with two women who know with certainty that he cannot be guilty: his daughter Anna, and the household servant Vibeke. As with *The Wife of Martin Guerre*, there are two kinds of knowledge in this book—the knowledge of reason and reasoned faith (including not only faith in God, but faith in the social institutions of justice and the ordered household); and the knowledge that comes from the intimate encounters of creatures who care deeply for one another. The law—both human and divine—"wins" in *The Trial of Sören Qvist*, as it does in *The Wife of Martin Guerre*, and in *The Trial of Sören Qvist* this winning brings happiness to the protagonist-victim. Qvist is, by his own account, "happy"[44] as he faces death, because his universe still makes sense to him. But the horror of Anna and Vibecke, who know from long acquaintance with the pastor that he cannot be guilty—that somehow, something in this case does not make sense—represents a form of knowledge that ultimately impugns the pastor, his faith, and the members of the community who fall too readily under the sway of putatively rational circumstantial evidence. Evil triumphs in *The Trial of Sören Qvist*, but it is not only the evil of Morten Bruus; it is the evil of Qvist's own excessively narrow belief, his diminished view both of the power of human evil and the power of human good. And it is the evil as well of justice, which accepts the surface of events simply because, as surfaces, they make sense.

The Ghost of Monsieur Scarron extends, not the hopeful possibilities of interconnection and intuitive morality, but rather the darkest elements of Lewis's earlier work. It is a ponderous, trenchant novel. It punishes not only its characters, bringing them all to ruin, but also the idea of eros itself. Whatever earlier links there may have been between eros and Manibohzo are severed. Passion, which once appeared in Lewis's work as an appropriate manifestation of human health, is a diabolical force, full of danger. Characteristically, however, it is a danger that men set in motion; it is the men who are venal. Paul Damas, a journeyman bookbinder of considerable skill, comes from Auxerre to Paris in 1694 to find work, and ultimately takes a position with the binder Jean Larcher. Larcher's wife, Marianne, also works in the shop; as time goes on she and Damas become friendly. One day, while Damas is helping her with the laundry, "She froze, holding her breath, and then she felt a kiss, not on her throat, which the loosened kerchief left bare, but upon her shoulder, on the kerchief itself. The kiss was light. She barely felt the touch. It was such a kiss as might rank as stolen, unobserved; or, if she chose, she might acknowledge it."[45] Thus the affair begins, with Marianne nurturing the illusion of choice. After a time, however, her interest in Damas becomes passionate, and the question of choice vanishes. She wraps her life around him.

For her, this affair is no immoral dalliance, but the fulfillment of an entirely understandable desire—the desire to be cherished as she never has been by her husband. To Damas, however, she is a delightful challenge, a potential conquest. His toying with her ultimately leads to horrifying consequences. Arranging to run off with her, he takes the opportunity to rob Larcher of his entire life's savings; he then leaves incriminating pamphlets, insulting to Louis XIV, half-hidden on a shelf in Larcher's workshop. When the police come to gather evidence about the robbery, they find the pamphlets, arrest Larcher, and take him to prison, where he is ultimately sentenced to death.

Some months later, returning from England, Larcher's son Nicolas learns of his father's execution and surmises what happened. His father leaves him a clue in the form of a tiny message—"DAMAS"—embedded in a scapular that Larcher handed to the executioner at the last moment. Seeking to avenge his father's false accusation and wrongful death, Nicolas tracks down his mother and Damas, planning to force a confession from Damas. When he hears from his mother's lips her complicity in the affair, however, his rage overpowers him, and he kills them both. Shortly thereafter, he slips into a fatal illness; his own death signals the end of the novel.

Ironically, the greatest virtue in this novel is the virtue of silence. Jean Larcher, called upon to identify anyone connected with the offensive pamphlets, refuses to denounce either Paul Damas or his own wife. Although he is in fact the victim of a stupid and vicious crime, he takes full responsibility for what has occurred in his shop; his silence leads directly to his death. In this novel, silence is fidelity; speech is betrayal. Larcher remains faithful to his wife and his own sense of duty, even when his wife is unfaithful to him and duty can lead only to a form of suicide. He is betrayed by the speech of others: by the published words of the unknown pamphleteers whose work Damas initially brings into the shop more or less as a curiosity; by the words of love Damas speaks to Marianne; and by the speech-act of Damas's placing the pamphlets in Larcher's shop where the authorities will discover them. Both silence and speech are punished in this novel. The power of silence, which in a sense draws Larcher away from the ordinary conditions and judgments of life, leads to death; the power of speech, whose erotic content links words and desires in explosive proportions, also leads to death. Yet silence at least is honorable. Larcher's deed implies that where unjust persecution is inevitable, speech can only cause further harm. Silence is thus more than human, a kind of grace bestowed upon other humans by a fragile mortal. It is, in the end, better than speech. It is better, however, only within a crippled system of values.

The Ghost of Monsieur Scarron defines a universe cut off from the creaturely morality of Lewis's earlier work. Yet it is difficult to read the novel apart from its poetic precursors. The contrast between the poems and all three of the novels is great, but the common hand behind them demands acknowledgement. Shaping that acknowledgement, however, is a more difficult matter. One does not wish, as a biographer and a critic, to fall prey oneself to circumstantial evidence. Is the universe of the novels ultimately more "real" than the realm of Lewis's earlier poems? Is *The Ghost of Monsieur Scarron* the final cry of defeat for a worldview that could not accommodate the evils Lewis saw in human behavior? Or is it simply a thoroughly workmanlike performance, the work of a "professional," as Winters said, which takes up fundamental themes in a way that leaves an appropriately disturbing answer? One might answer "yes" to any of these questions—or one might if Lewis's career had stopped with this final novel (as indeed it appeared that it might in the late 1960s). For the voice behind the novels, which grows increasingly dark, mechanical, and even hateful over the course of this career, is a voice set against itself; in its professionalism it seems ultimately devoid of soul in the same way the middle poems were. If H.D.'s novels were written by "someone else"—that is, a different H.D., fully attuned to the workings of her life and determined to make them yield meaning—then Lewis's novels were also written by "someone else"—a woman whose own identity or voice as a writer becomes increasingly masked, until death is the *deus ex machina* and silence is the only virtue. These writers both turn to fiction as an alternative to poetry, but their purposes and ends are profoundly different. Two forms of silence heralded Lewis's career as a novelist—the silence of the poet, and the apparently compensatory "silence" of her distance as a novelist from Winters. Yet this compensatory silence does not, ultimately, lead to a new voice; on the contrary, the silence of the poet ultimately descends around Lewis's novels as well.

———

"For the Father of Sandro Gulotta," written three years after Winters's death, is the first poem of the last section of Lewis's *Poems Old and New, 1918–1978:*

When I called the children from play
Where the westering sun
Fell level between the leaves
        of olive and bay,
There, where the day lilies stand,
I paused
        to touch with a curious hand
The single blossom, furled,
That with morning had opened wide,
The long bud tinged
        with gold of an evening sky.

All day, and only one day,
It drank the sunlit air.
In one long day
All that it needed to do in this world
It did, and at evening precisely curled
The tender petals to shield
From wind, from dew,
The pollen-laden heart.
Sweet treasure gathered apart
From our grief, from our longing view,
Who shall say if the day was too brief,
For the flower, if time lacked?
Had it not, like the children, all Time
In their long, immortal day?[46]

In some ways the first stanza suggests that Lewis has picked up where she left off over thirty years earlier. A scientist's or naturalist's perspective inhabits the stanza. The speaker is curious about the furled blossom, and one might expect some relatively dispassionate reflection on the life cycle of a flower. But the second stanza shatters this view—or rather, it does something much more interesting: it demonstrates Lewis's ability to incorporate certain techniques and interests that dominated her Winters years into themes that are unmistakably and irrevocably her own. The second stanza has a reasoned forcefulness that recalls Lewis's best work during her middle period. Yet that reason, that argument, also heralds the return of Manibozho, and along with him the critical paradox of human mortality and immortality. Combining reason with neglected and powerful revelation, the poem attempts to move beyond the tragedy of human ending. Written for the father of a boy who was dying of leukemia, the poem begins and ends with children. But the children are not the sole focus of the poem.

The close observations of the first stanza—the "olive and bay," the day lilies, the "long bud tinged / with gold of an evening sky"—imply thoughtfulness, even dispassionateness, rather than saccharine feeling. This heightens the effect of the second stanza, which, based on an attentive rather than a sentimental view, becomes an ardent appeal to interpret nature—to find meaning that in some way conforms to the actual circumstances of nature, rather than simply ascribing pleasant or demonic values to it. In that act of interpretation the old voice, the voice of Manibozho, becomes clear once again, as one might hear it in "Nightfall Among Poplars," a poem from the 1920s:

> As light grew horizontal,
> I, among bracken,
> Felt the cold ripples
> Among bracken stems.
>
> The quick dry spider
> Ran across my hand.[47]

Like the sudden shock of the spider, Manibozho is both in and out of time. His presence seems as vivid as if it lasted an eternity, yet it still passes. His variance is at variance with his constancy. In the fact of this paradox of mortality and immortality, one may find shelter from the storm of chaos—at least one may hope for shelter. But the key to shelter here, as elsewhere in Lewis's best poems, is not so much the quality of reason as the quality of love that the poem manifests. In regard to love, "For the Father of Sandro Gulotta" is unequivocal. It insists that love is an act of interpretation, a way of learning and thinking past nature, which gives us the strength to say "In one long day / All that it needed to do in this world / It did." This insistent linking of love for the world and love for the variant principle of life is the eros of creation in its essence. Perhaps the purest statement of this resurgence of Manibozho, this dance, comes with one of Lewis's more recent poems, "Snail Garden."

> This is the twilight hour of the morning
> When the snails retreat over the wet grass
> To their hidden world, when my dreams, retreating,
> Leave me wondering what wisdom goes with them,
> What hides in mouldering earth.
>
> Softly they go, the snails,
> Naked, unguarded, perceptive

Of the changing light, rejoicing
In their slow progress from leaf to stem,
From stem to deeper darkness.
Smoothness delights them.

What do they hear? The air above them
Is full of the sharp cries of birds.
Do they see? The lily bud,
Three feet above the soil on its leafy stalk,
Is known to them at midnight
As if it were a lighthouse. Before sunrise
They have gnawed it half in two.
Toothless mouths, blind mouths
Have turned the leaf of the hollyhock to lace,
And cut the stem of the nasturtium
Neatly, just below the blossom.

The classic shell, cunningly arched, and strong
Against the hazards of the grassy world
Is nothing before the power of my intention.
The larks, also, have had their fun,
Crashing that coiled shell on stone,
Guiltless in their freedom.

But I have taken sides in the universe.
I have killed the snail that lay on the morning leaf,
Not grudging greatly the nourishment it took
Out of my abundance,
Chard, periwinkle, capucine,
Occasional lily bud,
But I have begun my day with death,
Death given, death to be received.
I have stepped into the dance;
I have greeted at daybreak
That necessary angel, that other.[48]

In "Snail Garden," nature is the other world, the unknowable. Yet Lewis still affirms some link with the unknowable. Her dreams retreat with the snails toward a "hidden world," which they inhabit without self-awareness and which she cannot inhabit precisely because of her capacity for curiosity, reflection, wonder. Dreams and snails alike retreat to Manibozho. But Manibozho is not a romantic figure. He is not the Wordsworthian sign of greater reality. Incarnate, he is obscene as well as sacred. Demanding love, he does not live by love alone—or, rather, he lives by love if that love includes a clear-sighted recognition of life's danger. The dance is not a minuet, but something far harsher and more beautiful.

Lewis is quite matter-of-fact about this. A close observer and admirer of nature, she nevertheless has her way: "The classic shell. . . . Is nothing before the power of my intention." She kills snails; she takes sides in the universe. The power of intention, and of death, is strong in this poem, as it is in Lewis's novels, but the difference is critical. In the novels, intention and death overwhelmed any sustaining creaturely necessity or instinct. In this poem, that sustaining instinct finds its place within a universe which death and human intention cannot overwhelm.

In her late poems Lewis harkens back to her early work, and her early mythologies of revelation, quite explicitly—in her 1979 chapbook "The Ancient Ones," for example, which chronicles her more recent visits to the American Southwest and its important sites of Navaho, Hopi, and other American Indian cultures. In these poems the variant principle of life arrays itself in reflections on time and sacredness, on the multiple names for water and the multiplicities of its sustenance, on the human role as she conceives it in "The Ancient Ones: Betatakin."

> We do not recreate, we rediscover
> The immortal form, that, once created,
> Stands unchanged
> In Time's unchanging room.[49]

Here a truce has come to pass. Reason is a useful human tool, but the past reveals other forces as great and greater. In these poems, of course, the past is the collective past—the pasts of Native American tribes as Lewis has come to perceive them; but it is also Lewis's personal past as she rediscovers the form and motion of her own early work, which, "once created, stands unchanged." Her poetic career permits considerable philosophical interpretation, yet it is once and for all a career of seeing and listening—listening for what is distinct and cherishable, seeing what may be too easily overlooked. Though her middle poems and novels show a kind of uncenteredness one does not see in the other work, her poems always start with the phenomena of the world; from them her work moves toward reason or revelation, seeking the route that yields harmony. To watch and listen is to attend to life, which is the first task and the most important. This idea is confirmed in the first poem of *Poems Old and New, 1918–1978,* "The Indians in the Woods":

Ah, the woods, the woods
Where small things
Are distinct and visible,

The berry plant,
The berry leaf, remembered
Line for line.

There are three figures
Walking in the woods
Whose feet press down
Needle and leaf and vine.[50]

The distinctness of things, the relation of things to movement and process, and the importance of seeing, all combine nearly sixty years later to reappear in the last poem of the book, "The Wonder of the World":

From the old stone
The carven words reproach me,
Beside the rows of quiet dead:

The wonder of the world,
The beauty and the power,
The shapes of things,
Their colors, lights and shades,
These I saw.
Look ye also
While life lasts.

Earth, air and upper air,
Earth, air and water I knew,
And the sun on my face.
The voices of women and men,
The shouting of children,
These I knew.
Harken ye, also.
Drink while life lasts
The wine of astonishment.

So spoke the stone.[51]

Lewis borrows the seven lines of the second stanza from an inscription on an old Swedish gravestone in Wyoming. They "reproach" her, who, born in 1900, stands among the monuments of death at an age few people reach. In the presence of death, life is the necessary force; the inanimate stone speaks this. Once again the mythology of revelation holds, and the past returns in objects and words to redeem the present life. The past here is not, however, a specific tradition of knowledge; it is not equivalent to the Logos, the *animus,* which so powerfully shaped Winters's life. The past is a way of seeing and a set of personal experiences that confirm the unique lives of those who are now dead. The past, properly understood, reinforces those dead as subjects in their own right. They matter to Lewis, not because they *knew,* but because they *were.*

Such confidence in Manibozho and his constant reincarnations suggests that one of Lewis's strongest qualities is her patience. Though she chooses sides in the universe, the universe revises itself and even shifts the borders of those sides through its own "geometries," as Lewis notes in a later poem by that name. To be on one side at one time is conceivably to be on another side at some other time. To take sides is to experiment; if the experiment does not succeed, the variant principle of life will eventually either change the experiment or compel one to move away from it. This patience is in no way equivalent to passivity; yet the sense of selfhood that arises from patience has a peculiarly quiet eroticism, a passionateness that knows it will come into its own and can bide its time.

Like Manibozho in his ursine incarnation, Lewis hibernates as Winters enters his most influential stage as a critic and mentor. She does not rebel, because she understands too well that, as Allen Tate has said, "Winters made the mistake of judging people by their poetry."[52] His judgment of her poetry, cited earlier, suggests that he found her talent as a novelist admirable but somewhat remote; he knew the fineness of her gift for rhythm and meter; and he found her domesticity and sentimentality cherishable yet minor. To continue to produce works of art that defied the values of the mentor, however—except in the guise of fiction, where the demands of plot and narrative might make conflicting values less apparent—would have been to place an intolerable burden on the relationship. The passion of Lewis's vision of Manibozho could not easily coexist with the profound intellectualism of Winters's vision of poetry. Yet to lose the mentor would have been to lose the husband as well—in this case an unacceptable loss.

Thus she waited. Whether she outlived her husband, whether she recovered the passion of her earliest work, whether she reasserted her identity as a poet was not so much her responsibility as it was a matter of psychic geometries. The forms of being that had led her into her earlier vision, her earlier mode of speech, would perhaps recombine, and she would be ready once again. As it turned out, she did outlive Winters and did recover her voice. But since, at some level, she had known her poetic identity all along, the issues of rebellion or liberation were never central to her self-presentation. She appeared to the world as an artist who could move from experimental early work to formal middle work to fiction; there was no reason to expect that one form would not work as well as the other. Yet, from a reader's point of view, the risks Lewis ran were considerable. The excellence of the later poems makes Lewis's silent years resound with unfulfilled possibilities: the echoes suggest that, from a purely human standpoint, one may wait too long, and may have to rely too much on good fortune. Perhaps for one who believes as strongly in Manibozho as Lewis does, that kind of risk seems simply irrelevant. But to have died in silence would have been too terrible an homage to the mentor.

Notes

1. Yvor Winters, *The Poetry of Yvor Winters,* ed. with introduction by Donald Davie (Manchester, England: Carcanet, 1978), p. 126.

2. John Donne, *The Complete English Poems,* ed. with introduction by A. J. Smith (Harmondsworth, England: Penguin, 1973), p. 54.

3. Janet Lewis, *Poems Old and New, 1918–1978* (Athens: Swallow Press/ Ohio University Press, 1981), p. 41.

4. Yvor Winters, letter to Hisaye Yamamoto, Apr. 7, 1951, the Yvor Winters and Janet Lewis Papers, Special Collections, Stanford University Libraries.

5. Winters's books of poetry include *The Proof* (1930), *The Journey* (1931), *Before Disaster* (1934), *Poems* (1940), *The Giant Weapon* (1943), *Three Poems* (1950), *Collected Poems* (1952), and *The Early Poems of Yvor Winters, 1920–1928* (1966).

6. Lewis's books of poetry include *The Indians in the Woods* (1922), *The Wheel in Midsummer* (1927), *The Earth-Bound, 1924–1944* (1946), *Poems, 1924–1944* (1950), *The Ancient Ones* (1979), and *Poems Old and New, 1918–1978* (1981). Her novels are *The Invasion* (1932), *The Wife of Martin Guerre* (1941), *Against a Darkening Sky* (1943), *The Trial of Sören Qvist* (1947), and *The Ghost of Monsieur Scarron* (1959). She published a children's novel, *Keiko's Bubble,* in 1961, and a collection of stories, *Goodbye, Son, and Other Stories,* in 1946. She has also written libretti for several contemporary operas. See Brigitte Hoy Carnochan, *The Strength of Art: Poets and Poetry in the Lives of Yvor Winters and Janet Lewis* (Stanford: Stanford University Libraries, 1984), pp. 46–47.

7. See note 27, p. 118.

8. Yvor Winters, *Forms of Discovery* (Chicago: Swallow Press, 1967), p. 331.

9. For more on "the great conflagration," see Carnochan, p. 32.

10. Janet Lewis interview with Thomas Simmons, Dec. 10, 1986.

11. Janet Lewis interview with Brigitte Hoy Carnochan, *Canto* 4, no. 4 (1981): 57.

12. See Charles Crow, *Janet Lewis,* Boise State University Western Writers Series No. 41 (Boise: Boise State University, 1980), p. 7. Janet Lewis's novel *The Invasion* (Chicago: Swallow Press, 1932) also gives a valuable sense of these experiences.

13. Quoted in Kenneth Fields's "Motion and Quiet Reconciled," jacket notes for *Janet Lewis Reading at Stanford* (Stanford: Stanford Program for Recordings in Sound, 1975). I am indebted to Kenneth Fields for first calling my attention to the function of Manibozho in Lewis's poetry.

14. Lewis, *The Invasion,* p. 4.

15. See Carnochan, pp. 19–21.

16. Lewis, *Poems Old and New,* p. 4.

17. Lewis, *Poems Old and New,* p. 11.

18. Ezra Pound, "A Few Don'ts," *Literary Essays of Ezra Pound* (New York: New Directions, 1968), p. 4.

19. Ezra Pound,"In a Station of the Metro," *Selected Poems of Ezra Pound* (New York: New Directions, 1957), p. 35.

20. Lewis, *Poems Old and New,* p. 31.

21. Jessica Benjamin, *The Bonds of Love: Psychoanalysis, Feminism, and the Problem of Domination* (New York: Pantheon, 1988), p. 41.

22. Long before I did, Howard Baker used the revelation-reason terminology in his article on Winters in *The Southern Review* 17, no. 4 (1981). My sense of the application of these terms is somewhat different from his, however, since I did not encounter his article until I was well along in the writing of this chapter.

23. See A. J. Ayer, "Critique of Ethics and Theology," *Language, Truth and Logic* (New York: Dover, 1952), pp. 114–20.

24. Theodore Roethke, review of *The Earth-Bound* by Janet Lewis, *Poetry* 69, no. 1 (1947): 220–23.

25. Lewis, *Poems Old and New,* p. 54.

26. Lewis, *Poems Old and New,* p. 67.

27. Lewis interviews with Thomas Simmons, Feb. 24, 1987, and October 17, 1987 (the latter interview was conducted in the company of Dave Sylvester, *San Jose Mercury News*).

28. Tillie Olsen, *Silences* (New York: Delacorte Press, 1978), pp. 6–46.

29. Lewis interview with Carnochan, *Canto,* p. 67.

30. Lewis interview with Carnochan, *Canto,* p. 67.

31. Lewis's novels have all gone through several printings, most with distinguished publishers. *The Wife of Martin Guerre,* originally published by the

Colt Press in San Francisco, was reprinted in a jointly sponsored anthology by the Swallow Press and William Morrow & Co. in 1947 (the work was titled *Anchor in the Sea: An Anthology of Psychological Fiction,* edited by Alan Swallow); it was reprinted again by Alan Swallow in 1950 and 1959, and in several subsequent releases through 1987. It was also published in London, most recently by Penguin Books, whose 1977 edition has gone through four reprints. In addition, the novel has been translated into French, Italian, and Spanish, and has served as the basis for an opera libretto.

The Trial of Sören Qvist originally appeared from Doubleday in 1947; it was a Book-of-the-Month Club selection in Canada for that year. Alan Swallow reprinted the book in 1959, and Victor Gollanz in London reprinted it in 1967. The joint venture of the Swallow Press and the Ohio University Press reprinted the novel in 1983, and Robin Clark in London reprinted it in 1986. In addition, a French edition appeared from the Presses de la Cité in 1968.

The Ghost of Monsieur Scarron appeared in 1959 from Doubleday in New York and Victor Gollanz in London; it was reprinted by Alan Swallow in 1965 and again by the Swallow Press/Ohio University Press in 1981.

Lewis's earlier novel *The Invasion* was published in 1932 by Harcourt, Brace & Co., and was reprinted several times by Alan Swallow (as well as by the University of Denver Press); the 1943 *Against a Darkening Sky* was published by Doubleday, and reprinted by Swallow Press/Ohio University Press in 1985.

I am indebted to Margaret Furbush of Los Altos, California, Janet Lewis's bibliographer, for these details.

32. Winters, *Forms,* p. 331.

33. Yvor Winters, letter to Hisaye Yamamoto, Apr. 7, 1951, reproduced in Carnochan, pp. 36–37.

34. Yvor Winters, letter to Pearl Andelson Sherry, Apr. 30, 1923, reprinted in Carnochan, pp. 18–19.

35. Lewis interview with Carnochan, *Canto,* p. 71.

36. Janet Lewis, *The Wife of Martin Guerre* (Athens: Swallow Press/Ohio University Press, 1985), unnumbered foreward.

37. See Alan Swallow, ed., *Anchor in the Sea: An Anthology of Psychological Fiction* (New York: The Swallow Press and William Morrow & Co., 1947).

38. Lewis, *Wife,* p. 13.

39. Lewis, *Wife,* pp. 13–14.

40. Carol Gilligan, *In a Different Voice: Psychological Theory and Women's Development* (Cambridge: Harvard University Press, 1982), p. 33.

41. Janet Lewis, *The Trial of Sören Qvist* (Athens: Swallow Press/Ohio University Press, 1983), p. 143.

42. Lewis, *Trial,* p. 149.

43. Lewis, *Trial,* p. 164.

44. Lewis, *Trial,* p. 239.

45. Janet Lewis, *The Ghost of Monsieur Scarron* (New York: Doubleday & Co., 1959), p. 143.

46. Lewis, *Poems Old and New,* p. 77.

47. Lewis, *Poems Old and New,* p. 6.

48. Lewis, *Poems Old and New,* pp. 102–103.

49. Lewis, *Poems Old and New,* p. 89.

50. Lewis, *Poems Old and New,* p. 3.

51. Lewis, *Poems Old and New,* p. 112.

52. Allen Tate quoted in Thom Gunn, "On a Drying Hill," *The Southern Review* 17, no. 4 (1981): 692.

5

Who Shall Deliver Me from the Body of This Death?

The Mentorship of Louise Bogan

With both Yvor Winters and Ezra Pound, the dangers of mentorship had much to do with the will to master. In Winters's case, mastery was the logical extension of a cultural tradition that prized the legacy of reason as a wall against chaos. To leave an effective intellectual legacy, a teacher must master his discipline by submitting to it; as a "master" he must exert his influence on his pupils to preserve his own experience of submission. In Pound's case, the will to master extended from a different source—the spiritual need, perhaps healthy in essence but also megalomaniac, to escape the incarceration of the single self. Both mentors wrestled with a powerful awareness of their will—even their obligation—to master. This self-conscious inheritance of a traditional mentorship made them in some ways attractive, in other ways dangerous to their apprentices. The attraction that the powerful mentor—the interpreter who has seen answers to life's most disturbing questions—exerts over the apprentice is not unlike the attraction any powerful figure exerts over those whose sense of identity, for whatever reason, is fragmentary or inchoate. The apprentice desires recognition; the master offers it, for a price. "Domination does not repress the desire for recognition," Benjamin writes; "rather, it enlists and transforms it. Beginning in the breakdown of the tension between self and other, domination proceeds through the alternate paths of identifying with or submitting to powerful others who personify the fantasy of omnipotence."[1] Benign though they might have seemed (when compared to extremes of erotic domination), neither Pound nor Winters expected a nonhierarchical relationship with their apprentices. Nor nor was there ever any question of the importance of ending the relationship of inequality or basing the mentorship on "service to the lesser party," as Miller has said. To end the unequal relationship with either mentor was in some way to betray the mentor. While it may well be argued that both Pound and Winters served their apprentices, their service was predicated on a sense of mission that could accommodate interdependence between mentor and apprentice only with the gravest difficulty.

As H.D. suggested, for a work of art to contain a child, an erotic spark, it had to evolve from a union in which each party maintained his or her discrete identity. In both Winters's and Pound's stories one finds evidence of a tendency to absorb or circumscribe identities. With Louise Bogan, however, comes a distinctly different notion of mentorship—a notion that preserves the role of the lover-teacher, yet presses hard against the inevitability of dominance. In part her will to equality, rather than mastery, stems from her own experience as a subordinate player. Her two failed marriages, one to a novelist and poet who openly criticized her work, showed her the embarrassments and greater emotional dangers of subjugating one's talent to any other human being. For Bogan to reach this concept of mentorship, however, was for her to return from a descent into several levels of hell. From her two nervous breakdowns in the early 1930s she emerges utterly convinced of the importance of following one's own sense of selfhood as an artist. That journey is the subject of this chapter.

———

According to Elizabeth Frank, Louise Bogan in her later years laughed at the solemnity of *Body of This Death,* the title she chose for her first published book of poems in 1923.[2] Yet the quotation from *Romans* 7:24, high-minded as it seems, has more than mere solemnity to say about the young, convent-educated Louise Bogan. "O wretched man that I am!" writes Saint Paul. "Who shall deliver me from the body of this death?" Paul's cry comes near the end of a chapter in which he expounds on the paradoxical necessity of both sin and law. "For without the law sin was dead," he says; for Paul it is the law that confirms human sinfulness. In this self-enclosed, self-entrapping world, the grace of Christ is Paul's exit. But what of those who do not seek Christ, or God? What of those for whom the typology of sin-law-Christ is itself a trap—and at the same time a kind of temptation, a will to order?

About seven years after *Body of This Death* was published, Bogan composed an interview with herself. Unknown until Ruth Limmer found it among Bogan's private papers, the piece was included in *Journey around My Room.* Among the questions and answers are these:

> *Did you ever seek God?*
> No.
> *What is it that you sought?*
> I sought love.
> *And you sought love for what reason?*
> Those about me, from childhood on, had sought love. I heard and saw them. I saw them rise and fall on that wave. I closely overheard and sharply overlooked their joy and grief. I worked from memory and example. . . .
> *You wished—?*
> To live without apology. . . . To live my life, at last delivered from ambition, from envy, from hatred, from frightened love, to live it until the end *without the need for philosophy;* that is all I ask. I fear the philosopher as I fear the ambitious, the seeker for God, the self-satisfied proud. In them lies evil. . . .[3]

Clearly in this later work, this version of a diary entry, Bogan rejects any kind of orthodoxy, Christian or otherwise. Yet even here she seeks the *form* of something, seeks it so ardently that she is willing to "overlook" the grief of those who lose it. That form is love. Love may be original and creative enough to sustain a personality in the process of forming itself. On the other hand, love may itself become a trap, a kind of Pauline typology. In terror of the traumas of human life, one turns from wretchedness to—God? Love? The difference is essential, yet all too easily obscured. The love Bogan identifies in the diary entry is rooted in personality. It forcefully identifies and celebrates the person in the exactitude of his or her human condition. That is not the love Saint Paul professes in *Romans,* nor is it the kind of love one finds in Bogan's first book.

Why do Saint Paul and the varieties of love matter to Bogan's first book? Why is the Pauline title so appropriate? Because, although *Body of This Death* takes as its themes human ensnarement and the perils of liberation, it treats them with a kind of typological force that is at once highly charged spiritually and remarkably self-concealing. *Body of This Death* is brilliant both technically and rhetorically; yet from an artistic viewpoint it is curiously limited—limited, one might say, in the same way that Paul is limited in his typological approach to nontypological problems. The craft of typology is essentially legalistic. It validates conditions of the soul only in their relation to a process. Thus lust or self-aggrandizement or depravation or bereavement or undeserved suffering cease to be themselves, becoming instead components of a larger event. Damnation or salvation may result, but it is the process itself that matters, not the specific human condition. Typology can thus be seen as a way of converting people into formulae in order to save their souls. Its view of the person as an object of revision or redemption might seem to confer on it a kind of grace; yet this view demeans the notion of personhood and obviates interdependency. What is left is precisely a hierarchy of power and submission, in which the powerful gain power by virtue of their skill in distinguishing between absolute "subject"—the type itself—and absolute "object"—the messy human being in need of salvation.

The first poem in the collection, "A Tale," is cast in the form of a lesson about life, but the terms of the lesson are somewhat odd. The protagonist, a young man, is weary of "a land of change"; he seeks to free himself from the exigencies of life—and at the same time have a genuine adventure—by seeking what is perfect, Platonic, immutable. The poem implies that this adventure is doomed to failure:

> But he will find that nothing dares
> To be enduring, save where, south
> Of hidden deserts, torn fire glares
> On beauty with a rusted mouth,—
>
> Where something dreadful and another
> Look quietly upon each other.[4]

What is perfect is not accessible to human consciousness. It manifests itself rather as stasis, horror. The poem urges its protagonist to go back to change—go back to the adventure of passionate, mutable life. Yet the poem is curiously cast in the negative, for it does not celebrate this passionate life. Rather, it presents a dreadful picture of the alternative, so that mutability becomes the lesser of two evils. We do not see the protagonist turning toward anything positive; rather, we see him turning toward what he *thinks* will be positive, but what in fact will turn out to be terrifying. How do we know this? Because the narrator—the "I think" of the ninth line of the poem—is prescient and possesses the wisdom to envision the young man's tragedy. As Elizabeth Frank says, "The poem's riddling tone belongs to someone who sounds somehow *returned* from a sight too terrible for ordinary human eyes, and there is a reproach in the last stanza."[5] For Frank, this "reproach" is aimed at Bogan's first husband, Curt Alexander, who swept her off to Panama; by implication, "something dreadful and another" are Louise and Alexander, though of course—as Frank is careful to point out—this autobiographical possibility is so carefully concealed as to be almost entirely conjectural. This concealing, and this prescience, create a narrator to whom wisdom has been revealed; but the force of the wisdom actually conceals the narrator. The poem thus operates with a shadow-narrator who herself creates a shadow-protagonist.

Why do both the narrator and the protagonist seem so unreachable, so concealed, in this poem? The answer does not lie simply in Bogan's fear of confessionalism. Rather, the answer can be found in the fragmented character both of the speaker and the one spoken of. The youth who goes "to see what suns can make / From soil more indurate and strange" is already divided against himself. He is right to seek adventure, but wrong to set out toward Plotinus instead of Homer. His destiny foretold, he becomes, not an actual figure of tragic miscalculation, but a type of that figure. The point here is not to make him a person, but rather a vehicle for the wisdom of the poem. That wisdom is, of course, that those who seek perfection by whatever means are doomed to horror. But can it be that one who has experienced this doom can return merely as an observer—as this narrator does, observing the young man about to descend to tragedy? This is surely the method of the narrator, but the method is at odds with the poem. For the poem encourages, even if by implication, the life of passionate involvement in mutability. The narrator advocates an involvement to which she will not commit herself.

The poems in *Body of This Death* swing through their own fragments, their own acceptance and renunciation of passion, their vying voices. "Knowledge," for example, rejects even the passion whose value is implied in "A Tale":

> Now that I know
> How passion warms little
> Of flesh in the mould,
> And treasure is brittle—
>
> I'll lie here and learn
> How, over their ground,
> Trees make a long shadow
> And a light sound.[6]

In "The Alchemist," by contrast, knowledge is not enough. The passion that leads to death, that "warms little / Of flesh in the mould," is nevertheless unquenchable.

> I burned my life, that I might find
> A passion wholly of the mind,
> Thought divorced from eye and bone,
> Ecstasy come to breath alone.
> I broke my life, to seek relief
> From the flawed light of love and grief.
>
> With mounting beat the utter fire
> Charred existence and desire.
> It died low, ceased its sudden thresh.
> I had found unmysterious flesh—
> Not the mind's avid substance—still
> Passionate beyond the will.[7]

This poem could well be the final or ideal autobiography of the adventurer in "A Tale." Having sought the perfections of Platonism, he learns of counterforces that cannot be quelled. "The Alchemist" is an important poem because it both suggests the locus of Bogan's later work and shows the difficulty of getting there. Though it does not constitute the voice of personality—it is too schematic, too neatly divided and arranged for that—the poem nevertheless poses an alternative vision to the typologist's celebration of the intellect. "The mind's avid substance" cannot be the hero of this poem, because it is the stuff of alchemy—a bogus science, a shadow of truth. Alchemy is a way of typologically reorganizing the matter of the universe because that matter is too taxing to be understood in itself. Bogan comprehends both the brilliance and the limitations of alchemy in this poem; its downfall is not further mystery, but rather the fact of "unmysterious flesh." The process is still important here—the movement from mind back to matter, from will to passion—and this preoccupation with process remains a hallmark of the limitations of the early poems. And yet this poem works away from traditional typologies, or rather truncates them. In so doing it derives a distinctly different moral lesson, a lesson verging on the personal.

"Memory" is another poem showing the dual tensions of typology and personality.

> Do not guard this as rich stuff without mark
> Closed in a cedarn dark,

Nor lay it down with tragic masks and greaves,
Licked by the tongues of leaves.

Nor let it be as eggs under the wings
Of helpless, startled things,
Nor encompassed by song, nor any glory
Perverse and transitory.

Rather, like shards and straw upon coarse ground,
Of little worth when found,—
Rubble in gardens, it and stones alike,
That any spade may strike.[8]

The poem both fulfills and distorts conventional typological expectations. In a Pauline context, human memory is coarse and fraudulent;
its chief value is to focus on human sinfulness and—aided by grace—
the possibilities of divine inspiration. Bogan conveys this coarseness, but
her aim and her tone are quite different from what one might expect.
Yes, memory is "like shards and straw upon coarse ground"; but this in
no way diminishes its value. Rather, it redeems memory from the more
commonplace stereotypes under which it functions. Indeed, the elaborate diction in the first two stanzas almost mocks these commonplace
visions: memory as a repository for tragedy, memory as the offspring of
helpless predestination, are teased into embarrassment with "tragic masks
and greaves" or "perverse and transitory" glory. One begins to hear the
voice of the poet demanding an original perception of this human tool—
a perception that will permit her the foraging she needs without automatically converting it into an experiential type. "Rubble in gardens" is
what she seeks, rubble "that any spade may strike."

Elizabeth Frank points out that "Memory" was first published in the
New Republic in May 1922, and may well have been written a few
months earlier while Bogan was undergoing psychoanalysis in New York
with Dr. Samuel Tannenbaum. The sessions lasted only a short while;
Bogan was in Europe—Vienna, in fact—by the time the poem made it
into print. "Considering her lifelong aversion to direct reminiscence,"
Frank writes, "she may well have reached a point where the work of pro-
ducing memories had become too painful to bear, and the subsequent
disaffection and homesickness she experienced in Vienna may have been
part of a desolation following this evasion. The shards, straw, and rubble may have struck the fastidious and frightened young woman as un-
bearably messy and unclean."[9] The shabbiness of memory horrified

Bogan; her other biographical papers suggest good reasons for horror. Certainly the final stanza of "Memory" has a biting self-deprecation to it—an assertion of "little worth"—that suggests a speaker divided against herself. And yet the poem has its strength. It defies commonplace expectations of the nature of memory, and in that way distinguishes itself from a crowd of types.

At the same time, this assertion of difference leads nowhere. What are the shards, the rubble, the straw? As Frank suggests, even Bogan herself found the answer to this question unmanageable, and the poem— or subsequent early poems—cannot begin to incorporate an answer. "Memory" is not about the function of one specific human memory so much as it is about a strategy for defining memory; though couched in emotional rhetoric, it is essentially an intellectual exercise. Again, it finds shelter in the typological fold, though it peers out under the eaves toward a wider reality.

Reading these early poems, one comes to understand the need for suffering as a precursor to personality. But one also sees the strangely dual nature of typological writing. What is typed can emerge either from legitimate suffering or deceiving conjecture, and the difference is not always easy to detect. The function of a type is usually to redefine human reality according to some received wisdom—and thus to transform or even mute human reality. In Pauline Christology, for example, the sufferings of Christ are of use primarily as a reminder of the intensity of his salvation; Christ becomes both a model of faith and a type of the human experience. Wretchedness may well be a blessing, for according to Paul wretchedness is a precursor to the revelation that Christ "will deliver me from the body of this death." Ultimately wretchedness equals blessedness, sorrow equals joy, and pain equals redemption.

While the promise of this kind of typology may seem pleasant, in fact the effect is to negate the actual value of each discrete experience. With such negation, who can tell what is truly felt? The wretchedness of Paul, under these circumstances, might as well be any other form of human experience, except that this particular vocabulary of experience leads to the other, all-important vocabulary—that of freedom or redemption. Under such conditions the only possible self is fragmented, for a unified self could not be so at odds with the actuality of its feeling. But though the fragmented self necessarily suffers from its fragmentation, it does not necessarily comprehend the value of that suffering; instead it sees the fragmentation—not the pain—as the essential object of concern. The problem, of course, is that this fragmentation is foretold by whatever received wisdom operates, so that the fragmented self becomes one with the mediocrity of the foretold. In a sense, then, the fragmented self deceives itself by misunderstanding the real force of its alienation—that is, alienation from the potential strength of the integral personality. This deception becomes apparent to some degree when the self devotes inordinate effort to positing a typological system by which it is saved.

The legitimate suffering of the self stands in contrast to this deception. Such suffering can be determined primarily through the language of exposition, when the exact human condition begins to supplant the saving, exterior vision. This kind of suffering begins to appear in the later poems of Bogan's first book, when the fragmented self leaves the secular iconography of types and starts to explore its own emotional terrain. Ironically, this suffering—and not the deceiving self, with its will to typology that shadows suffering—marks the beginning of the personality, and the self-referential power that finds its expression in confident, novel fusions of mind and passion. The acknowledgement of this suffering, which becomes crucial in Bogan's relationship with Roethke, requires sufficient courage to confront sharply conflicting attitudes toward fundamental human problems—sexuality, family, professional identity, personal freedom. For all her alleged fear of the past, Bogan begins to demonstrate this courage in her life even as she is composing the poems that comprise *Body of This Death*.

To go back into Bogan's early years is to enter a world of almost-concealed psychic collisions. The second child of Daniel and May Bogan, Louise came into what might be described as a white-collar world; her father, after all, was a mill foreman, "a boss," as Edmund Wilson once archly described him.[10] Yet even here the terminology conflicted with reality. The Bogans, though not poor, were hardly well-off. They inhabited that twilit middle ground of people with just enough security to know how much of the world eluded them. This was particularly true of May, Louise's mother, who after Louise's birth found herself more frequently seeking solace and excitement in a kind of passionate life that conventional lower-middle-class society rejected. The family moved around; May had affairs. On some of these occasions the young Louise had to accompany her mother to the site of the tryst. She explained it this way: "The door is open, and I see the ringed hand on the pillow; I weep by the hotel window as she goes down the street, with *another*."[11]

At other times, when her mother went "to the city," Louise was left with Mrs. Parsons, a neighbor and "a pillar of the Congregationalist church."[12] Once, May vanished for several weeks;[13] her deeply contrite return did not prevent the inevitable parental fight from breaking out. Recalling the family violence in her journal years later, in 1954, Bogan wrote:

> I must have experienced violence from birth. But I remember it, at first, as only bound up with *flight*. I was bundled up and carried away. . . . The curved lid of the trunk is thrown back, and my mother is bending over the trunk, and packing things into it. She is crying and she screams. My father, somewhere in the shadows, groans as though he has been hurt. It is a scene of the utmost terror. And then my mother sweeps me into her arms, and carries me out of the room. She is fleeing; she is running away. Then I remember no more, until a quite different scene comes before my eyes. It is morning—earliest morning. My mother and I and another woman are in a wooden summerhouse on a lawn.[14]

These visions of domestic infidelity and rage followed Bogan throughout her childhood. At the age of nine she was sent to a convent—Mount Saint Mary Academy, in Manchester, New Hampshire—so that her mother would be free for a year to drive to California with another "admirer." Her home life certainly was not all bleakness and tumult, but its tribulations impelled her toward the first sign of escape, which showed up in her nineteenth year in the form of Curt Alexander. Alexander quickly dashed both her romanticism and her quest for escape. He expected her to be his servant and refused to sleep with her after she gave birth to her only child.[15] Only his early death following an operation saved her from initiating a divorce. Thus, by the age of twenty-three, Bogan had traded one traumatic domestic life for another, only to find herself free of both for a time. Though she visited her parents regularly—especially since they were taking care of her daughter, Maidie—Bogan was no longer tied to them, or to anyone. At twenty-three she began her independent life. But the freight she carried with her was heavy.

One begins to see just how heavy in a letter Bogan writes to Edmund Wilson in 1925, four years after Alexander's death. At the time Bogan is involved in her first extramarital affair; her reading of Henry James prompts her to some sophisticated reflections on the subject of marriage, love, and fidelity: "I think [James's] sense that all sexual play is essentially evil is an extremely important detail. The array of innocent enough people who are made subtly monstrous because they have slept with someone outside the banns of holy matrimony—it's a child's sense of evil."[16]

Bogan's letter suggests that her painful, conventional family life may have actually liberated her from the damnations of cultural spooks. Guilt, jealousy, anger—these evolve from the belief that extramarital sex is "subtly monstrous," and Bogan had stashed that thought away among other anachronisms of hypocrisy. Yet even as she was writing this letter, Bogan was beginning a relationship with Raymond Holden that would invoke her hidden reservoirs of envy and rage. Holden represented much of what Bogan wanted, and most of what she could not have. A poet and novelist of moderate yet noticeable talent, he was handsome in that slightly awkward way that invites endearment. From an established New England family, he grew up with all the advantages of Harvard and the Continent that Louise had lacked. He fancied himself a ladies' man, and apparently had his share of success. The only recorded failure, in fact, was with Bogan's daughter Maidie, who once broke his glasses and kicked him in the eye when he tried to spank her.[17] Edmund Wilson offered a characteristically sharp summation of Holden in a letter to John Peale Bishop in January 1924, when he noted that Holden "heroically left his wife and family and is now living in sin with Louise Bogan." If Holden were successful in obtaining a divorce, Wilson wrote, "all the remarkable women of the kind in New York will be married to amiable mediocrities."[18]

Holden was more than amiable; he was ardently in love with Bogan, and regularly showered her with a lover's tenderness. And, while he managed to insult her poetry behind her back to her friends—he thought he was the better poet[19]—he generally supported Bogan's work, and tolerated if not encouraged her own journeys to Europe in search of peace and inspiration. Yet, with Bogan, his good qualities were his downfall in a way that his faults could never be, bad as his faults sometimes were; for with her unresolved experience of domestic violence and jealousy, Bogan constructed ample enough faults of her own for Holden. Elizabeth Frank describes one such fault-finding this way:

> She once invited a friend from Massachusetts to stay overnight with them as a houseguest. No sooner did the guest arrive than Louise announced

that she had an errand to do, and disappeared for two whole days, returning only to confront Raymond with triumphant accusations of infidelity (which, though sorely tempted, he had not, in his opinion, *technically* committed). . . . Louise's storms, rages, and cruelty were inseparable, to Raymond, from her intellectual fire and sexual ardor, and he found himself living in increasing emotional bondage to her.[20]

For Bogan, love was a form of power, and power was always unmanageable. It was thrilling, but it could harm or hurt as quickly as a changing mood. If Bogan subjugated Holden, she also subjugated herself through her own certainty of his infidelity—and her gut-level horror at the thought, despite her earlier comments to Edmund Wilson. To grasp the passionate allure of the world was also to mistrust and hate that world; this had been Bogan's model of living since her earliest years. And while this model virtually guaranteed suffering, it made love more and more impossible.

After Bogan married Holden in 1925, their battles came more frequently. He himself exacerbated the situation by apparently having an affair while Bogan was abroad on a Guggenheim fellowship in 1933.[21] He may well have had previous affairs, but whether or not he did, Bogan was convinced that he did, and that made all the difference. As Frank explains, "Aware as she was of her tendency toward hysterical jealousy, Louise could not help believing that her fears had a foundation in reality. Certain that he had had occasional affairs since the early stages of their relationship, she had, more than once, suffered from hating and fearing a woman she considered her rival. Holden's denials did little to assuage her suspicions; his protestations of adoring love sounded hollow and rhetorical to her ears."[22]

Holden is an intriguing character in part because, when he took refuge behind the veil of fiction, he could be an astute analyst of motives and methods—both his own and Bogan's. In his 1935 autobiographical novel *Chance Has a Whip,* he offers an insightful portrait of Bogan's complex social standing—an attractive woman who nevertheless has "assumed the moral, the social stature of a man."[23] At the same time, his portrait is also impressively bitter: he observes Bogan's "wide and contented pity" for men, suggesting that she felt "they were vessels too small for great emotion."[24] In the early 1930s, however, Holden's rhetoric in his letters might be seen as evidence for the point of view he ascribes to Bogan. Expressing his disappointment at her—apparently justified—suspicions in 1933, Holden opens with calculated benevolence but ends with simple outrage:

I've been building so much on the hope that you really have gotten over those self-centered notions that have been (with the help of a little resentful stubbornness on my part) so disastrous in the past, and then you, who are vacationing abroad amidst the things you have wanted to see and who ought to be having at least an interesting experience, write to me who remains at home in the same narrow environment, for whom no benevolent foundation or governments are lifting a finger, as if I and the silly, empty-headed people I see were drinking champagne out of silk-hats and slippers while you fried in hell![25]

But in some ways Holden was simply the central symptom of Bogan's long-standing suffering—her inability to detach herself from the tangle of love and violence. In 1931 and 1933 she experienced some form of a breakdown; on both occasions she voluntarily sought help, the first time at the New York Neurological Institute and the second at the Westchester Division of the New York Hospital. Her journal account of the time between her return from Europe in September 1933 and her breakdown in November is torturous. Mixing her self-deprecations with anger at her entrapment to what she calls the "confused and mindless bundle of unresolved emotions"[26] that is Raymond, she attempts to order her thoughts about her life in a way that will still allow her to control them; but the hand on the tiller is that of a sailor who senses an inevitable capsize. Bogan eloquently accepts her suffering, and attempts to arrange and re-arrange it like some shamanistic sticks. It keeps her company in a way Holden cannot, as her description of him makes clear:

> . . . the reason for his continued romantic unfaithfulness is this: he has no intellectual interests. He cannot read, he cannot judge, he cannot analyze or plan. So he waits for the newest wind of romantic love to blow over him, and again and again writes a new series of sonnets, in which the stars bend from heaven and sink into his beloved's eye. His life is again rescued, blessed and refreshed by a new woman. Nothing, in his actions, seems to him strange, or disloyal, because he cannot detach himself from the adolescent image he has of himself: the passionate lover, the poet drowned in his lover's arms.[27]

Bogan cannot conceal the sting her version of his actions brings. In disgust and envy she watches an ancient pattern emerge, in which the man is rescued by acting out his "adolescent" fantasy. Within the context of marriage, this route is psychically forbidden to Bogan, who watched her mother live out her fantasies and felt the violent horror of domestic upheaval. What Bogan wants is not revenge, or freedom, or adolescent fantasy, but love—the kind of love she describes in her journal entry of 1932. Yet to seek or accept love is to descend from the one hold she has on her world—the hold of the brilliant clinician, the somewhat distant analyst who keeps track of all her misery as a way of preventing it from overwhelming her. Bogan refuses to descend; the filthy, sordid, loving world moves farther from her. She describes it like this in the *New Yorker,* one month before her second breakdown:

> Going in is like this: one morning you finally make up your mind that no one in the world, with the single and certain exception of yourself, has a problem, utters a groan, or sheds a tear. The entire habitable globe, to your distraught imagination, is peopled by human beings who eat three meals a day, surrounded by smiling faces, work with a will in offices, fields, factories, and mines, and sleep every hour of the night. . . .
>
> You look back over history and it presents to your biased eye nothing but records of glamour and triumph. O happy happy Aztecs; O splendid Punic Wars; O remarkably situated medieval serfs. . . . As for you, the most miserable person in any age, you sob and clutch your breast and reject with a sneer all consolations of religion and philosophy. You kick, you snarl, you spit, and you scream.[28]

Bogan continues with a kind of distant, terrifying accuracy, identifying what a sufferer can reasonably expect after "recovery": "You can choose several roads to happiness and a useful career," she says in the grim lingo of healthy-mindedness. "Let us examine these roads as briefly as possible."[29] In fact, though, Bogan does not get to these career choices; her article stops with an evocation of "one lucid moment," in which the sufferer sees clearly the scope and power of human horror. This vision of horror in the midst of daily life overwhelms the effort at sardonic humor. At about the same time, writing in her journal, Bogan expands the thought:

> At the newsreel theatre—
>
> I said to myself: Very well, why should I not let down and become part of this? . . . Here stands Mussolini, already grizzled, an aging bullet-headed man. Convicts have wrecked a prison. The fleet shoots off guns. The rayon, silk, and woollen textile workers are ordered to stand by for further instructions. Children laugh at monkeys. Here are residents of Papua, clasped in a beautiful and friendly dance, with impassive faces and linked arms; the officers of the cruise ship give them jars of jelly which they receive with great deference.
>
> Let down—believe—be part of it. O disordered, meaningless life! Let down! But I could not.[30]

"Who shall deliver me from the body of this death?" Here is no typology, no strategic quest for opposites or paradoxes, no conversion of
experience into striated forms of meaning. Here is the black circus of
experience itself—the commonplace evoked so easily and justly as a
nightmare, the supposedly entertaining and edifying newsreel seen as a
purposeless melange of unrelated and unrelatable moments. No scope,
no form, no meaning—nothing but a kind of bright, flickering ugli-
ness only abject love could love. But to love is to let down—to accept
"the punctual rape of every blessed day"[31]—and to let down is to lose
that last control, that last distance, over the horrors of betrayal and lost
devotion. Bogan is being perfectly straightforward when she says she
cannot do this; her description of her earlier breakdown holds true for
this one as well. "I refused to fall apart," she wrote John Hall Wheelock in 1930, "So I have been taken apart, like a watch."[32] The crucial
difference is this: in 1930 Bogan averred that "I still can love,"[33] while
in 1933 no such affirmation can be found. Under intensive psychiatric
care for the second time in three years, Bogan looks on in horror both
at her own malady and at the prospect of becoming—as she writes in
her poem "Evening at the Sanitarium"[34]—"again as normal and selfish
and heartless as anybody else."

And yet, with its treatments and its unthreatening invitations to concentrate on the absolute particulars of life—leaves, light, furniture, colors, faces, conversations—the psychiatric hospital in White Plains began to let Bogan down into that world of love that her old self could
not accommodate. In her letters and journals, Bogan confirms the life-
giving power of these particulars, which themselves begin to draw her
away from her typologizing intellect toward something more profound,
more integrating—something that preserves in its wholeness the soli-
tary, discrete moment of meaning. In a letter to her sixteen-year-old
daughter Maidie, Bogan provides an account of her hospital stay that is
not merely familial or conversational but remarkably self-revealing:

> It is really quite pleasant here, in a way. Everything is done to make
> the "patients" comfortable; the food is quite good, now and again; the
> air is delicious and some of the females are really very charming. . . .
>
> My metabolism, my teeth, my bony structure, my eyes, ears, nose and
> throat have all been gone over carefully. . . . I weigh *129* pounds, stripped,
> or did when I came, so you can see what a diet of beer and light wines
> did for me. . . .
>
> I'm making a whole bevy of baskets for your buttons, needles, thread,
> waste and trinkets. They tried to get me interested in book binding but

I said no. I don't believe in binding books. I'm knitting a grand sweater, dark green on one side and light green on the other: one dark and one light sleeve![35]

The poet whose first book *Body of This Death* was so highly praised by critics, whose poems and essays frequented the *New Yorker,* whose friends included the literary icons of New York, now stays away from books, or at least from binding them—that is, preserving them. But what she adheres to is far more important to the books—her books—that follow. The "bevy of baskets for your buttons" is a good alliterative line of verse; more important are the details themselves, the implications in this letter—and in other writing that Bogan does at this time—that "needles, thread, waste and trinkets" matter, really matter. These hard structures whose multiple functions all have their meaning are the fundamental structures of Bogan's talent; they help redeem her mind from the vortex of measureless passion as much as they redeem it from its own tendency toward the abstract, the typological. As she looks more closely at these particulars of place and people, she begins to speak, not only of specific creations, but of her own ability to embrace those creations. Through such an embrace "love calls us to the things of this world,"[36] for love is in the detail, the actual moment unconfused by doubt or hatred. This detailed observation becomes more a part of Bogan's writing—as she describes, for example, the afternoon walk at the hospital:

All that winter in the afternoon at four o'clock precisely the voice ran through the halls. "Walking, walking," it cried, with a sort of falsely cheerful note of invitation, an affected note of persuasion. Everyone promptly appeared, a few moments after the call, their hats and gloves already on, and more or less warmly clad, according to the state of the weather. The young women from the Physical Education Department were invariably young, brisk, and slender; they wore short skirts, leather jackets, bright mittens, and bright woolen socks. They walked into the rooms of the laggards. The laggards got into their hats and coats and came along. . . .

At this moment of the walk Miss Andrews heard again inside her heart her father's voice; he admonished her; he looked at her with love. Little Mrs. Harburg felt the fear that nothing could happen again; that everything was over; that life had closed up against her. . . . At this point Miss Gill heard the voice that told her she must run away. Her plan, to get rid, forever, of her sagging and unused body. Some heard or saw nothing, but felt again that pang, nameless and centered below the throat, of sorrow which had become part of them, like an organ in their flesh.[37]

The pang of sorrow, "nameless and centered below the throat," might have appeared in an earlier poem or prose piece of Bogan's; it possesses that same lovely definition of the general at the expense of the specific. But the specific, the new voice, is also here: the voice describing, and specifically identifying, Miss Andrews and Mrs. Harburg and Miss Gill. Implicit in this voice is a kind of touching and even tragic love, a willingness to "let down" and acknowledge the inseparability of love and loss and pain. In one of those essential ironies of human life, however, this acknowledgement breathes strength into the sufferer, into Bogan. She begins to free herself both from the fear of loss that leads to jealousy and the fear of worthlessness that leads to domestic violence. This is not a sudden transformation, of course. But as Bogan recovers in 1934 she also begins a kind of liberation. By July she is legally separated from Holden, and in less than a year she is writing triumphantly to Edmund Wilson that she is in the midst of a delicious affair—a fling apparently, and seemingly devoid of the earlier traps of jealousy and self-subjugation.

> I, myself, have been made to bloom like a Persian rose-bush, by the enormous love-making of a cross between a Brandenburger and a Pomeranian, one Theodore Roethke by name. He is very, very large (6 ft. 2 and weighing 218 lbs.) and he writes very very small lyrics. 26 years old and a frightful tank. We have poured rivers of liquor down our throats, these last three days, and, in between, have indulged in such bearish and St. Bernardish antics as I have never before experienced. . . . Well! Such goings on! A woman of my age! . . . He is just a ripple on time's stream, really, because he is soon going to Michigan to write a text-book on electrical fields. . . . I hope that one or two immortal lyrics will come out of all this tumbling about.[38]

Bogan's comment about Roethke's "very very small lyrics" is endearingly condescending, a lusty insult such as Roethke might well have loved; he himself indulged in them about himself, as when he responded to a less-than-admiring Yvor Winters review in 1953 by telling Winters, "My book, compared to yours, seems the slobberings of a child."[39] Nevertheless, Bogan's letter to Wilson reveals little evidence of her later esteem for Roethke as a writer. Taken by itself, it is simply a testament to a passing pleasure. But what this pleasure says about Bogan's ability to liberate herself, at least in some ways, from her past is striking. For a woman haunted by the double need to subject herself to unsuitable lovers and to terrorize herself about their inability to love her, the passage to a less strident conception of love is a great achievement. But a further achievement is Bogan's less divided view of life, her new ability to see beyond the typological dichotomies of reason versus passion, love versus betrayal, self-reliance versus subjugation.

This does not mean that her understanding of life was somehow more positive or hopeful in its complexity; on the contrary, Bogan—who had seemingly suffered so fruitlessly in her earlier years—now had a grasp on the essential, tragic necessity of suffering, of life's "facts [and] their dreadful implications,"[40] as she wrote in her journal. Yet this recognition of suffering brought with it a sense of power—a will to live in the moment, in the particular present, since that present is inevitable. Bogan chose the inevitable, and in choosing—rather than resisting or simply being carried along—she discovered a voice both more forceful and more particular than any in her first book of poems. It would be fair to say that she discovered the classic voice, if "classic" refers to the essential character of an ego poised in a world of time and fate. This was the voice of personality, not typology. The difference becomes clear in Bogan's third book, *The Sleeping Fury*, published in 1937 by Charles Scribner's Sons. Bogan was working on poems in the book as early as 1930, in the midst of her first crisis. Both the crisis and the will toward a less divided sense of life run throughout the book.

"Song," the first poem in *The Sleeping Fury*, begins by referring to a kind of turning away, a dividedness that recalls the typology of the early poems.

> It is not now I learn
> To turn the heart away
> From the rain of a wet May
> Good for the grass and leaves.[41]

The echo of "April is the cruelest month" is here, certainly. What brings forth the redeemed season, the "grass and leaves," is too painful to be trusted. The intelligent soul learned long before this to turn from these signs of renewal, knowing how bitter they grow in the absence of spring. Like a good Paulist, who sees the futile end of all things human and knows what hope that end foretells, the speaker here

> . . . watched the long slow scythe
> Move where the grain is lined,
> And saw the stubble burn
> Under the darker sheaves.[42]

The metaphor here is not of harvest but of a kind of culturally sanctioned violence: what is left after the necessary reaping is mere stubble, fit only for burning. Yet that stubble was once the source of abundance; its fate is the fate of a heart in a predatory society. To see, and turn from, this elemental fact connotes the relief of teleology. Yet right in the midst of this typological craftsmanship the poem itself turns: "Whatever now must go / It is not the heart that grieves."[43] The weary heart, which guides the willing soul away from futility toward some redemption not of the earth, is itself an honored type; but here the speaker explicitly rejects it. Grief lies somewhere other than "the heart." Indeed, the heart—the real heart, the speaker's suffering self—has seen too much to be able to return to this narrow language. For the first time in a Bogan poem, words stutter and stumble with an obvious rage:

> It is not the heart—the stock,
> The stone,—the deaf, the blind—
> That sees the birds in flock
> Steer narrowed to the wind.[44]

The comma after "stone" suggests a grammatical continuity that the dash wrecks; the lack of a comma after "blind" signals an even more abrupt pause. Yet the movement here is utterly deliberate. The heart—which the poet has not yet dismissed—is linked first to particular, solid objects in a way that may make sense: the heart has grown cold, perhaps, and needs redeeming. But no; for real rage follows, rage that could not come from a cold source. The heart is one with the deaf and the blind; it is not merely weary, but cut off from the world. This surely is dismissive: this cannot be the heart we rely on to turn us to the true path.

At the same time, "It is *not* the heart" that grieves, or that perceives "the birds in flock / Steer narrowed to the wind." This is not only a change in temperament, but a change in definition. What we call the heart is no longer the heart, but a kind of sham. True feeling—whether or not it promises some kind of redemption—lies elsewhere. True feeling includes the grief which absorbs the poem, but which appropriately eludes an agent. The source of the grief remains nameless, because to name at this point is to regress. The narrowing at the end of the poem, the pulling in, has a kind of hard sacredness to it that invokes the notion if not the fact of Yaweh. The identity of the grieving soul is not to be desecrated by names, as it once was. Then, too, there is one Yaweh here, not a profusion of gods; the pantheon of claims against the speaker's soul has been banished, and the narrowed silence is ironically a kind of prayer to what is new and real. It is a hard prayer, not a prayer of joy or typological redemption. Yet in its hardness lie its grace and cogency, its personality.

"Song" sets out the initial terms of the spirit/matter or destructive lust/redeeming love dichotomies, only to defy them with a sweeping dismissal of the typological language that sustains them. A similar process occurs in "Henceforth, From the Mind," which seems to establish the primacy of mind only to require its allegiance to "sea and earth."

> Henceforth, from the mind,
> For your whole joy, must spring
> Such joy as you may find
> In any earthly thing,
> And every time and place
> Will take your thought for grace.
>
> Henceforth, from the tongue,
> From shallow speech alone,
> Comes joy you thought, when young,
> Would wring you to the bone,
> Would pierce you to the heart
> And spoil its stop and start.
>
> Henceforward, from the shell,
> Wherein you heard, and wondered
> At oceans like a bell
> So far from ocean sundered—
> A smothered sound that sleeps
> Long lost within lost deeps,
>
> Will chime you change and hours,
> The shadow of increase,
> Will sound you flowers
> Born under troubled peace—
> Henceforth, henceforth
> Will echo sea and earth.[45]

There is a crucial difference between the method of this poem and the method of an earlier poem such as "The Alchemist." In this poem, though mind and matter are clearly opposites, they are complementary; they are not enemies. The pendulum no longer swings between extremes. Rather, a rapprochement, a diplomatic arrangement, must be made between the intellect and the material world to forestall typological tyranny on the one hand or despair on the other. The metaphorical mind finds meaning in the body's links with earth. These links, for Bogan, are a fundamental fact of health and art, not a construct or abstraction with a romantic or neo-romantic label. They are the harsh adventure, the "Putting to Sea":

> Who, in the dark, has cast the harbor-chain?
> This is no journey to a land we know.
> The autumn night receives us, hoarse with rain;
> Storm flakes with roaring foam the way we go.
>
> Sodden with summer, stupid with its loves,
> The country which we leave, and now this bare
> Circle of ocean which the heaven proves
> Deep as its height, and barren with despair.
>
> Now this whole silence, through which nothing breaks,
> Now this whole sea, which we possess alone,
> Flung out from shore with speed a missile takes
> When some hard hand, in hatred, flings a stone.
>
> The Way should mark our course within the night,
> The streaming System, turned without a sound.
> What choice is this—profundity and flight—
> Great sea? Our lives through we have trod the ground.
>
> Motion beneath us, fixity above.
>
> "O, but you should rejoice! The course we steer
> Points to a beach bright to the rocks with love,
> Where, in hot calms, blades clatter on the ear;
>
> And spiny fruits up through the earth are fed
> With fire; the palm trees clatter; the wave leaps.
> Fleeing a shore where heart-loathed love lies dead
> We point lands where love fountains from its deeps.
>
> Through every season the coarse fruits are set
> In earth not fed by streams." Soft into time
> Once broke the flower: pear and violet,
> The cinquefoil. The tall elm tree and the lime
>
> Once held out fruitless boughs, and fluid green
> Once rained about us, pulse of earth indeed.

There, out of metal, and to light obscene,
The flamy blooms burn backwards to their seed.

With so much hated still so close behind
The sterile shores before us must be faced;
Again, against the body and the mind,
The hate that bruises, though the heart is braced.

Bend to the chart, in the extinguished night
Mariners! Make way slowly; stay from sleep;
That we may have short respite from such light.

And learn, with joy, the gulf, the vast, the deep.[46]

The Sleeping Fury contains some of Bogan's best poems, and "Putting to Sea" is one of them, although it is not widely known. It is not easy to interpret without some knowledge of Bogan's own growth as a poet. What is the relation of the paradisal vision to the rest of the poem? Why, if this paradise is so lovingly described, does it not receive the speaker's adoration? Why, if the country being left is so appalling, is the voyage appalling as well? And why, given the horrors of the voyage, should it be undertaken with joy? The answers to these questions not only confirm the excellence of the poem, but demonstrate the power of a human being in the process of liberating herself from the beautiful and treacherous typologies of her past.

The paradisal vision, though not intimately linked with *The Revelations of St. John the Divine,* nevertheless captures that book's teleological mingling of form and spirit. Love is the creative force: it "fountains from [the] deeps," sustaining the entire vision from beach to palms. Wallace Stevens's "Palm at the End of the Mind" may have a bird with "fire-fangled feathers," but that seems a paltry prize compared to Bogan's paradisal palms, with "the Way" and the "streaming System" to sustain them. The only way this vision can remain effective, in fact, is if it remains seductive. Bogan understands the need for a vision of hope for pilgrims, a vision so sensuous that it bathes away the body's icy fears.

And yet this seduction is a great deceit. Beautiful as it is, it masks the reality of the voyage. For teleology is ultimately irrelevant to humans, and the types of experience—the despair, the setting out, the vision of paradise—which embrace teleology also come to negate themselves as they tolerate their absorption into the larger vision. Concerned with ultimates and ends, with redemption and paradise, that larger vision invokes eternity. For Bogan, that loss of time signals the primary danger to human beings. "Soft into time / Once broke the flower: pear and violet, / The cinquefoil." Bogan expresses the urgency of this fact through the quiet precision of her diction, moving from fruit to common flower to less-well-known flower—insisting on the exactitude of the moment of creation that time demands. On earth there is no paradise; on earth "the flamy blooms burn backward to their seed." These blooms are not visions spun from the hopeful mind; they are substances whose origins and whose passage through time urge the reality of perception.

The earth tragically validates mortality and its imperfections—its hatreds, its sterility, its language that loses meaning. Yet even these risks are preferable to the sullied vision of paradise, "Putting to Sea" suggests; for any confrontation with the real at least gives life, whereas a confrontation with a dream produces sterility. Paradise is sterile; the implacable and confidential future is sterile because unknown. What is known is the language of things perceived, and the exactitude of the present. These comprise the chart, to which the mariners must bend; in this night of the voyage they must use it well, and pray for "short respite" from the light of the authentic. As in "Song," there is no name for this authenticity, no description of its experience—only an acknowledgment of its crucial and difficult presence. To find it is to find oneself; to find it is to find "joy, the gulf, the vast, the deep." For Bogan to be able to assert this—to identify herself as a fellow mariner, to reject the dichotomies of earth and heaven for the integrity of the voyage itself—is to assert a force of personality that types or teleologies do not bind. The end does not give life, and may not in fact exist. What gives life is the action, in time, of the incarnate mind.

To encounter the incarnate mind, and through it to abandon the paradisal vision, is one escape from dichotomy; but it is only a partial escape. For the escape from dichotomy is itself a dichotomy, requiring the poet to recognize and defeat not only paradise but also its hellish opposite. But what is that hellish opposite? And how does one describe the power that observes it, commands it? The title poem of the book, "The Sleeping Fury," reveals this. A rare free-verse poem in Bogan's oeuvre, it evolved from Bogan's reflections on her addiction to self-punishment through sexual jealousy—her simultaneous will to power and self-subjugation, as she became both the lover and the child whose sense of familial guilt is so great that it spills back upon herself. Bogan's manu-

script pages for the poem include a number of notes, including a reference to "Megaera"—the jealous Fury, avenging sexual crimes—and this
paragraph of research and commentary:

> It [Magaera] was so loved, so feared, but now it lies in a symbol before
> us, fixed and asleep. The hair, wet with grief, lies upon its cheek, no longer
> in the semblance of serpents lifted in the gale of its movement. It, too,
> slumbers like a mortal; it can be approached, gazed upon, even touched.
> It can draw pity from our hearts, and tenderness, as it lies in its solitude.
> It has scourged us, with its vituperation, hounded us with its cries,
> dropped us from the ignoble dream, whipped us through a thousand cit-
> ies, and made horrible a thousand resting places. But now it is alone, and
> asleep, beautiful as a child whose hair, wet with rage and tears, now clings
> to its face. It has peace, and we look upon it with mercy, although it has
> never been merciful to us, and with love.[47]

This, of course, describes not a process, but a result. The scourger sleeps,
and in its exhausted rest it appears pitiable, even loveable. This is Bogan's
past—back to Holden, to Curt Alexander, to her mother and father and
their torturous fights over infidelity. This is the enemy, the hell of wanting love and knowing somehow that love means weakness and manipulation and violence as well as power. In many ways this is also the essential
prefeminist torture of passionate women. All routes to mastery in love
appear closed, since to be a woman is to be told what one cannot do.
Even when one manages to do what one "cannot" do—assert one's need
for a love beyond convention, a bold love—one suffers, as Bogan did,
because one is a kind of eccentric. The power to experiment lies with men,
not women. This is the cultural mythology, the waking Fury, which rules
Bogan's life through the early 1930s. Her liberation from it comes in a
form of self-recreation, a remaking in which she begins by seeing herself
in relation to the particulars of life—the hard details of her world—until
these details begin to frame the identity she knows to be hers. In this way
she comes out from under the self-subjugation that is also societal. She
no longer tortures herself by doing and fearing what she cannot do—loving those whom she "cannot" love—because the fragmented voice that
restricts her is no longer within her; the shattered superego that spawned
it reconstitutes itself in the sleeping Fury.

> You are here now,
> Who were so loud and feared, in a symbol before me,
> Alone and asleep, and I at last look long upon you.

Your hair fallen on your cheek, no longer in the semblance of serpents,
Lifted in the gale; your mouth, that shrieked so, silent.
You, my scourge, my sister, lie asleep, like a child,
Who, after rage, for an hour quiet, sleeps out its tears.

The days close to winter
Rough with strong sound. We hear the sea and the forest,
And the flames of your torches fly, lit by others,
Ripped by the wind, in the night. The black sheep for sacrifice
Huddle together. The milk is cold in the jars.

All to no purpose, as before, the knife whetted and plunged,
The shout raised, to match the clamor you have given them.
You alone turn away, not appeased; unaltered, avenger.

Hands full of scourges, wreathed with your flames and adders,
You alone turned away, but did not move from my side,
Under the broken light, when the soft nights took the torches.

At thin morning you showed, thick and wrong in that calm,
The ignoble dream and the mask, sly, with slits at the eyes,
Pretence and half-sorrow, beneath which a coward's hope trembled.

You uncovered at night, in the locked stillness of houses,
False love due the child's heart, the kissed-out lie, the embraces,
Made by the two who for peace tenderly turned to each other.

You who know what we love, but drive us to know it;
You with your whips and shrieks, bearer of truth and of solitude;
You who give, unlike men, to expiation your mercy.

Dropping the scourge when at last the scourged advances to meet it,
You, when the hunted turns, no longer remain the hunter
But stand silent and wait, at last returning his gaze.

Beautiful now as a child whose hair, wet with rage and tears
Clings to its face. And now I may look upon you,
Having once met your eyes. You lie in sleep and forget me.
Alone and strong in my peace, I look upon you in yours.[48]

Bogan's life lies whole in the seventh stanza: the "false love due a child's heart," the "kissed-out lie," the two "who for peace tenderly turned to each other," record in a kind of shorthand the drastic hopes and self-sacrifices that comprise Bogan's experience of love. Here at the hearth lie the worst abuses of the heart. And because these loves are self-defeating, because they are divided against themselves in their simultaneous will to mastery and to self-subjugation, they cannot exist in real peace; they exist in the domain of the Fury, who must drive the lovers to see what it is they love, as Bogan suggests in the eighth stanza.

The result of this slave-driving is not necessarily hell itself, but "truth and solitude," and "expiation"—the one force to which the Fury gives mercy, *unlike* men. Men congratulate or console themselves; they are not at odds with the superego, "The Sleeping Fury" suggests, at least where romance is concerned; they seem to need no expiation. This male mastery may well be the worst self-set snare for men. But because there is no socially-sanctioned impulse for men to confront it, they do not need, or do not know that they need, to be merciful to themselves with regard to it. For to need mercy is to cut through the mastery of conformity into the horrible world Bogan described in her saga of the newsreel—it is to "let down," to love what is tawdry and unmasterable, to love the self. To give up control, to seek redemption from the dichotomies of mastery and subjugation, to condemn and to love oneself at the same time—this is the process that the Fury herself sets in motion. The sadomasochist pair of jealousy and need, this poem suggests, may finally shatter and recombine into the self-protection and self-regard of the lover, the woman of personality. The Fury sleeps, then—or rather, the emerging woman puts her to sleep; "Alone and strong in my peace, I look upon you in yours." As at the end of a long battle, the victor looks with relief and respect upon the vanquished. Without the enemy the victor would not have achieved what was far more important than the victory—the identity, the sense of self, which the victory conferred.

The personality that evades types and ideologies, that chooses love and does not fear it, that escapes the antithetical pulls of jealousy and need, that embraces the hard particulars of life, is the personality of the mature artist—the artist who knows the strength of herself as subject, and who knows that that strength diminishes the possibility of romantic or artistic subjugation. This is the emerging identity of Bogan in the mid-1930s, an identity that two poems in "The Sleeping Fury" in particular confirm. Unlike the poems previously described, these two—"Roman Fountain" and "To My Brother Killed: Haumont Wood: October 1918"—have little to do with the process by which Bogan works out her personality. Instead, they present that personality in its flowering—in its experiential wisdom and its delight in its own power.

> Up from the bronze, I saw
> Water without a flaw

Rush to its rest in air,
Reach to its rest, and fall.

Bronze of the blackest shade,
An element man-made,
Shaping upright the bare
Clear gouts of water in air.

O, as with arm and hammer,
Still it is good to strive
To beat out the image whole,
To echo the shout and stammer
When full-gushed waters, alive,
Strike on the fountain's bowl
After the air of summer.[49]

Nature inspires mimesis here, but mimesis is not all there is to art. It is good "to echo the shout and stammer" of the water, but even that imitation shows more art than replication; for *that* shout and stammer come from the rise and fall of water in a fountain, a man-made object. Left to its own devices, water passes back and forth from sky to earth to sky, from fall to winter to spring, and invites no judgment of its motion. The artist is metaphor-maker, artificer: with a small quantity of water and a device, a fountain, he captures the cyclic motion of nature and displays it. More than that, he revises it. According to his vision and craftsmanship, he creates a metaphor of value; he demonstrates at once the lustiness of striving and the enduring miracle of the pause, the moment of "rest."

And yet, of course, the fountain is not the only artistry here. To identify the fountain and its meaning, to link that meaning to human effort, and to celebrate the link between nature and human power, is the work of the poet. More specifically, it is the work of a poet who loves art because she perceives confidently the power she wields. Human hands made the fountain, but the poet is the final artificer, the one who "Shapes upright the bare / Clear gouts of water in air." If the fountain is a metaphor in bronze, the poem is one in the mind; based on bronze, it nevertheless exists apart from it, drawing its strength from its author's ability to transform physical particulars into mental images—"bronze of the blackest shade," "full-gushed waters, alive," "the fountain's bowl." Without losing their particularity, these become images of a permanent relation between humankind and nature, in which death and decline occupy an appropriate place without siphoning off the greatness of creation, of the human will. In "Roman Fountain" a forceful personality celebrates her kinship with other, unknown personalities—those of artists and craftsmen—whose own forcefulness endures, and is transformed in her hands.

The same emphasis on the course of a particular in "Roman Fountain" shows up in "To My Brother Killed: Haumont Wood: October 1918," which Bogan wrote to commemorate her brother's death in the First World War. Interestingly, Bogan did not write the poem in the 1930s, but much earlier—less than a decade after the event itself.[50] Yet she chose not to keep the poem; she apparently sent it off to Rolfe Humphries without retaining a copy. When, in 1935, she asked him to return any poems of hers she included with past letters, he sent "To My Brother"; but Bogan could not remember writing it.

This seemingly casual disregard for a great poem suggests two things about Bogan: she possessed a powerful personality, given to keen appraisals of herself and the world, long before her crises of the 1930s; and she could not recognize the strength of this dormant personality, even when she herself created evidence for it, before the mid thirties. The poem's particularity, its directness, marks a great advance over the other work Bogan produced in the twenties, but it took her years to see it.

> O you so long dead,
> You masked and obscure,
> I can tell you, all things endure:
> The wine and the bread;
>
> The marble quarried for the arch;
> The iron become steel;
> The spoke broken from the wheel;
> The sweat of the long march;
>
> The hay-stacks cut through like loaves
> And the hundred flowers from the seed;
> All things indeed
> Though struck by the hooves
>
> Of disaster, of time due,
> Of fell loss and gain,
> All things remain,
> I can tell you, this is true.
>
> Though burned down to stone
> Though lost from the eye,

I can tell you, and not lie,—
Save of peace alone.[51]

The poetic commonplace is that verse offers humans eternal life; "To My Brother" seems, at first, to perpetuate this commonplace. But the poem quickly defies this expectation by listing those things that endure— not heroes, or great exploits in battle, or even the quiet aftermath of war, but the raw materials whose very absorption into war signals indecent anger, waste, decay: the marble, the iron, the broken spoke, the mangled haystacks. What precedes this vision of horror? A veiled reference to the miracles of Jesus, the "wine and the bread," a phrase which appears in many New England hymnals of the nineteenth and early twentieth centuries. The road even of the purported son of God leads straight through the swath of war, "struck by the hooves / Of disaster." This is the real tragedy, the harshest demand—to witness, and not to turn away, to remember what it is that prevents the advent of peace.

Where "Roman Fountain" celebrates the thrill of human creation, "To My Brother" acknowledges the precision of tragedy—the other side of "Roman Fountain," the side confirming that, even though death cannot defeat human creation, it is in every sense an enemy. In this poem Bogan's grief is explicit, ungeneralized. It carries none of the weight of typology, nor is there any *deus ex machina* teleology that sweeps the poem to safety or some kind of redemption. The poem comprises grief, and love, and great personality. For Bogan to perceive this about her earlier, lost poem—and for her to include it in the 1937 volume—suggests her own recognition of her essential wholeness. "To My Brother" no longer needed to be lost, because it was no longer a threat. The integrated personality it implied—the personality free of typology and liberated from the fragmentations of jealousy and desperate need—was one that Bogan began to recognize as her own.

By the time Bogan encounters Roethke in the mid-1930s, she is well along in a vivid and painful self-transformation. She herself no longer moves from type to type—the tortured child, the irrepressible romantic, the thwarted lover, the self-destructive ingenue, the lonely woman decrying the fate of her sex. Because each of these types represents a form of subjugation—a means of "submitting to powerful others who personify the fantasy of omnipotence"[52]—Bogan also begins to liberate herself from the identity of the victim. Love cannot punish her, men cannot punish her, because they cannot grab hold of some fragment of her being and wield it against her like a weapon. To be a victim is always to hold some fragment of oneself so dear, so inviolable, that the horrors of the world cannot touch it. This precious child, this innocent, invites abuse, not only from the world but from oneself; for in seeking to protect the child within, the fragmented person automatically consents to his or her own fragmentation and alienation. Any jealousy, any anger, any fear, any abuse is tolerable, so long as the person can hold something in abeyance—can avoid "letting down," can avoid consenting fully to love the world of suffering and sorrow. Ultimately, in creating this illusion of safety, the person risks losing real love and real suffering by numbing the reality—and thus the value—of suffering and by giving love no opportunity to alleviate the horrors of reality. With neither love nor suffering, the person becomes an ideal candidate for some kind of subjugation—either personal or artistic, or both.

To "let down" into this misery, and endure it; to suffer at heart, and to give up one's claim to the old self—even the protected fragment, the innocent child, of selfhood; to consent, finally, to love what one finds on the other side; this is the beginning of the integrated personality. This is the self that resists subjugation both because it knows what a victim is and because it draws its strength from within, not without. The conflicts of the external world are no longer its source of life. This does not imply that the integrated personality is a kind of Nietzschean superhuman; its actual power depends on the depth of its new-found love, and the extent of its previous suffering. As Bogan's letters to Roethke will reveal, however, Bogan's new-found love for herself was great, and—as we have already seen—her suffering was immense. What she possessed, then, was a force of personality that—aside from her achievements as an artist—placed her in a master's role. Yet the notion of the master and the subjugated, with its resonant sexual stereotypes and past miseries, held little appeal for her.

Bogan would not be the "essential angel," as Tillie Olsen writes in *Silences*—the nurturer upon a pedestal who nevertheless nurtures from below, who takes vicarious pride in the accomplishments of her apprentices because she can take no pride in her own work.[53] She would, however, draw upon the essential strengths of connection and reciprocity within a morality of care whose roots may lie in women's experience. "The ideal of care is . . . an activity of relationship," Carol Gilligan writes,[54] yet for Bogan this ideal could not take form without a strong sense of self-regard—her own, and that of her apprentice. To be a "thing," by contrast, was not to enter into a relationship; it was not to care; it was to be self-destructive, angelic.

Although she did not reserve a critical language for these values, Bogan embraced them both in her work and in her relationship with Roethke. Her time with Roethke was a success, both personally and artistically, because the master had loved and suffered enough to learn that wisdom did not mean typology, and mastery meant neither submitting to a "superior"—a tradition of knowledge—nor dominating a "lesser," an apprentice. The act of mastery, of mentorship, meant the pursuit of excellence with "a person of as much intrinsic worth as the [so-called] superior."[55] It was Roethke's good fortune to be that second subject, that person.

Notes

1. Jessica Benjamin, *The Bonds of Love: Psychoanalysis, Feminism, and the Problem of Domination* (New York: Pantheon, 1988), p. 219.

2. Elizabeth Frank, *Louise Bogan: A Portrait* (New York: Alfred A. Knopf, 1985), p. 54.

3. Louise Bogan, *Journey around My Room: The Autobiography of Louise Bogan: A Mosaic by Ruth Limmer,* ed. Ruth Limmer (New York: Viking, 1980), pp. 53–58.

4. Louise Bogan, *Body of This Death* (New York: Robert M. McBride, 1923), p. 1.

5. Frank, p. 57.

6. Bogan, *Body,* p. 13.

7. Bogan, *Body,* p. 19.

8. Bogan, *Body,* p. 22.

9. Frank, p. 70.

10. Edmund Wilson, *A Winter in Beech Street,* in *Five Plays* (New York: Farrar, Straus and Giroux, 1954), pp. 242–43. Quoted in Frank, p. 9.

11. Bogan, *Journey,* p. 172.

12. Bogan, *Journey,* p. 4.

13. Bogan, *Journey,* p. 35.

14. Bogan, *Journey,* pp. 24–26.

15. Frank, p. 41.

16. Louise Bogan, *What the Woman Lived: Selected Letters of Louise Bogan, 1920–1970,* ed. with intro. by Ruth Limmer (New York: Harcourt Brace Jovanovich, 1973), p. 20.

17. See Frank, p. 102.

18. Edmund Wilson to John Peale Bishop, Jan. 15, 1924, *Letters on Literature and Politics, 1912–1972*, ed. Elena Wilson (New York: Farrar, Straus and Giroux, 1977), p. 118. Quoted in Frank, p. 78.

19. See Frank, p. 96.

20. Frank, pp. 83–84.

21. Frank, pp. 184–187.

22. Frank, p. 136.

23. Raymond Holden, *Chance Has a Whip* (New York: Charles Scribner's Sons, 1935), p. 226.

24. Holden, *Chance*, p. 227.

25. Holden to Bogan, June 7, 1933, The Louise Bogan Papers, Amherst College. Quoted in Frank, pp. 172–73.

26. Bogan, *Journey*, p. 76.

27. Bogan, *Journey*, p. 76.

28. Bogan, *Journey*, pp. 79–80.

29. Bogan, *Journey*, p. 81.

30. Bogan, *Journey*, pp. 83–84.

31. Richard Wilbur, "Love Calls Us to the Things of This World," *The Poems of Richard Wilbur* (New York: Harcourt Brace Jovanovich, 1963), p. 65.

32. Bogan, *Letters*, p. 57.

33. Bogan, *Letters*, p. 57.

34. Bogan, *Journey*, p. 85.

35. Bogan to her daughter Maidie, Nov. 20, 1933, Archives of Charles Scribner's Sons, Princeton University Library. Quoted in Frank, p. 190.

36. Wilbur, p. 65.

37. Bogan, *Journey*, pp. 85–88.

38. Bogan to Wilson, June 22, 1935, *What the Woman Lived*, pp. 84–85.

39. Theodore Roethke, Letter, Dec. 10, 1953, in the Yvor Winters–Janet Lewis Collection, Box 1, Folder 1, Rare Book and Manuscript Division, Stanford University Libraries.

40. Bogan quoted in Frank, p. 198.

41. Louise Bogan, *The Sleeping Fury* (New York: Charles Scribner's Sons, 1937), p. 3.

42. Bogan, *Fury*, p. 3.

43. Bogan, *Fury*, p. 3.

44. Bogan, *Fury*, p. 3.

45. Bogan, *Fury*, p. 4.

46. Bogan, *Fury*, p. 36.

47. Bogan, manuscript of "The Sleeping Fury," The Louise Bogan Papers, Amherst College. Quoted in Frank, p. 258.

48. Bogan, *Fury*, pp. 27–29.

49. Bogan, *Fury*, p. 26.

50. See Frank, p. 256.

51. Bogan, *Fury*, pp. 24–25.

52. Benjamin, p. 219.

53. Tillie Olsen, *Silences* (New York: Delacorte Press, 1978), p. 35.

54. Carol Gilligan, *In a Different Voice: Psychological Theory and Women's Development* (Cambridge, Massachusetts: Harvard University Press, 1982), p. 62.

55. Jean Baker Miller, *Toward a New Psychology of Women,* 2d ed. (Boston: Beacon Press, 1986), p. 5.

6

My Secrets Cry Aloud
Theodore Roethke as Apprentice

Louise Bogan's development as a poet is unusual for several reasons, but perhaps the most prominent of these is her legacy of displacing the role of a mentor onto two male lovers, one of whom—Raymond Holden— brought all her jealousies and self-doubts to a flashpoint. From this thralldom to a romantic ideal of the poet, she emerged a fundamentally strong woman who applied that strength to her art; this constituted her liberation, not only from the worst self-deceptions of love, but also from the miseries of apprenticeship. Throughout her career as a poet she had literary peers and friends, including Edmund Wilson, Rolfe Humphries, Morton Zabel, and John Hall Wheelock, but she evaded overt apprenticeship. Yet her experiences with Holden—who, after all, fancied himself a better poet than Bogan and gave her his advice more than willingly—were enough to alert her to the dangers of conferring one's needs and desires on anyone. In a vivid letter to Roethke in September 1935, barely ten months after they first met, Bogan warns Roethke that he must preserve his dignity even though the world denigrates his work:

> The loss of face is the worst thing that can happen to anyone, man or woman. I know, because I have lost mine, not once, but many times. And believe me, the only way to get it back, is to put your back against the wall and fight for it. You can't brood or sulk or smash around in a drunken frenzy. Smashing around gives the world's insects and worms the upper hand, and if you smash yourself dead, they won't give a damn; it won't impress them in the least; they'll get up every morning and gar-

gle with Listerine, just as though you had never been. . . . When one isn't free, one is a *thing*, the *thing* of others, and the only point, in this rotten world, is to be your own, to hold the scepter and mitre over yourself, in the immortal words of Dante.[1]

This letter most of all suggests Bogan's own hope for Roethke's independence. If the apprentice himself realizes this need, he takes a step toward liberation and toward an identity of his own as an artist; but it is only one step, and by no means implies success. What is equally important is for the mentor to make the same move. As Jean Baker Miller suggests, to be a mentor is by definition to enter a relationship whose greatest success lies in its closure.[2] This closure, however, is what Ezra Pound and, in a different way, Yvor Winters found exceptionally difficult to accomplish. Though they shaped their apprentices in identifiable ways, their capacity for possession also threatened the artistic independence of those most intimately connected with them.

For Bogan, however, the power of possession was already familiar, and dangerous. She knew the stealthy temptations of this kind of power, and her letters to Roethke show that she could not always avoid the temptation. She had her ways of taunting and cajoling him, even of manipulating him. Yet on the whole Bogan used her mentorship as a means of establishing a rich bond of difference with Roethke, insisting on mutual "attention and response," as Gilligan says.[3] The network of attention and response she and Roethke wove touched every aspect of the younger poet's life, yet it did not make him dependent on her. Nor did it violate her demand for freedom. On the contrary, it reinforced Roethke's own sources of confidence: his genius for serious play, particularly in language, his keen critical judgment, his determination and stamina. And it reinforced Bogan's sense of her freedom to choose her relationships, her other subjects, rather than being the object of someone else's subjugation. What Bogan saw—the behavioral experience that Miller, Gilligan, and Benjamin were to explore explicitly four decades later— was that interdependence did not weaken either the apprentice or the mentor. Because the qualities of love and care, which underlay this interdependence, also affected the work of the two poets, such a relationship could be far more sustaining than the conventional hierarchies of power and influence that Bogan had confronted earlier. In consciously rejecting the more conventional role of the mentor, Bogan enabled Roethke to develop his faith in the latitudes of imagination. From this development, as essential as Bogan's attention to the details of his poetry, Roethke established his identity as a poet.

———

In 1958, long after the ardent phase of his relationship with Bogan had ended, Roethke was an established poet with an occasionally debilitating manic depressive illness. On several occasions in the forties and fifties he had sought professional help; now, after a bad attack in late 1957 and a three-month stay in a hospital and a sanitarium, he underwent further psychoanalysis.[4] Among his regular correspondents at the time was the Princess Marguerite Caetani, founder and editor of *Botteghe Oscure,* who had invited him to contribute to the magazine in 1948 and who over the course of the decade had become a close friend. In a November letter, Roethke explains to her a recent revelation from his treatment:

> In the verse appreciation class we have been ranging around following associations and somehow René Char's name came up. I talked about him briefly as a poet and told one story that I knew to be true about his heroism. Then the next day in my session with the doctor I began relating this and suddenly without my seeming to understand it a great flood of emotion burst loose. I kept talking about him and his poetry and quite literally weeping, in a sense tears of joy, during the whole hour. I said to the doctor, "I suddenly realize that René Char is an older brother symbol for me." I am always looking for a father, it would seem, but this is the first time I realized that emotionally I've always wanted an older brother. Someone who's strong and powerful yet gentle and innocent and gifted.[5]

Roethke is a sentimentalist, and one sees the sentimental touch in "innocent"; otherwise these attributes of an older brother describe Louise Bogan. Bogan urges him to be independent, exhorts him to write, and warns him of the dangers of excessive drinking. Yet, even as she emphasizes his need to stand on his own, she invites him to take comfort in the fact of her care. If her strength is her confidence in Roethke, her power appears in the words that rise from that confidence: her letters to Roethke brim with power like a restorative tonic. At the same time, she appreciates his frailties. She is often gentle with him, and her gentleness is as much her gift as her poetry.

When, in late 1935, Roethke was hospitalized at Mercywood Sanitarium in Michigan for what turned out to be his first vivid bout with manic depression, he knew that he might well have shattered his nascent career. The academics in charge of his progress were only too happy to use this illness as a way of easing him out of Michigan State.[6] But Bogan, who had recently passed through her own mental traumas, was comforting and, after some initial euphemism, honest and encouraging:

> I am so sorry that you are still under the weather, but I am glad that you're having good, sensible, professional care. There's nothing like it, when one gets really down, and isn't able to make the motions by oneself.—Believe me, my dear, I've been through it all, not once, but many times (twice, to be exact!) And after the first feelings of revolt and rage wear off, there's nothing like the peace that descends upon one with routine, lovely routine. At the Neurological Center, here in town, I went at one time through three weeks of high-class neurology, myself. I had a room all done up in non-corrosive greens, and a day and a night nurse, and a private bath, and such food as you never ate, and hydro-therapy, including steam cabinets, and a beautiful big blond doctor by the name of McKinney. . . . The good old normal world is really a lot of fun, once you give into it, and stop fighting against it. Fight with your work, but let the world go on, bearing you and being borne by you: that's the trick.[7]

This, then, is Roethke's "brother," a powerful woman whose gentleness and whose personal and artistic gifts soothe his psyche and aid his career. But why a woman? And why Bogan? After all, Roethke spent plenty of time in his early career cultivating or attempting to cultivate the interest of a number of established male poets and editors: Morton Zabel, the second editor of *Poetry;* Horace Gregory, poetry editor of *New Masses;* George Dillon, third editor of *Poetry;* and Rolfe Humphries and Stanley Kunitz, who as slightly older and more successful writers ought to have been more obvious candidates for Roethke's unconscious bestowal of brotherhood.[8] At the same time—in the late 1930s and early 1940s—Roethke was clearly much in love with Katherine (Kitty) Stokes, a librarian he had met during his years of teaching at Pennsylvania State College from 1936 to 1943. By 1940, after spending much of his free time with her, he moved into an apartment in her building, and came as close as was decent at the time to moving in with her: he wrote poems, corrected student papers, and conducted his life in her home.[9] His letters to her in these Penn State years reveal an intimacy at once passionate and cavalier. If she was his reigning passion, where did Bogan fit in? If Humphries and Kunitz and the others were his unconscious brother figures, how did Bogan come to play the role so well?

The answer is that Bogan crossed roles in a way none of the others could. Her authoritative voice, unwilling to tolerate the constraints of any stereotypical role, ironically echoed a masculine mask that Roethke would have recognized: her trial-tempered strength and independence had the ring of *animus,* and yet she was also woman, lover, and poet. To Roethke's Telemakhos she was Mentor within Athena. Roethke could not ascribe this combination of identities to any of the other key characters of his life. It seems clear that he could maintain his passionate regard for Bogan at the same time he was in love with Katherine Stokes precisely because she was a completely different *kind* of person from Stokes—a hard-drinking artist, an established force in poetry rather than (as Stokes was) simply an intelligent, romantic peer. There was no question of infidelity; there was only a question of difference. At the same time, Bogan was more magnetic to Roethke than Humphries or Kunitz because of her passion. She placed a heterosexual topspin on the idea of the brother figure that Roethke—unconscious as he was of his brother-quest at that time—may have instinctively cherished. Though by no means all things to him, she was enough different things to him to seem, at least early on, almost godlike. He admits as much to Humphries in November 1934, shortly after his first personal encounter with Bogan. Roethke is in anguish over what seemed to him a boorish performance on his part coupled with a rather arch performance on hers:

> I was, as I said, too completely overwhelmed [by Bogan]. A case of hero-worship I guess. I was like a country boy at his first party,—such an oaf, such a boob, such a blockhead. I don't think I was ever much worse.
>
> And then when she [Bogan] asked me whether I figured out for my-self that Taggard was no good—that was the pay-off. Damn her anyway. She and her Irish digs. . . .
>
> Please give me her address. I'd like to write her a note at least. Some time I hope to gain her respect.[10]

Roethke, of course, got over this anguish, in part because his wor-shipful approach to Bogan soon subsided. This was a crucial transition—this move from a worshipful apprentice, enthralled with the mentor, to a lover and younger brother whose mentor is both a demanding guide and a compassionate friend. What made this transition possible for Ro-ethke was the very quality of character in Bogan that made it possible for her ultimately to be both a brother figure and a lover.

And what was that? It seems to have been Bogan's ironic appreciation of the kind of strength that lay behind male role-playing. Bogan
took pleasure in the male mask. She could commute between its strength
and her own without forsaking either. This might seem an odd assertion about a woman who—once liberated from the traumas of jealousy
and marital dependence—so clearly relished her female sexuality. Yet
Bogan's efforts to break free of the stereotypical role of the female poet
had led her to see that real strength was not a moated castle belonging
to men; that castle belonged to the strong of either sex. Moreover,
Bogan's lower-middle-class background gave her a lifelong appreciation
of strength and dignity in the face of constant crises. To be tough, to
appreciate the pain and necessity and triumph of hard work, to drink
and curse and carouse and enjoy it—to celebrate traditionally blue-collar values, and willingly set their virtues up against the more elegant and
arcane values of the white-collar world—this for Bogan was strength,
including the masks of male strength. It even carried a potent mystery
of caring, as Bogan learned in childhood. One of her earliest memories
was of old Leonard, an eerily tough and poor neighbor, who came to
the kitchen from time to time for a bit of warmth in winter and something to eat:

> It was bitter weather, too cold for storms, too rigid and silent for the
> wind, when old Leonard first came to the kitchen door. . . . He lifted his
> head and saw me and grinned down into his beard. If he had put out his
> hand to touch me, I could not have been more frightened; with half a
> room between us, I stood transfixed by that smile. "It's Mr. Leonard,"
> my mother said, and lifted the stove lid, shifting the kettle to one side.
> "It's a cold night, and I'm giving him a nice hot cup of tea to warm him
> up." . . . Then I heard him speak the first words that were not curses. "We
> must be wise," he said to my mother. "We must be as wise as the serpent
> and as gentle as the dove. As the serpent, as the dove," he said, and picked
> up the cup of tea from its saucer.[11]

More than thirty years later, writing to Rolfe Humphries about Bennington College, Bogan explicitly contrasts her vision of the hard and
tender virtues of this wounded man in her blue-collar community with
the seemingly unreal world of the Vermont college:

> I wouldn't have missed Bennington for anything, but it is a bad, fan-
> cy, three-times-removed-from-reality kind of place, and I pity the girls
> and fear for their futures. The faculty is almost without exception a bunch

of neurotics and would-be's. . . . They sell cocktail mittens with bells on them and little pieces of china and the latest books and God knows what else, in the Commons building, and they listen to Horace Gregory and Josephine Herbst hand out the old rantings, but do they go down and look at the mill in town; do they ever see a proletarian—no. I saw a few proletarians, nice beery ones, in the station, when I was waiting for my ticket, and I just wanted to go back to the college with same, and push them into the Commons room, and shout, "Go ahead and make a speech! They need you!"[12]

The dichotomy here—beery proletarians versus effete Benningtonians—might suggest that Bogan, who herself had only one year at Boston University, envied the prospects of these students. Yet her acute description of the distance the college kept from the world at its own borders indicates that Bogan keenly felt the legacy of a serious social rift. Her words here and in other letters imply a confidence in blue-collar resiliency and humanity that other writers from less harsh backgrounds tend to convert too easily to a harmless romanticism. Strength, including male strength, meant something more to Bogan than making great proletarian speeches at cocktail parties.

But Bogan was too cagey not to see that this ideal of strength had a dark side as well. The more powerful the ideal became, the less feeling entered into it. When taken as an immutable reality rather than a mask, male strength buried the emotions. It justified this burial with the mistaken belief that feelings weakened one's armor against an exploitative world. To escape the pattern of infidelity and rage her parents had laid down, it was important for Bogan not to feel—not to feel when Curt Alexander carted her off to Panama and refused to sleep with her, not to feel when Holden left clues to affairs and lied about them, not to feel when she walked at large into a world whose tawdry complexity seemed to negate her own reasons for living. Her breakdowns in 1931 and 1933 are so heartrending, and so important, because they illustrate the consequences of this lack of feeling and show what possibilities for health arise when feeling—even angry, self-pitying feeling—returns. Bogan, who so well understood the value of male role-playing, understood its dangers even better; this enabled her to exert a powerful influence on Roethke.

For Roethke loved all the masks of male strength, and regularly sought the stages where they might play. His own vast bulk gave him an appreciation for physical strength and grace, along with an awareness of how the body could both coerce and intimidate. The body was a tool, a weapon, a beloved self-affirmation, a presence parallel to the presence of the mind. Moderation was not an idea he much understood. He was a showman, and to perform was to go all the way. He preferred tough guys and tough talkers to the denizens of the academic world he inhabited, although his manic depression kept him classified as 4F during World War II and although once, when his early flame Mary Kunkel struck a man who had insulted him, he did not take up the fight.[13] Biographer Allan Seager recounts a story, set in Roethke's early days at Bennington College in 1943, which tells much about Roethke's love of dramatic male role-playing:

> Ethan Allen was a local man and the only notice I ever heard Ted pay to these famous [Revolutionary War] victories was his gleeful repetition of Allen's behavior at Ticonderoga. The history books say that Allen beat on a door of the fort and intoned, "Open in the name of God and the Continental Congress." The local tale, however, which may have come down by word of mouth, is that Allen beat on the door and shouted, "Open the door, you god-damned British sons-of-bitches, or we'll kick it in." This delighted Ted.[14]

At the outset of his career, poetry was scarcely enough for Roethke—or rather it was an adjunct or complement to his other careers as tennis coach, steak cook, and seducer of women.[15] This is not to suggest that Roethke was not serious about his art from the first. On the contrary, he believed in the power of poetry to reveal and persuade with all the fierceness he usually mustered for more obviously physical pursuits. But what could it reveal and how could it persuade? To anyone acquainted with his middle or late work, Roethke's early poems give surprisingly constrained answers to those questions. Poetry should persuade us to be strong, his early work suggests; it should persuade us to find a flaw in a point of view and attack it; it should persuade us to stand against the crowd when necessary. It should do this by revealing the outrageous inconsistencies of a common point of view, or by revealing through overwhelming rhetoric the miserable cupidity and mendacity of an opposing view.

Roethke's vision in the early 1930s of what poetry could do is of course intimately linked with his own understanding of what *he* as a man could do; he could be strong, resilient, and defiant in the face of mediocrity. But anyone with both common sense and compassion, the essential qualities of a good psychologist, would see that these were poses. Why Roethke demanded these poses from himself, and what they concealed, were essential questions from a psychological point of view; they were essential questions from an artistic point of view as well. For Roethke's career as a poet is a study of the art of opening the reservoirs of feeling without having them gush out in some tedious sentimentality. At his greatest—in the 1964 "North American Sequence," for example— he manages to combine some intellectual structure or insight with a vivid sense of the meaning of feelings that lie beyond words. This kind of meaning threatens him early on in part because he is so familiar with the idea of feeling as sentimentality: to feel is to be sentimental, and to be sentimental is of course unbecoming in a man. Ironically, this view itself is itself a kind of masculine sentimentality, but Roethke does not see it that way. Roethke's emotional life in the early thirties incorporates a distinct dichotomy between thought and feeling: thought is synonymous with manhood and strength, and is therefore acceptable; feeling is its opposite, and unacceptable.

This dichotomy does not derive merely from some contrived sense of masculine virtue. Roethke's early bouts with manic depression left him open to extraordinary excesses of feeling, which jeopardized his academic career and brought him, as he thought, to the brink of lunacy. The events leading up to his 1935 hospitalization at Mercywood illustrate this danger. On the night of November 11, 1935, while out for a walk in the woods around Michigan State, Roethke had what he described as "a mystical experience with a tree" in which he learned "the secret of Nijinsky."[16] After shedding one boot to stimulate circulation in his freezing foot, he walked several more miles; he finally turned around and hitched a ride back to Lansing in the middle of the night. In a letter to Mary Kunkel he described the rest this way:

> I took a long hot bath to take the chill out. Then the next morning I decided to cut my eight o'clock class deliberately just to see how long they would stick around, then go to see the Dean to explain one or two things about this experiment. (He hadn't asked to see me) Well, I decided I'd take a little walk in the country again without a coat before doing so. It was damp and quite cold, and I got so chilled and so frightened that when I finally reached the Dean's office, I was a mess. I was so cold and chilled and frightened that I was delirious, I suppose, although they didn't have sense enough to realize it. They finally called the ambulance and a doctor who led me to the damned car, just groggy as hell.[17]

This relatively mild extravaganza, coupled with some hectic moments at the hospital during which Roethke barricaded himself naked behind a mattress, refused medication, and demanded a beer,[18] encouraged the cautious Dean Emmons to begin proceedings to dismiss him.[19] With such consequences attendant on his bouts of vision and disorientation, it seems entirely reasonable that Roethke tried to keep all but the most conventionally male emotions out of his poems. He was strongest, most masculine, and most reliable when he was at once intellectually and physically imposing. Indeed he celebrates these values countless times in his early poems—for example in "Song for Hemingway," which he enclosed in a letter to Rolfe Humphries in August 1935, three months before his first breakdown.

> The season wakes within my side.
> The pulse leaps to command.
> The push of May, the stallion's pride
> Informs my thrilling hand.
>
> Old cunning stirs behind the brow,
> The blood begins to shove,
> I'm stuffed with sun; the time is now
> For turning to my love.[20]

And just in case Humphries misses the tone—which would be hard to do in a poem as blatant as this—Roethke adds a last postscript: "Kick me in the ass the next time you see me."[21]

The diction of the poem is uneven, ranging from the coolly intellectual "informs my thrilling hand" to the awkwardly Brueghelian "I'm stuffed with sun." But behind these problems lies the essential sentimentality of conception. The Hemingway of Roethke's poem rises like a stallion to the commands of the season; his masturbatory erection follows "the push of May." A creature so addicted to the wildness of instinct is hardly likely to make the highly refined gesture of "turning to my love." Until the last line, Roethke is making fun of Hemingway; in the end, however, his tone is both more intimate and harder to read. Roethke, as well as parody, is the subject here—particularly Roethke's faith in the male role that will save him from a self he dares not examine too closely. But as a poet, this limited self-conception could well be his downfall.

This danger of self-destruction by posing is exactly what Bogan understands. For the kind of posing Roethke attempts in his art is akin to Bogan's own self-protective posing in her early poems. In the early Bogan

poems one finds types—damned women, daring women, women walking the edge of damnation and salvation. These types acutely describe
the condition of the prefeminist woman in early twentieth-century
America, and no one would assume that Roethke's early poems could
resemble this kind of typology. Yet Roethke's poems are typological as
much as Bogan's, and as appropriate for their generation: for Roethke
creates again and again in his early work a Promethean image—the image of a strong man whom fate has abused but not conquered. What
saves this man from tragedy is precisely his stereotypical manliness—
his confidence in reason, his rejection of all feeling except rage or or-
gasmic ecstasy, his sense of some innate and inviolable toughness. Roethke's early poems damn feeling even as they celebrate an enraged
bravado. In this divergence between complex feeling and powerful posing, Roethke describes the emotionally circumscribed condition of a
man.

It might be argued that Roethke ultimately lacked the precision of
language and experience for great subtleties of feeling, but his feelings—
once drawn out—made his poetry inestimably better. One can credit
Bogan to a great degree with this development, which occurs from their
first encounters in the mid-1930s to the publication of *Open House* in
1941. In 1935 Bogan can write to John Hall Wheelock that Roethke's
talent is "slight, but unmistakeable."[22] In 1941 one no longer hears from
Bogan such vaguely dismissive admiration, and boldness and emotional as well as technical proficiency have replaced the slightness.

If Roethke's other work in the mid-1930s is any guide, "Song for
Hemingway" is indeed a serious effort, despite (or perhaps because of)
its bravado. Roethke often included drafts of poems with his letters, and
these augment the assortment of early poems that appear in *Open House.*
In most of these poems—with three or four important exceptions—one
hears the typologically masculine voice of stoicism and rage at work.
Though often deft, the writing is narrowly focused; the achievement is
intriguing yet disappointing. In a January 1936 letter to Rolfe
Humphries, for example, Roethke encloses an untitled poem along with
an apology—"it's nothing very profound, God knows."[23] Though the
poem is not included in *Open House,* it shares some essential characteristics of the work in that book.

Assailants lurk behind the door.
This is a treacherous time. Beware
The shadow darkening the floor,
The foot that scuttles on the stair.

Escape the paralytic hand
That fumbles at your sleeve, the spies
Who mark you for a sudden end.
Be quick to pierce the fool's disguise.

You hesitate to step beyond
The narrow room; congeal with fear.
Your indecisions will confound
Your friends, while enemies draw near.

The knuckles of the spine betray
The heart: the marrow's drained away.
You need to resurrect the will
To fight when backed against the wall.[24]

The potential story here, the "you"'s implied capacity for feeling, provides the intrigue in this poem. Yet this story is denied. Instead the reader finds confusion and evasion. Who is the "you"? In a poem so highly wrought, so filled with crisis, one expects a lightning rod; but the storm in this poem swirls across a rodless field. The "you" is not a center, but a blur. Experimental, even Frankensteinian, the "you" objectifies certain conflicts that interest the poet—will versus fear in the face of uncertain enemies, self-doubt versus the exigencies of danger.

But by distancing himself from these conflicts, Roethke also diminishes the impact of the poem. The contrived quality becomes even more apparent if one substitutes "I"—which the intensity of the poem implies—for the more decorous and evasive "you." "I need to resurrect the will / To fight when backed against the wall" sounds both too elaborate and too passive for the action it describes, as if a coward were to console himself by compiling lists of what he *should* do. This trick of replacing "you" with "I" also makes another problem in the poem increasingly obvious—the split voice. If an "I" is hesitant and fearful in the last two stanzas, then whose is the voice of wisdom—the imperative voice—in the first two stanzas? It may be possible for one voice both to command and to describe the failings of the one whom he commands, as Roethke does; but this leaves the identity of the speaker even more in doubt. "You" is a clever ruse to conceal this confusion, but the larger issue remains unresolved: who is feeling a fear so great that it congeals him—and why? The poem will not address these issues.

The rhetoric of this poem, on the other hand, is deliciously sharp and epigrammatic. The first two lines, though bordering on cliché, escape the prison of triteness primarily through their sound. The incisive shortness—even breathlessness—of the regular iambic tetrameter line works well here, and perhaps explains why Roethke was loath to abandon this charming but deceptive poem. Almost two years later, on November 20, 1937, Roethke sent Humphries a revision of the poem.

> Assailants lurk behind the door.
> This is a treacherous time. Beware
> The shadow darkening the floor,
> The foot that scuttles on the stair.
>
> Avoid the paralytic hand
> That fumbles at your sleeve, the eyes
> That mark you for a sudden end.
> Be quick to pierce the fool's disguise.
>
> You hesitate to step beyond
> The narrow room; congeal with fear.
> These imbecilities confound
> Your friends, while enemies draw near.
>
> The knuckles of the spine betray
> The heart; the marrow's drained away.
> You need to resurrect the will
> To fight when backed against the wall.
> The fingers limp upon the wrist
> Must clench the palm in hardened fist.[25]

Most of the changes are conservative. Roethke substitutes "Avoid" for "Escape" in the second stanza, with an interesting prophylactic implication; he also changes "spies" to "eyes" in the same stanza, thus quieting some of the cloak-and-dagger tone of the poem. One of the most interesting changes appears in the third stanza: the relatively mild "Your indecisions" becomes the harshly judgmental "These imbecilities." It might be encouraging to think that, in this revision, one begins to see the author's frustration with feelings too long ignored or misunderstood. But it makes more sense to infer that Roethke was simply reinforcing the willful, masculine typology of the poem. The change has a militaristic intolerance to it: all weakness is "imbecility," and therefore ought to be jettisoned or overcome.

The ending of the revised poem most clearly shows that Roethke is heading into a dead-end. He can make the poem longer, but he cannot make it better, because he does not adequately confront the source of its paranoic fear. Instead the new lines add confusion. A poet as sensitive to language as Roethke could hardly have avoided recognizing that, by placing "limp" and "wrist" as he does, he flirts with a homophobic cliché. One might think that, in this revision, the poet reveals with touching awkwardness his own doubts about his masculine identity—the kind of doubts that roam freely through the underworld of male role-playing. Yet again, the revision is coy. Because the narrator vanishes into a pronominal wasteland, the poet Roethke discreetly ducks the issue.

Aside from this flirtation with a homophobic image, the last lines of the revised version of "Assailants lurk behind the door" add nothing new. They do not link the feeling of the poem more clearly to the circumstances of a real person, unless—ignoring the acts of concealment in the poem—one reads it simply for its accidental autobiographical revelations. As posed as a Clint Eastwood publicity shot, this poem is irretrievably flawed. It seeks to construct an impenetrable suit of armor, an iron will. But when one opens the visor one finds no one inside.

This effort to define feeling only in typological terms—imbecilic stasis or crippling fear versus willful strength—shows up often in Roethke's early poems. In "Exhortation," for example, which appeared in the November 1934 *American Poetry Journal,* Roethke writes:

> Infertile quietude
> Now dominates the blood,
> The barrenness of pause
> From passion and its vows,
> Bleak juncture of distress,
> The mind's blank loneliness.
>
> Thou gusty hope, release
> Me from this sodden ease,
> Rouse my quiescent will
> With sudden miracle![26]

Here Roethke again acknowledges the possibility of complex feeling—"passion and its vows," the "bleak juncture of distress." But what do these conditions mean for him? We never know, and apparently are not expected to care much, for Roethke himself lumps them all together as mere "sodden ease" in the second stanza. This regressive and psychologically unhealthy view of depression and psychic disorientation remains distressingly common, and Roethke buys into it fully here: the successful human being is the one who rejects all emotional pain as sloth and simply lifts himself up with a hopeful will. A fool's view of the mind, it carries its own implicit warning. It will bring tragedy to whomever has the hubris to believe that the will can cure all. Roethke, for a time, sustained this hubris, and suffered the attendant tragedy of mental breakdown; he also suffered the artistic tragedy of a narrowed and rhetorical sensibility. But this liability did not go unnoticed.

In a long, newsy letter dated August 23, 1935—about three and a half months before Roethke's first major breakdown—Bogan included this striking analysis of her new lover:

> The difficulty with you now, as I see it, is that you are afraid to suffer, or to feel in any way, and that is what you'll have to get over, lamb pie, before you can toss off the masterpieces. And you will have to *look* at things until you don't know whether you are they or they are you. The lack of fundamental brain-work, so apparent in most lyrics, is not apparent in yours; you have a hell of a good mind, and real intelligence; real, natural, rich, full (in the best sense) intelligence. Your mind isn't a piece of ticker tape, going from left to right, like many minds, and it isn't full of gulfs and blank spots and arid areas. But it *is,* half the time, hiding from itself and its agonies, and until you let it do more than peek out, from time to time, you aren't going to get much done.[27]

An aversion to feeling, and a careless eye: these are Bogan's astute criticisms of Roethke. They come from a woman whose own typological poetry, a decade before, had pitted excessive feeling against hardly any feeling at all. Bogan knew personally the crippling consequences of these extremes. But how is it possible to persuade a poet nearly consumed in masculine myths that feeling—as well as careful observation, a distinctly unstereotypical activity—really matters? Bogan succeeds in part by praising the poems in which Roethke begins to take off his tough-guy mask; but she also succeeds by weaving together the roles of mentor, lover, and brother. These roles are already apparent in the language of the August 23 letter to Roethke, and become clearer in subsequent letters.

In the August 23 letter, the mentor voice is obvious: Bogan identifies a general problem in Roethke's work, sets it against his obvious and unique strengths, and ends with a specific recommendation for improvement. The mentor knows that "fundamental brain-work" is absent from many lyric poems of her time, which too often concentrate on soporific feeling or simple-minded ideologies. She gives her apprentice reason to be proud of his mind. Furthermore, she provides examples: as the letter continues, Bogan the mentor shoves Roethke the apprentice toward Rilke:

> Now in these Rilke poems (said she, ascending the podium) you get two things. You get a terrific patience and power of *looking*, in the Blue Hortensia one, and in the other you get a magnificent single poetic concept carried through with perfect ease, because it is thoroughly informed by passion, in the first place. In the latter poem Rilke is terribly upset about his inability to get away from it all,—you know that without my telling you, but let me maunder on. So he starts to write a poem, and he turns the lack of freedom into a perfectly frightful metaphor: he is unable to see any distance, any horizon (lovely word!), and he is so unable to see any, that he feels himself *inside* a mountain, like a vein of ore. Everything is nearness, and all the nearness stone. Magnificent. And then what happens? Well, he can't stand it, so he turns to someone for help, and he drags the person into the metaphor. *I* am no adept at pain, he says, but if *you* are, make yourself heavy (isn't that schwer ["heavy"] wonderful?) and break in, so that your whole hand may fall upon me and I on you with my whole cry.[28]

Without insulting Roethke's intelligence, which she has already taken pains to praise ("you know that without my telling you"), Bogan explicates the second Rilke poem to show how a sense of psychic imprisonment has a felt component—indeed is nothing without that feeling. The explication is excellent, and if it were merely an explication it might still be useful; but it is not merely an explication. It also contains the kind of familiar asides that lessen the mentor's augustness and maintain a sense of loving play. Bogan parodies her own apparent mentorship in the first sentence; her parenthetical self-deprecation places her virtually on an equal footing with her correspondent. Her second self-deprecation comes only two sentences later, when she asks Roethke to "let me maunder on." Given Roethke's profound admiration, Bogan could easily play the lord to his vassal. But she adopts no royal tones with him. Instead she writes with an incisive, knowing wit that encourages the very kind of speculation and emotional experimentation she hopes for from her apprentice.

But this language of the mentor differs sharply from the language of the lover or brother figure in the earlier paragraph. In a single sentence Bogan compresses the language of lover and brother: her term of endearment, "lamb pie," bangs up against the casual cant of the office or the barroom—"before you can toss off the masterpieces." In this paragraph, too, Bogan swears—"you have a hell of a good mind"—and refers to "ticker tape," the (at the time) archetypally male symbol of power. To all appearances she is the feisty woman Roethke enjoys, an intellectual match and a horse-playing lover to boot; but in fact her language also incorporates a compassionate boyishness that characterizes Roethke's repressed wish for a brother. It is in this paragraph—where her own emotional stance is most vivid—that Bogan turns Roethke's attention to one of his few poems with successfully-realized feelings: "TO MY SISTER is a swell poem, because, as I said, you are right in it, mad as hell, and agonized as hell, and proud as hell."[29] Again, Bogan's language is both familiar ("swell") and stereotypically masculine ("mad as hell"). It reinforces her closeness to the twenty-seven-year-old Roethke, with whom she—the distinguished poet in early middle age—can afford to let down her guard; but it also reinforces her toughness. Given such a combination of voices, a young poet might well plan to study any poem these voices agree on as successful. "To My Sister" is worth that kind of study, for several reasons.

> O my sister remember the stars the tears the trains
> The woods in spring the leaves the scented lanes
> Recall the gradual dark the snow's unmeasured fall
> The naked fields the cloud's immaculate folds
> Recount each childhood pleasure: the skies of azure
> The pageantry of wings the eye's bright treasure.
>
> Keep faith with present joys refuse to choose
> Defer the vice of flesh the irrevocable choice
> Cherish the eyes the proud incredible poise
> Walk boldly my sister but do not deign to give
> Remain secure from pain preserve thy hate thy heart.[30]

"To My Sister" is deceptive because, at first glance, it seems much like Roethke's other earlier work: it warns against the overflow of romantic feeling and defends the virtues of pride and boldness. Unlike those other early poems, however, it has a clearly locatable narrator and a clear line of feeling. The speaker is the brother, and the brother knows fear and anger as well as nostalgia. Indeed his nostalgia threatens to consume him, revealing the poem to be more profound than one might expect: the speaker is in love with his sister and the displaced eroticism of their past, and as he eyes the future he sees that he will be eclipsed. The poem is not generous but selfish; toward the adult world at large it directs contempt, which it disguises as the sister's ("preserve thy hate thy heart.")

The speaker's rage at the anticipated loss of "each childhood pleasure" is as palpable as his powerlessness to prevent it. The elaborateness of the nostalgia itself implies that what has passed cannot be recovered, and the speaker overtly acknowledges this impossibility when he refers to his sister's "incredible poise." To resist the rising lusts and loves of the adult body is to resist the whole direction of human life, which is outward—out into the world, into the realms of adventure and risk and heresy and mutuality and forgiveness. A pose, a poised pose, against this outward motion is incredible; and yet it is a delicious thought as well, to resist the inevitable. Georges Bataille is not the first philosopher to equate eroticism with death (and murder—the murder of the self),[31] but even in his sophisticated analysis of the subject one sees the deep embedding of a primarily selfish implication. The self is all, it is most perfectly attuned to the world when it is least conscious of sexuality, birth and death, and in this state of latency it discovers the best the world can offer. The alleged tragedy, of course, is that this "best" is an illusion. It is also very much a model of the fear of difference—of the inability to see any meaningful value in "states in which distinctness and union are reconciled."[32] Applied to Roethke's poem, this observation suggests that Roethke has begun to commit a fundamental anxiety—a concomitant of his masculine myth-making—to paper, as he has not previously been able to do.

While these ideas underlie "To My Sister," they do not overwhelm it, because Roethke's control of tone is so sophisticated. The more impossible his advice becomes, the more one perceives the futility of his hopes. Who can remain "secure from pain"? Who, finally, can "not deign to give"? For how long can "hate" and "heart" be synonymous? "To My Sister" is the Alamo of adolescence, and as such it becomes an elegy—not only to the past the speaker shared with his sister, but also to the speaker's own past, when he believed in "the pageantry of wings the eye's bright treasure." This selfish poem also shows the limits of selfishness—the point at which selfishness begins to parody itself, and becomes both pointless and destructive—but at the same time it makes that selfishness compelling, and the sense of loss tragic.

Bogan had good reason to be impressed and touched by this poem. She herself knew the double identity of selfishness. She knew its false allure, its mystique of invincibility and typological salvation; she also knew its real value, on the far side of despair. Dignity, as she implied in her letters, was a form of selfishness—but a selfishness stripped of the fantasies of superhuman power. The dignified person could not preserve the lovely past, as the speaker of "To My Sister" seeks to do; nor could he prevent the miserable consequences of human mendacity and careless lust. Yet the dignified person fully knew the value of the self; the self was refuge, comfort, and identity. Bogan suggests this to Roethke in her letter of September 4, 1935: "You are thoughtless and unhappy and spoiled, and I wish I had $10,000. Perhaps I could shake you out of it, on that sum. You could shake yourself out of it, for much less. And, take the word of one who has lain on the icy floor of the ninth circle of hell, without speech and will and hope, it's the self that must do it. You, Ted Roethke, for Ted Roethke. I, Louise Bogan, for Louise Bogan."[33]

To be shaken out of one kind of selfishness—egotistical self-absorption, with the disappointments that implies—and to attain that other kind of selfishness, was in Bogan's view to arrive at adulthood. Although the emphasis in Bogan's language might seem to be on the kind of will-fillness Roethke celebrates earlier, the actual fact of her method—her emphasis on one person urging another to embrace himself as subject, to refuse the role of object—is sophisticated and helpful. In a similar vein, she would continue to cajole and hector Roethke toward adulthood for some time. As late as 1941, when *Open House* first appeared, she wrote Roethke, "Auden respects you and likes you thoroughly. . . . He thinks you a good poet, a good teacher, and a fine person generally; but we both agree that you should GROW UP, and stop pretending that your childish side is melancholy, WHICH IT ISN'T. Now worry over that one![34]

But Bogan also encourages Roethke's discovery of adult selfishness, or self-awareness, by praising those few early poems that themselves indicate that nascent insight. "To My Sister" is one of these, in part because it is honest about its fear of eroticism. Adulthood is the enemy, but the very qualities of anger and memory that define adulthood this way are themselves very adult, very sophisticated. In another poem that Bogan praises, "Epidermal Macabre," Roethke pulls a strange trick: he attempts to envision physical life on *his* terms, rather than on the terms the adult body presents.[35] "I hate my epidermal dress," he writes, disparaging the body; what Roethke wants is a body of another kind, full of pleasure but designed by somebody with taste.

> And willingly would I dispense
> With false accouterments of sense,
> To sleep immodestly, a most
> Incarnadine and carnal ghost.[36]

Yet, while this poem seems a little foolish, it has a hard edge: its portrait of the mortal body is sketched by one who knows well its pain and misery. This knowledge, which is present to a lesser degree in "To My Sister," implies a depth of feeling which Roethke's more rhetorical poems lack.

This depth of feeling appears again in "The Premonition." Here Roethke reveals the Bataillian phantom behind eros, which is death.

> Walking this field I remember
> Days of another summer.
> Oh that was long ago! I kept
> Close to the heels of my father,
> Matching his stride with half-steps
> Until we came to a river.
> He dipped his hand in the shallow:
> Water ran over and under
> Hair on a narrow wrist bone;
> His image kept following after,—
> Flashed with the sun in the ripple.
> But when he stood up, that face
> Was lost in a maze of water.[37]

Like "To My Sister," this poem has a clearly identifiable narrator and a clear line of feeling. Yet it is even more explicitly personal than the previous poem. Its use of a simple narrative structure creates at least the fiction of artlessness, a rare fiction indeed in Roethke's early poems. Like the earlier poem, this one reminisces. Unlike "To My Sister," however, this poem includes the poet's adult persona. In the first and second lines Roethke establishes his distance from his childhood; but he also establishes the power of memory to reinforce the quiet terror of time. With startled weariness—"Oh that was long ago!"—he looks back to what is almost the panorama of a pet, a puppy, which stays "close to the heels" of its master. The master is infallible, immortal, perfect—as is the father. But this is the sweet lie of childhood; the adult understands that "when he stood up, that face / Was lost in a maze of water." What comes from the world of earth and water returns to it, and this is true for infallible humans as well as for mere creatures of the dark. The adult speaker of the poem knows this: life looks toward dissolution. Nature does not reflect the immortality that humans feel; only humans reflect these feelings to each other, and inconsistently at best. If the tragedy of love is that it can endure far longer than the beloved, the tragedy of adulthood is to understand this. But the final lines of the poem are ambiguous. We do not know if the child who perceives the vanished reflection merely notes that curiosity or actually has a premonition of adult wisdom. The title, of course, implies that sudden rush of confused adult feeling, but this again may be the speaker imputing motives and interpretations to the child. Whichever of these interpretations one chooses, the point is clear: adulthood is the locus of this poem, and its speaker. In this respect it extends an advance already made with "To My Sister."

If "The Premonition" acknowledges the terror of death that haunts human love, "For an Amorous Lady" subverts that terror with the weapon of humor. Bogan, who usually reserved her comments on Roethke's poems for the middle or end of her letters, opens her April 10, 1938, letter with rare, unqualified praise for the poem. "I loved the Amorous Lady verse," she writes. "I hope the notation means that the New Yorker has bought it."[38] Though the poem might seem silly or insignificant, it is both highly accomplished and extremely unusual for the young Roethke. Here one finds the boisterousness that characterized his romance with Bogan. But one finds as well a fully adult acceptance of joy and pleasure. In its coy and clever mix of high and low diction, and in its daring, almost reckless brush with parody, the poem breathes an orgiastic air. Its silliness is its genius for life.

> *"Most mammals like caresses, in the sense in which we usually take the word,*
> *whereas other creatures, even tame snakes, prefer giving to receiving them."*
> *From a natural-history book*

> The pensive gnu, the staid aardvark,
> Accept caresses in the dark;
> The bear, equipped with paw and snout,
> Would rather take than dish it out.
> But snakes, both poisonous and garter,

In love are never known to barter;
The worm, though dank, is sensitive:
His noble nature bids him *give*.

But you, my dearest, have a soul
Encompassing fish, flesh, and fowl.
When amorous arts we would pursue,
You can, with pleasure, bill *or* coo.
You are, in truth, one in a million,
At once mammalian and reptilian.[39]

One hears in this poem the nascent voice that booms so loudly through "Four for Sir John Davies," poems that Roethke composes over fifteen years later. "The living all assemble! What's the cue?— / Do what the clumsy partner wants to do!" writes Roethke in the second of those poems, "The Partner."[40] "For an Amorous Lady" has in common with "The Partner" a tolerance for the awkwardness and bizarreness of adult love—a tolerance that is absent from "To My Sister." Like the later poem, "For an Amorous Lady" reflects a sophistication that the jocular language only partly disguises.

"To My Sister," "Epidermal Macabre," "The Premonition," and "For an Amorous Lady" are by no means the only early poems of Roethke's that Bogan praises. But her praise for them is important because it is consistent with her emphasis on his need to feel, and because—with hindsight—one sees that these efforts to develop a vocabulary for feeling pay Roethke handsome returns in his later poems. Without denigrating his sheer rhetorical talent, Bogan steers Roethke away from the typologies of masculinity—from poems that celebrate a blatantly male stand against some form of disaster or misery. What she steers him toward is a poetry capable of exploring precisely the kind of erotic relationship they themselves created. As it turns out, the essential characteristics of this relationship are passion and a sense of closure; for the lust-feast of the Roethke-Bogan affair was startlingly brief, consuming the month of June 1935 and recurring only infrequently after that.[41] What remained from the affair, however, was a strong erotic bond between the mentor and apprentice—a bond that Bogan put to good pedagogic use. In her letters in the mid and late thirties, she revises this bond into a kind of metaphor for mortality and desire, and then subtly converts it once again into a lesson: life is not long, the brief passion to create is great, and the artist must pursue that passion as he pursues his carnal loves. Through these acts of conversion, Bogan weans Roethke of his apprenticeship: she coaxes him into internalizing the values that enabled her to stand free of the miseries of her past. These values—the primacy of the mind, the need for the mind to know and understand its feelings, and the symbiosis of physical and intellectual passion (both within one self and beyond the self to other subjects)—run beneath the witty, sardonic, yet deeply engaged tone of her letters.

Caressing and cajoling Roethke out of his blackest moods, urging him to work, Bogan pursued that goal of teaching Roethke to take himself seriously as an artist. In her long letter of September 4, 1935, she gave Roethke a great deal of explicit advice and encouragement—advice about the importance of self-esteem, and about the dangers of drink, as well as some welcome pats on the back: "If you didn't have such a good, happy and sensitive mind, I'd say, go on and drink, if you want to. Lots of excellent people have drunk and drunk and produced. But drinking seems to have you down, at the moment, and to hell with anything that gets a person of your potentialities down. If, as someone once said, Kenneth Burke is one of those providential characters put into the world to show how the human mind should not be used, you may well be a person put into t. w. to show how it should."[42] This is high praise for a young poet who has not yet published a volume of poems. But it is not an accident—not an isolated moment of exuberance for Bogan. At the end of the letter she writes, "Forgive me if I sound melodramatic, my pickled pear. I am fond of you, and I think there are so few of our kind that you should stay in the ranks."

To a young poet stranded in the depressed Midwest, with an iffy position as a teacher and a sense of isolation almost as vast as the prairie, the idea of being "in the ranks" could only be thrilling. It meant that, by virtue of his talent and determination, Roethke had earned a place in the society of artists, as opposed to the mere would-be's or hangers-on. Though this view of things is undeniably sentimental, it accurately describes Roethke's approach to writing. The house of artists may have many mansions—many genres and ideological feuds—but to one on the outside it has only two features, an inside and an outside. In the early thirties one sees Roethke on the outside struggling ardently to get in, as in this telling 1931 letter to Harriet Monroe of *Poetry:*

> Could I be assured, in just this one instance, that you yourself pass judgment on these poems?
> It has been some time since I have submitted anything to your office.

When I first began to write verse, I was much discouraged by your immediate and impersonal rejections. Recent acceptances, however, by such
magazines as *The New Republic, The Commonweal, The Sewanee Review*
have led me to hope that perhaps I do write a poem occasionally. . . . For
this reason, if for no other, may I be pardoned for making this request?[43]

Behind Roethke's inside-outside view of the artists' world lay his profound eagerness to *belong*. He was ambitious, and—despite his claims
to the contrary—was capable of hard work. He was also clearly capable
of the kind of interdependence—the tolerance of difference, the awareness of the necessary paradox of distinctness and union—which characterized membership in ranks of serious writers. This was true despite
his early love of masculine myth-making; it was a characteristic that
Bogan herself quickly perceived. For a poet of Bogan's stature to autho-
rize Roethke's membership was a critical imprimatur of success.

In inviting Roethke to stay in the ranks—a tacit compliment to him
for already having arrived—Bogan also cleared the way for the kind of
hard, professional work Roethke would have to do to consolidate and
extend his gains. She exhorted him to take criticism well—"You must
realize that Rolfe and I do this sort of thing all the time with each other's works," she wrote on September 9, 1935—and proceeded to offer
him detailed critiques of a good twenty of his poems over the next two
years. Though Elizabeth Frank argues that Roethke "listened well" to
these criticisms,[44] he adopted Bogan's suggested revisions only infrequently; in a late 1935 letter to Roethke, Bogan implied her awareness of his
touchiness on the subject when she wrote, "Take [my criticisms] amiss
and ascribe bitch hood to me if you like. I don't really care."[45] Bogan
protected herself, and Roethke, from any possible anger he might feel
toward her by insisting on a mentorship that assumed trust in the judgment of the apprentice. True, Bogan was not above manipulation: to
tell an obviously devoted apprentice that she didn't "really care" how he
took her criticisms was to place his role in doubt. Perhaps he was not
important enough to warrant a position "in the ranks" after all. And
yet, in the context of her other letters to Roethke, this comment takes
on a wider, noncoercive meaning.

Bogan cared greatly for Roethke, but could not run his career for him.
She intended to make sure he understood that he *was* a serious poet.
She would offer criticism, but would not go out of her way to coerce
him to take it. Her occasional peevishness or casualness—indeed, the
kind of cavalier approach she claimed to adopt for "all gents"—when

criticizing Roethke's work may be seen as coercive, but it does not create the kind of elaborate dependence that some mentors foster in their apprentices. Indeed, by 1940 Roethke is, as Elizabeth Frank says, growing "up and away."[46] When Bogan accuses him of echoing Joyce in his manuscript of *The Lost Son,* he responds in an April 25, 1947, letter: "Thanks for the solicitude about 'The Lost Son.' But for once, pet, you're wrong, really you are. I wrote that poem out of real suffering: cut myself off from people; went into my interior. The only 'influenced' line is an exact quote from the bible: 'Hath the rain a father:' ⅓ of a line, honey."[47]

What's extraordinary about this passage is its combined confidence and lack of posing. Though the "honey" in the last phrase could be read sardonically, as a new note of condescension, the overall tone of the passage is not defensive. Instead one hears the voice of a maturing artist who appreciates the value of suffering as a source of insight—and who is willing to argue, without rancor or contrived toughness, for the rightness of his method. This is the image of the artist Bogan suggests in her earliest letters to Roethke. The intimate use of a term of endearment, "pet," offsets Roethke's somewhat combative phrasing at the end of that sentence—"you're wrong, you really are"—and the net result is a confident tone. Roethke no longer writes ingratiatingly to Bogan, even when he disagrees with her. His disagreement, though affectionate, is genuine yet unthreatening—both to him and, apparently, to Bogan.

Given the risks of the apprentice's quest, one would be hard pressed to find a more provocative example than Roethke's apprenticeship to Bogan. From her he desires, and receives, love and guidance, sympathy and rousing encouragement, criticism and praise. Bogan begins, not with a tradition of knowledge that she feels obligated to pass along, but with Roethke the man and artist. She binds him to her own experience of doubt, exploration, and happiness even as she draws close to his experience. Although traditions of art certainly exist behind Bogan's judgments of her work and Roethke's—as, indeed, they exist behind Roethke's own judgments—these traditions do not subsume either poet; neither becomes the object of a tradition.

Under Bogan's tutelage Roethke becomes a more careful observer and writer, and his poems begin to command their own audience, until his public reputation rivals and finally surpasses his mentor's. More importantly, he learns through her keen insight into his personality how to drop some of his protective masks or poses. Bogan confirms for Roethke that suffering is not only inevitable but essential; this helps deflate Roethke's male role-playing and his fear of showing real feeling in his poems. Bogan also helps Roethke understand how not to fear the powerful but uncharted regions of impulse and self-doubt. She points out to him that his apparent vices of lust and gluttony and sloth can also be seen as healthy appetites and the inevitable lulls between important work.

To the young man uncertain of the caliber of his soul, the established older poet offers calibration; the instrument that results is far more finely tuned to the rhythms of the self than it ever was previously. If Bogan on occasion teases Roethke, plays with his affections, or taunts his stubborn will, she never descends to more elaborate forms of manipulation. Throughout her affair with him one hears the echo of her early warning to him: "When one isn't free, one is a *thing*, the *thing* of others, and the only point, in this rotten world, is to be your own."[48] If Bogan does not become the romance of Roethke's life, she nevertheless supplies a crucial combination of romance and instruction; and as the erotic bond is real, not feigned or contrived, the instruction too gains the power and depth that sincerity confers upon it. The young, anxious, ambitious apprentice in 1935 is destined to be an established poet within a decade. But part of what enables him to accept center stage so gracefully is his mentor's graceful bowing out.

Notes

1. Louise Bogan, letter to Theodore Roethke, Sept. 4, 1935. The Theodore Roethke Collection, Box 3, Folder 15, University of Washington Libraries. Quoted in Louise Bogan, *What the Woman Lived: Selected Letters of Louise Bogan, 1920–1970*, ed. Ruth Limmer (New York: Harcourt, Brace Jovanovich, 1973), pp. 98–99.

2. Jean Baker Miller, *Toward a New Psychology of Women*, 2d ed. (Boston: Beacon Press, 1986), p. 4.

3. Carol Gilligan, "Remapping the Moral Domain: New Images of Self in Relationship," *Mapping the Moral Domain*, ed. Carol Gilligan et al. (Cambridge, Mass.: Harvard University Graduate School of Education, 1989), pp. 8–9.

4. Allan Seager, *The Glass House: The Life of Theodore Roethke* (New York: McGraw-Hill, 1968), pp. 244–46.

5. Theodore Roethke, *Selected Letters of Theodore Roethke*, ed. with introduction by Ralph J. Mills, Jr. (Seattle: University of Washington Press, 1968), pp. 222–23.

6. Roethke found himself dealing with W. W. Johnston, head of the English department at Michigan State, and Lloyd Emmons, Dean of Humanities and Sciences and a mathematician by training. Both men moved swiftly and smoothly to ease Roethke out of the department; their secret correspondence is documented in Seager.

7. Louise Bogan, undated letter to Theodore Roethke (probably late Dec. 1935). The Theodore Roethke Collection, Box 3, Folder 15, University of Washington Libraries. Quoted in *What the Woman Lived,* p. 122.

8. Humphries would have been a particularly good candidate for the older brother figure: as Seager writes, "Humphries was the first poet of ability with whom Ted could have a continuing association." Humphries's letters to Roethke were thoughtful and instructive; they criticized his work frankly but not harshly. See Seager, pp. 76–78.

9. Seager, pp. 118–19.

10. Roethke, p. 25.

11. Louise Bogan, *Journey around My Room: The Autobiography of Louise Bogan: A Mosaic by Ruth Limmer,* ed. Ruth Limmer (New York: Viking, 1980), pp. 7–8.

12. Bogan, *What the Woman Lived,* p. 131.

13. Seager mentions the 4F classification on p. 122; the fight Roethke does not take up is discussed on p. 75.

14. Seager, p. 131.

15. Seager suggests that, while Roethke liked to pose as a Don Juan, he actually became passionately involved with few women (p. 84). Roethke was an ardent tennis coach at Lafayette College in 1934 (see his letter to William Mather Lewis, *Selected Letters,* p. 26; and his letter to D. L. Reeves, in Seager, p. 72); and his love for steak was legendary (Seager, p. 175).

16. See Seager, p. 90.

17. Seager, p. 91.

18. Seager, p. 92.

19. See note 6.

20. Roethke, p. 34.

21. Roethke, p. 34.

22. Bogan, *What the Woman Lived,* p. 114.

23. Roethke, p. 36.

24. Roethke, p. 36.

25. Roethke, p. 53.

26. Roethke, p. 24.

27. Louise Bogan, letter to Theodore Roethke, Aug. 23, 1935, the Theodore Roethke Collection, Box 3, Folder 15, University of Washington Libraries. Quoted in *What the Woman Lived,* p. 96.

28. Bogan letter, Aug. 23, 1935. The Rilke poems are "Blaue Hortensie"

and an early, untitled one—"Vielleicht, dass ich durch schwere Berge gehe." Quoted in *What the Woman Lived,* pp. 96–97.

29. Bogan letter, Aug. 23, 1935. The Theodore Roethke Collection, Box 3, Folder 15, University of Washington Libraries.

30. Theodore Roethke, *The Collected Poems of Theodore Roethke* (New York: Anchor/Doubleday, 1975), p. 5.

31. See Georges Bataille, *L'Erotisme* (Paris: Editions de Minuit, 1957), pp. 15–29.

32. Jessica Benjamin, *The Bonds of Love: Psychoanalysis, Feminism, and the Problem of Domination* (New York: Pantheon, 1988), p. 29.

33. Bogan, *What the Woman Lived,* p. 99.

34. Bogan, *What the Woman Lived,* pp. 220–21.

35. Bogan praises "Epidermal Macabre" in an undated 1935 letter to Theodore Roethke, the Theodore Roethke Collection, Box 3, Folder 15, University of Washington Libraries.

36. Roethke, *Collected Poems,* p. 18.

37. Roethke, *Collected Poems,* p. 6.

38. Louise Bogan, letter to Theodore Roethke, Apr. 10, 1938, the Theodore Roethke Collection, Box 3, Folder 18, University of Washington Libraries.

39. Roethke, *Collected Poems,* p. 22.

40. These poems appear in Roethke's 1953 volume *The Waking,* which is included in the *Collected Poems.*

41. See Elizabeth Frank, *Louise Bogan: A Portrait* (New York: Alfred Knopf, 1985), pp. 226–27.

42. Bogan letter (September 4, 1935), Box 3, Folder 15, University of Washington Libraries. Quoted in *What the Woman Lived,* p. 99.

43. Roethke, *Selected Letters,* p. 3.

44. Frank, p. 229.

45. Bogan letter (undated, 1935), Box 3, Folder 15, University of Washington Libraries.

46. Frank, p. 234.

47. Quoted in Frank, pp. 234–35.

48. Bogan letter (Sept. 4, 1935), Box 3, Folder 15, University of Washington Libraries. Quoted in *What the Woman Lived,* pp. 98–99.

Index

A Lume Spento (Pound): man's relation to the divine in, 34; source of the self in, 36; self and eros in, 38; will to master in, 39

ABC of Reading (Pound): male authors chosen for, 26

Abelard, Peter, 3, 7–12; characteristics as mentor, 11. *See also* Heloise

"Acon" (H.D.): classicism in, 62

Adams, Henry: Winters's essay on, 94–95

Aeneid (Virgil), 12–14

Against a Darkening Sky (Lewis): publication of, 136

Alain [Emile Chartier]: on nature of divinity, 5

"Alchemist" (Bogan): forecasts later work, 162; alternative to typology in, 163; compared to "Henceforth," 176–77

Aldington, Richard: husband of H.D., 44–45; on the label "H.D.," 50n29; use in H.D.'s writing, 53

Alexander, Curt: husband of Louise Bogan, 166

"Ancient Ones: Betatakin" (Lewis): principle of life in, 150

"Ancient Ones" (Lewis): Native American influence in, 150

"Anima Sola" (Pound): self as demigod in, 35–36

Apprentices and apprenticeship: Telemakhkos as archetypal, 4–7; control over master, 15; concerns addressed by mentor, 92; persuaded of inadequacy by mentor, 92; dangers of rational tradition and, 97; of Lewis, 97; hierarchy and, 111; Roethke's as model, 214. *See also* H.D.; Lewis, Janet; Roethke, Theodore

Aquinas, St. Thomas: importance to Winters, 94, 96

Aristotle: importance to Winters, 94, 96, 109

"Assailants lurk behind the door" (Roethke), 200–203; split voice in, 201; masculine typology in, 202–3; revised version of, 202–3

Athena: characteristics, in *Odyssey,* 5; power via Mentor, 5–7; Louise Bogan as, 194

Authority, cultural: and personhood, 7; and mentorship, Gilligan on, 13; and gender, 14

Autobiography: Pound's reluctance about, 52; importance to H.D., 53

Ayer, A. J.: on transcendence and cognition, 131

Baha, Abdu'l: Pound on, 31

Baker, Howard: on revelation and reason in Lewis, 154n22

"Ballad Rosalind" (Pound), 39

"Ballad for Gloom" (Pound): image of God in, 34

Bare Hills (Winters), 100, 105

Bataille, Georges: eroticism as death to, 207

Baudelaire, Charles: influence on Winters, 104

Benjamin, Jessica, 130, 136, 191; on authentic selfhood, 1; on "intersubjectivity," 5–6, 18n2, 54–55, 96, 139; on empowerment, 7; concept of "difference," 26; on erotic life, 27; on domination, 157

Bid Me to Live (H.D.): H.D.'s early life in, 53; romantic thralldom in, 57; late publication of, 58

Body of This Death (Bogan), 158–65; significance of title, 158; themes of, 159; critique of typology in, 159–60; well reviewed, 172

Bogan, Louise, 157–87 passim; use of masks, 63; mentorship contrasted to Winters, 114; Pauline typology and, 158, 159–60; unconventional mentorship of Roethke, 158, 187, 191–92, 204–5; on love, 159, 169–70; relationship with Curt Alexander, 161, 166; critique of typology in "The Alchemist," 162; psychoanalysis, 163; childhood, 165–66; importance of suffering, 165, 174; relationship with Roethke, 165, 187; on sexuality in Henry James, 166; relationship with Raymond Holden, 167–68, 173; sexual jealousy and, 168, 179–82, 190; mental breakdowns, 169–70, 171, 196; hospitalization, 171–73; changing conception of love, 172–73, 181–82; love affair with Roethke, 173, 211; moves beyond typology, 174–79, 185–86; artistic maturity, 182; identity through conquest of jealousy, 182; integrated personality, 185; Holden's portrait of, 189–90; liberation from apprenticeship, 190; as older brother to Roethke, 192–93, 206; advice to Roethke on hospitalization, 193; appreciation of male role-playing, 195–96; blue-collar background, 195–96; ideal of strength, 196; evaluations of Roethke's poetry, 200, 210–11, 213; criticizes Roethke's avoidance of feeling, 204–5; on two modes of selfishness, 208. *See also* Roethke, Theodore; *individual works by title*

Boston, Bruce: on the mentor, 15–16; critical responses to, 19n2

Bowers, Edgar, 93

Breslin, James: on traditional poetic forms, 63

Bridge (Crane): Winters's criticism of, 89, 115–17

Briggs, William Dinsmore: Winters on, 110–11

"Brink of Darkness" (Winters): influence of Rimbaud on, 101

Bryher [Winifred Ellerman], 43, 53, 69, 76

Bunting, Basil, 25

Caetani, Princess Marguerite: correspondence with Roethke, 192

Cantos (Pound), 26–27; mastery in, 48

"Canzon: The Yearly Slain" (Pound): will to master in, 39

Canzoni (Pound): Pound on progress of, 29–30; will to master in, 39

Carnochan, Brigitte: on Winters's correspondence, 98

Carpenter, Humphrey: on Pound's relationship with Dorothy Shakespear, 29; on Pound's relationship with H.D., 30; on the label "H.D.," as concession to Pound, 50n29

Carruth, Hayden: praise of Winters, 90

Castaneda, Carlos: Bruce Boston on, 15–16, 18–19n2

Cavalcanti, Guido, 32

Char, René: importance to Roethke, 192

Chartier, Emile [Alain]: on nature of divinity, 5

"Church Monuments" (George Herbert): Winters on, 91

"Cino" (Pound), 38

Collected Poems (Edwin Arlington Robinson): reviewed by Winters, 100

Collected Poems (Winters), 89

Crane, Hart: Winters's attack on, 89, 96, 115–17; Winters on decadence of, 107–8; reaction to Winters's attack, 116; relationship with Winters, 116–17; suicide, 117

Cravens, Drusilla, 30

Cravens, Margaret: Pound's letters to, 30–31; relationship with Pound, 30–33; suicide of, and Pound, 30; motives for suicide, 33

"Crazy Jane Talks with the Bishop" (Yeats): compared to Winters's "Song," 104

"Dark Spring" (Winters): human generation in, 105

Death: Pound's view of, 30; enemy, for Winters, 98, 122–23; presence of, effect on Winters, 99; as limit, to Winters, 101, Lewis's "Snail Garden," 150; as enemy, in Bogan's "To My Brother," 185

"Death Goes Before Me" (Winters): death in, 101–2

Decadence: Winters on modern poetry and, 107

"Dedication for a Book of Criticism" (Winters), 110–11; intellectual tradition in,

110; compared to Pound, *Spirit of Romance,* 111

Dekin, Timothy, 94

Dickens, Charles: satire of rationality in *Hard Times,* 110

Dickinson, Emily, 102–3; praised by Winters, 108

Divinity: Emile Chartier [Alain] on, 5; in *Odyssey,* 6; Pound's concept of, 34–36

Dominance: in Athena-Mentor relationship, 6; of Abelard, 10–11; sources on, 19n2; and "romantic thralldom," 55; of eros, in H.D.'s *HERmione,* 72; Benjamin on, 157. *See also* Mentorship; Submission

Donne, John: view of body compared to Winters's, 122

"Donzella Beata" (Pound), 39

Doolittle, Charles (father of H.D.), 55–57

Doolittle, Eric (brother of H.D.), 56

Doolittle, Hilda. *See* H.D.

DuPlessis, Rachel Blau: on H.D.'s "crisis of naming," 49–50n29; on "romantic thralldom," 54–55, 83n8; analysis of H.D.'s *Helen in Egypt,* 83n8

Earth-Bound (Lewis): treatment of wisdom in, 130; reviewed by Roethke, 132

Edwin Arlington Robinson (Winters), 89

Eliot, Henry Ware, 24, 28

Eliot, T. S.: academic career, 23; Pound's mentorship of, 23–25; praise of Pound, 23; marriage, 24; Pound helps to publish, 24; Pound's financial assistance, 25; fear of biographers, 52; self-mythologizing of, 82; published in *Poetry,* 87; called "obscurantist" by Winters, 108; views of poetry contrasted to Winters, 109; mentioned, 28, 68

Ellerman, Winifred. *See* Bryher

Ellmann, Richard: on Yeats's use of masks, 63

Emerson, Ralph Waldo: Winters's criticism of, 89, 108

Empedokles, 35

End to Torment (H.D.): and Pound, 42; eros in, 45; as autobiography, 53; posthumous publication of, 58; Pound names H.D. in, 62

"Epidermal Macabre" (Roethke), 208–9

"Essay on Psychiatrists" (Pinsky): portrait of Winters in, 93

"Evening at the Sanitarium" (Bogan), 171

"Exhortation" (Roethke), 203–4; unhealthy view of depression in, 204

"Few Don'ts" (Pound): influence on H.D., 54

Fields, Kenneth: coeditor of *Quest for Reality* (Winters), 93

"For an Amorous Lady" (Roethke): 210–11; Bogan on, 210; adult tolerance in, 211

Ford, Ford Madox: on Pound's diction, 40

Forms of Discovery (Winters), 106; outspokenness of, 89; critical appraisal of Janet Lewis in, 124; published during marriage, 124

"For the Father of Sandro Gulotta" (Lewis): 146–48; treatment of love in, 148

"For the Opening of the William Dinsmore Briggs Room" (Winters): intellectual tradition in, 110

"Francesca" (Pound): H.D.'s "Phaedra" compared to, 65; use of mythology in, 65–66

Frank, Elizabeth: on Louise Bogan, 158; on Bogan's "The Tale," 160–61; on Bogan's "Memory," 163–64; on Roethke's response to Bogan's critiques, 213

Freud, Sigmund: analysis of H.D., 53, 56, 59, 74, 75

Friedman, Susan Stanford: on H.D.'s classicism, 54; on H.D.'s self-analysis, 59

Frost, Robert: assisted by Pound, 25; published in *Poetry,* 87

Function of Criticism (Winters), 124

"Further in summer than the birds" (Emily Dickinson), 102–3; view of consciousness compared to Winters's, 102–3

Gelpi, Albert: on dualism in H.D.'s *Notes,* 69

Ghost of Monsieur Scarron (Lewis), 144–46; Lewis awarded fellowship to write, 124; publication of, 136, 155n31; power of the irrational in, 137–38; danger of passion in, 144; silence as loyalty in, 145

Gift (H.D.), 76–80; wartime autobiography, 53; H.D.'s father in, 56; experience of speaker in, 62; as response to World War II, 76; importance of father in, 77, 78–79; fear of abandonment in, 79

Gilligan, Carol: on *Aeneid,* 12–14; on the self, 12–14; on values of care and connection, 111; on values and power, 140; on relationship, 186–87, 191

Goldring, Douglas: on Pound, 25

Gray, Cecil (father of H.D.'s daughter Perdita), 45

Gray, William and Marilynne: on Bruce Boston, 19n2

Gregg, Frances: soulmate of H.D., 43; use in H.D.'s writing, 53

Gregory, Horace: on Pound, 52; mentioned, 193

Guerard, Albert, 89

Gunn, Thom, 96; influence of Winters on, 90–92; interest in hallucinogenic experiment, 93; on Winters's rigidity, 112–14; on Winters and discipleship, 114

H.D., 52–83 passim; assisted by Pound, 25; relationship with Pound, 41–48; Pound's naming of, 42, 62; bisexuality, 43; relationship with Frances Gregg, 43; unfulfilled sexual relationship with Pound, 44; Pound criticizes classicism, 47; break with Pound, 48; classicism of, 53–54, 62, 68; early poetry not autobiographical, 53; life as subject, 53; and imagism, 54, 59–60; use of public persona by, 54–55; differing approaches to prose and poetry, 58–59; prose as private self-exploration for, 58; classicism as response to identitylessness, 59; poetry as link to Pound, 59; constraints of classicism, 64; decline in work of, 69; Greece as refuge for, 69; self-portrait as "Hermione," 70–75; analysis with Freud, 75; crises during World War I, 75; questioning of poetic identity, 75; "war-terror," 75–76; and World War II, 76; fear of abandonment, 79; recovery of self-worth, 79–80; appearance in *Poetry,* 87; compared to Winters, 104; compared to Janet Lewis, 132, 146; on identity in art, 158; mentioned, 3, 33. *See also* Pound, Ezra; *individual works by title*

Haigh-Wood, Vivienne: marriage to Eliot, 24

Hallie, Philip: on cruelty and mentorship, 16–17

"Hangar at Sunnyvale: 1937" (Lewis): time and dream in, 133–35

Hartley, Marsden: Winters on paintings of, 98, 109

Hawthorne, Nathaniel: Winters's criticism of, 89

Hedylus (H.D.): Pound's criticism of, 68

Hegel, G. W. M.: master/slave dialectic of, 19n2

Helen in Egypt (H.D.): life as subject in, 53

Heliodora (H.D.), 66–68; constraints of classicism on, 64

Heloise, 3, 7–12; resistance to marriage, 8–9; initial submission, 10–11; self-knowledge, 10. *See also* Abelard, Peter

"Henceforth, from the Mind" (Bogan): mind and matter linked in, 176–77

Herbert, George, 91

"Hermes of the Ways" (H.D.): classicism in, 62; Pound on, 62; control in, 63

HERmione (H.D.), 70–75; image of Pound in, 43; exploration of H.D.'s early life in, 53, 56; romantic thralldom in, 57; posthumous publication of, 58; role-playing in, 73–74; ambiguous treatment of sexuality, 74; independence in, 74

Heroism: and Pound, 26, 28

Heydt, Erich: analyst of H.D., 44

Historia calamitatum (Abelard): as morality tale, 7, 9; defeat of masculine will in, 9

History of My Heart (Pinsky): moves away from reason in, 93

Holden, Raymond: Edmund Wilson on, 167; relationship with Louise Bogan, 167–70; marriage to Bogan, 168; portrait of Bogan, 168–69; Bogan on, 169; separation from Bogan, 173; mentioned, 190, 196

Hopkins, Gerard Manley: primitivism of, to Winters, 108

Humphries, Rolfe: friend of Bogan, 190; as potential brother figure to Roethke, 216n8; mentioned, 193, 194, 195, 199

Hymen (H.D.): constraints of classicism on, 64

Identity: quest for, in *Odyssey,* 4; of H.D., in *HERmione,* 70–71; problem of, in Lewis's "Wife of Manibozho Sings," 129

Imagism: Pound as founder of, 40; influence on H.D., 54, 59; Pound defines, 60, 61; Janet Lewis and, 125, 128–29

Immobile Wind (Winters), 101–2; poetic form in, 100; published, 100

In Defense of Reason (Winters), 106; attack on irrational in literature in, 89; basis in dissertation chapter, 107; theory of poetic morality in, 109; intellectual tradition in, 110; Crane studied in, 117; published during marriage, 124

"In Santa Maria del Popolo" (Gunn): as journalism, Winters on, 115

"Incarnate for our marriage you appeared" (Winters), 121–23; compared to Donne's "The Ecstasy," 122–23

Indians in the Woods (Lewis), 125, 151–52; principle of life in, 129–30

Indians, American. *See* Native Americans

Intellectual tradition: Abelard and, 11; necessary limits of, 11–12; in *Aeneid,* 12–14; Carol Gilligan on, 12–14; destructive potential of, 17; as mentor to Winters, 94–95. *See also* Mentors and mentorship; Winters, Yvor

"Intersubjectivity": Jessica Benjamin on, 5–6, 96; relation to Jung, 18n1; in Janet Lewis's novels, 139

Invasion (Lewis): Manibozho in, 127

James, Henry: Winters reads, 99; Louise Bogan on sexuality in, 166–67

Johnson, Samuel: "Vanity of Human Wishes" compared to H.D.'s *Walls,* 81

Journey around My Room (Bogan): self-interview in, 159

Joyce, James: assisted by Pound, 25; "anti-intellectualism" attacked by Winters, 115; mentioned, 28

Juan, Don: Bruce Boston on, 15–16, 18–19n2

Jung, Carl, 2. *See also* Psychoanalysis

"Knowledge" (Bogan): rejection of passion in, 161

Kunitz, Stanley, 193

"Laudantes Decem Pulchritudinis Johannae Templi" (Pound), 39

Laughlin, James: assisted by Pound, 25

Lawrence, D. H.: use in H.D.'s writing, 53; as "Federico" in *Bid Me to Live* (H.D.), 59; mentioned, 76

Lesemann, Maurice: Winters's correspondence with, 98

Levine, Philip: on Winters, 112–13

Lewis, Janet, 121–53 passim; burned correspondence with Winters, 52, 125; contracts tuberculosis, 88; marriage to Winters, 88, 123–24; and Poetry Club, 88; marriage and early formal poems, 96–97; artistic separation from Winters, 97; poetic silence of, 97, 125, 135–37; role as homemaker, 123, 135–36; Native American influences on, 124–25, 126–27, 150; imagism in work of, 125; turn to formal verse, 125; balance of cultural and personal identities, 126; choice of revelation over

reason, 126; importance of motherhood to, 126; use of mythology, 126; and Manibozho, 127, 128, 147–53 passim; treatment for tuberculosis, 127–28; stayed outside schools/movements of poetry, 129; conflict between revelation and reason, 131; compared to H.D., 132, 146; reviewed by Roethke, 132; publication of novels, 136; fiction as escape from Winters, 137; Winters's limited praise of fiction, 137; novels, failure of rationality in, 138; avoidance of psychoanalytic categories, 139; gender models of morality in novels, 140; "silence" as novelist, 146; importance of seeing to, 150–51; revelation, in "Wonder of the World," 151–52; patience of, 152

Lewis, Wyndham: on Pound, 25

"Like Summer Hay" (Lewis): imagism in, 129

Living Together (Bowers), 93; longing for completion in, 93–94; moves away from Winters's view of reason, 93

Logos: Winters on, in human relationships, 90

Lomax, Bertold: character in "Scriptor Ignotus" (Pound), 37

"Love Song of J. Alfred Prufrock" (Eliot): publication in *Poetry,* 24

Lowell, Robert: praised Winters, 90; Winters on, 113; guest of Winters and Lewis, 123

Magpie's Shadow (Winters): poetic form in, 100; published, 100

Mallarmé, Stéphane: influence on Winters, 104

Manibozho (Ojibway trickster deity): characterized, 127; importance to Lewis, 127; escapes death, 128; in Lewis's later poetry, 147–53 passim

Maule's Curse: Seven Studies in the History of American Obscurantism (Winters), 89

Melville, Herman: Winters's criticism of, 89

"Memory" (Bogan), 162–64; tensions of typology and personality in, 162–63; intellectuality of, 164

Mentor (character): in *Odyssey,* 4–7

Mentors and mentorship, 1–18 passim; relation to parenthood, 1–2; conflicts in role, 2–3; *Odyssey* and cultural concept of, 3; divided self, in *Odyssey,* 6; role contrasted to teacher, 7–8; of Abelard, 11; reliance on traditional knowledge, 11; problem of authority, Gilligan on, 13–14; problem of hierarchy, 14–15; emphasis on knowledge over relationship, 16–18; relation to eroticism, 17; defined, 18–19n2; and Hegel, 19n2; Winters as archetype of, 90; apprentice persuaded of inadequacy, 92; apprentice's concerns addressed by, 92; of Winters, perpetual inequality in, 96, 157; hierarchical model in Winters's "Dedication," 110–11; hierarchical relationship with apprentice, 111; the will to master and, 157–58; Bogan's concept of, 187; successful, Jean Baker Miller on, 191; Louise Bogan as, 194. *See also* Pound, Ezra; Winters, Yvor; Bogan, Louise

"Midnight Wind" (Winters): sexual frustration in, 105–6

Miller, Jean Baker: on ending mentor relationships, 14–15; on inequality, 19n2, 95; closure goal of successful mentorship, 96, 191; on basis of mentorship, 158

Momaday, N. Scott: as apprentice to Winters, 92, 93; differences with Winters, 114; mentioned, 102

Monroe, Harriet: Pound champions Eliot to, 24; editor of *Poetry,* 87; friendship with Winters, 99; Roethke writes to, 212–13; mentioned, 28, 62

Moore, Marianne: on Winters, 90; correspondence with Winters, 99; reviewed by Winters, 100; primitivism of, to Winters, 108

"Na Audiart" (Pound): erotic mastery in, 38–39

Native Americans: influence on Lewis's poetry, 124–25, 126. *See also* Lewis, Janet; Manibozho

"Nightfall among Poplars" (Lewis), 148–51

Nights (H.D.): exploration of sexuality in, 53

"No-Winter Country" (Lewis), 132–33; absence of revelation in, 133

"North American Sequence" (Roethke): controlled sentimentality in, 198

Notes on Thought and Vision (H.D.): dualisms in, Albert Gelpi on, 69

Observations (Marianne Moore): reviewed by Winters, 100

Oderman, Kevin: on sexuality in Pound, 27

Odyssey (Homer): archetypal mentor in, 3; mentor-apprentice relationship in, 4–7

Ojibway Indians, 124, 126–27. *See also* Lewis, Janet

Olsen, Tillie: on domestic silence, 136; model of "essential angel," 186

"On Teaching the Young (Winters), 111–12; intellectual tradition in, 110

Open House (Roethke): stoicism and rage in, 200

Ostriker, Alicia: on isolation and transformation in H.D., 84n18

"Palm at the End of the Mind" (Stevens): compared to Bogan, 178

Paquier, Estienne: source for Lewis's *Wife of Martin Guerre,* 138

Parkinson, Thomas: on Crane's response to Winters, 116

"Partenza di Venezia" (Pound): will to mastery in, 39

Pearson, Norman Holmes, 47; advice to H.D. on *End to Torment,* 48

Perdita (daughter of H.D.), 44, 69

Personae (Pound): use of masks in, 63

"Phaedra" (H.D.): conventionality of, 64–65; compared to "Francesca," 65–66

"Phasellus Ille" (Pound), 39–40

Phillips, Samuel March: source for Lewis's *Wife of Martin Guerre,* 138

"Picture" (Pound): Anglo-Saxon diction in, 40

"Piere Vidal Old" (Pound): will to mastery in, 39

Pinsky, Robert: moves away from reason, 93; praise for Winters, 93

Pisan Cantos (Pound): mastery in, 48

"Plotinus" (Pound): self as demigod in, 35–36

Poems (Winters): departure from symbolism, 89

Poems Old and New, 1918–78 (Lewis), 146–48, 150

Poetry Club (University of Chicago), 87–88

Poetry magazine: Eliot's publications in, 24; and Winters, 87, 99; Winters contributed reviews to, 100; Winters attacks Crane in, 115; Roethke reviews Lewis in, 132

Portrait of a Lady (James): compared to Lewis's *Wife of Martin Guerre,* 139

"Portrait d'une Femme" (Pound): plainness of diction in, 40

Pound, Ezra, 23–48 passim; edited *Waste-Land,* 23; mentor of T. S. Eliot, 23–25; assisted Eliot, 24, 25; assistance to artists,

25; early detractors, 25; troubled relationships with friends, 25–26, 46–47; masculine role-playing by, 26; and nature of sexuality, 26–28; problem of difference to, 26; written personae of, 28–29; and Margaret Cravens, 30–33; relationship with H.D., 30, 41–48; troubador persona, 30–33, 37–39, 40; concept of divinity, 34–36; escape from the single self, 38; problem of eros for, 40–41; naming of H.D., 42, 62; will to master, and H.D., 42; unfulfilled sexual relationship with H.D., 44; hospital incarceration, 45; on William Carlos Williams, 46; break with H.D., 48; will to master, 48, 157–58; reluctance toward autobiography, 52; use in H.D.'s writing, 53; use of masks in *Personae*, 63; disgust with H.D.'s classicism, 68; as "George Lowndes" in H.D.'s *HERmione*, 70–75; self-mythologizing of, 82; loneliness compared to Winters, 95; called "obscurantist" and decadent by Winters, 107–8; difficulty in closing mentor relationship, 191; mentioned, 3, 76. *See also* H.D.; *individual works by title*

Pound, Omar: on relationship of Pound and Cravens, 32; on Cravens's suicide, 33

"Premonition" (Roethke), 209–10; death in, 209–10

Pre-Raphelitism: influence on Pound, 40

Primitivism: Winters on modern poetry and, 107

Proof (Winters), 103–4

Psychoanalysis: and parent-child *eros*, 2; emphasis on archetypes, 58; H.D.'s experience with Freudian, 59; influence on H.D.'s later work, 69; method of, in H.D.'s *The Gift*, 80; Lewis's avoidance of categories, 139; Bogan's reaction to, 163; Theodore Roethke and, 192

"Putting to Sea" (Bogan), 177–79; danger of teleology in, 178–79; image of paradise in, 178–79

Quinzaine for This Yule (Pound): will to master in, 39

Rationalism: of Abelard, 10; failure in Lewis's novels, 138

Red Roses for Bronze (H.D.): constraints of classicism on, 64

Rhodes, Fred H.: on Pound, 25

Rilke, Rainier Maria: Bogan recommends to Roethke, 205

Rimbaud, Arthur: influence on Winters, 89, 100, 101, 104, 106–7; on requirements of being a poet, Winters's familiarity with, 101

Ripostes (Pound): consciousness of voice in, 39–40; will to master in, 39; changes in Pound in, 40

Roberts, Elizabeth Madox: and Poetry Club, 87–88

Robinson, Edwin Arlington: reviewed by Winters, 100

Roethke, Theodore, 190–215 passim; guest of Winters and Lewis, 123; reviews Janet Lewis, 132; relationship with Bogan, 165, 187, 190–91; affair with Bogan, 173; response to Winters review, 173; Bogan as older brother to, 192–93; hospitalized, 192–93, 198–99; influence of Bogan on, 192, 214–15; manic depression, 192–93, 197, 198; sentimentality of, 192, 198; academic career, 193; first encounter with Bogan, 194; Telemakhos to Bogan's Mentor, 194; male role-playing, 196–98, 198–200; on moral value of strength, 197–98; dismissal from Michigan State, 198–99, 216n6; Promethean typology in poetry of, 200; aversion to feeling, 203–4; feeling as typology in early work, 203; advised by Bogan, 204–5, 212; Bogan on, 204–5; steered away from masculine typology by Bogan, 211; artistic validation by Bogan, 213; growing maturity, 214; Bogan as calibration, 215; mentioned, 3, 114. *See also* Bogan, Louise; *individual works by title*

"Roman Fountain" (Bogan), 182–84

"Romantic thralldom": Rachel Blau DuPlessis on, 54; defined, 55, 83n8; H.D. and, 57; in H.D.'s *HERmione* and *The Gift*, 76

Romanticism, American: Winters on suicidal impulse in, 103

Saint Paul: typological view of sin, Louise Bogan and, 158–59; typology, 164–65

"Scriptor Ignotus" (Pound): eros and self in, 36–37

"Seafarer": Anglo-Saxon diction in Pound's translation of, 40

Sea Garden (H.D.), 64

Seager, Allan: on Roethke's male role-playing, 197

"Sea Lily" (H.D.): H.D.'s early life in, 61; echoes of, in *Walls*, 81

"Sea Rose" (H.D.): flaws of, 59–60; and imagism, 59–62

Shakespear, Dorothy: correspondence with Pound, 28–29; as disciple of Pound, 29; marriage to Pound, 29; mentioned, 33

Shakespear, Henry Hope (father of Dorothy): Pound and, 29

"Sheltered Garden" (H.D.), 61; and imagism, 62

Silences (Tillie Olsen): compared to Lewis, 136

Sill, Louise Morgan: Pound on, 31

Skinner, Marilyn: on the *Aeneid*, 14

Sleeping Fury (Bogan), 174–85 passim

"Sleeping Fury" (Bogan), 179–82; compared to H.D.'s *HERmione*, 75; jealousy and, 179–82

"Snail Garden" (Lewis), 148–50; dance of life in, 128–29

"Socrates" (Winters): intellectual tradition in, 110

"Song" (Bogan), 174–76; Pauline echoes in, 174; dismissal of typology in, 176

"Song" (Pound): self in, 38, 39

"Song for Hemingway" (Roethke): masculine values in, 199; representative of Roethke's 1930s work, 200

"Song of the Trees" (Winters), 103–4; follows Dickinson, 103; compared to Yeats's "Crazy Jane," 104; self in, 104–5

Sour Grapes (Williams): reviewed by Winters, 100

Spirit of Romance (Pound): historical study as submission, 28; compared to Winters's "Dedication," 111

Spoo, Robert: on relationship of Pound and Cravens, 32; on Cravens's suicide, 33

Stanford University: Winters's career at, 88–89

Stern, Daniel: understanding of eros, 18n1

Stevens, Wallace: compared to Bogan's "Putting to Sea," 178

Stokes, Katherine (Kitty): Roethke's relationship with, 193, 194

Strength of Art (Momaday): defense of Winters in, 114

Submission: in Athena-Mentor relationship, 6; and "romantic thralldom," 55. *See also*

Dominance; Apprentices and apprenticeship

Swallow, Alan: on Lewis's *Wife of Martin Guerre*, 139

Symbolism: influence on Winters, 101, 104; Winters adapts terminology, 107

"Tale" (Bogan), 160–61, 162; Elizabeth Frank on, 160–61; perfection as horror in, 160; autobiography in, 161; shadow-narrator in, 161

Tate, Allen: correspondence with Winters, 89; decadence of, to Winters, 107–8; on Winters's rigidity, 112–14, 152

Telemakhos: as apprentice, 3, 4–7

"Time and Music" (Lewis), 124

"Time and the Garden" (Winters): intellectual tradition in, 110; irrelevance of the body in, 112

"To a Young Writer" (Winters): intellectual tradition in, 110

"To La Contessa Bianzafior (Cent. XIV)" (Pound): will to master in, 39

"To My Brother Killed: Haumont Wood: October 1918" (Bogan), 182, 184–85; Bogan's experiential wisdom in, 182; composition, 184; acknowledgment of tragedy in, 185

"To My Infant Daughter" (Winters): intellectual tradition in, 110

"To My Sister" (Roethke), 206–8, 209, 210, 211; Bogan on, 206; selfishness in, 207–8

"To the Holy Spirit" (Winters), 112: Hayden Carruth on, 90

"Toward the Piraeus" (H.D.), 66–68; retreat from personal experience in, 67–68; compared to *HERmione*, 72

Tradition. *See* Intellectual tradition

Trial of Soren Quist (Lewis), 141–44; publication, 136, 155n31; power of the irrational in, 137–38; critique of reason in, 143–44

Tribute to Freud (H.D.): as autobiography, 53; published late in H.D.'s life, 58

Trilogy (H.D.): start of H.D.'s autobiographical poetry, 53; mentioned, 70

Tuckerman, Frederick Goddard: praised by Winters, 108

Uncle Tom's Cabin (Stowe): and H.D.'s childhood, 77

Valéry, Paul: decadence of, to Winters, 107–8
"Vanity of Human Wishes" (Johnson): compared to H.D.'s *Walls*, 81
Very, Jones: praised by Winters, 108; self-annihilation of, 108
Vorticism: Pound as founder of, 40

Walls Do Not Fall (H.D.), 80–83; response to World War II in, 76
Waste-Land (Eliot), 68
Wells, Julia, 31
Welscott, Glenway: and Poetry Club, 88
Wheelock, John Hall: friend of Bogan, 190
"Where My Sight Goes" (Winters): dangers of excessive consciousness in, 102–3
White Buildings (Crane): Winters reviews positively, 115
"Wife of Manibozho Sings" (Lewis): techniques of imagism in, 129–30
Wife of Martin Guerre (Lewis), 138–41; publication history, 136, 154–55n31; power of the irrational in, 137–38; circumstantial evidence in, 138; sources of, 138; as psychological novel, 139
Wilbur, Richard: on accepting the body, 110; mentioned, 48
Wilkinson, Louis: husband of Frances Gregg, 43
Williams, William Carlos: Pound on, 46; autobiography of, 52; on Helen Wolle, 55–56; reviewed by Winters, 100; primitivism of, to Winters, 108; "anti-intellectualism" attacked by Winters, 115; mentioned, 68
Wilson, Edmund: on Raymond Holden, 167; friend of Bogan, 190
Winters, Yvor, 87–117 passim; burned correspondence with Lewis, 52, 125; childhood, 87; Western landscape and, 87, 92, 97–98, 99; academic career, 88–89; contracts tuberculosis, 88; marriage to Lewis, 88, 123–24; attack on Hart Crane, 89, 96; publication history, 89; value of reason to, 89, 90, 112; characteristics as mentor, 90,

117; influence on Thom Gunn, 90–92; value of poetry defined by, 90; movements beyond reason by apprentices, 93–94; and Aristotle, 94, 96, 109; encounter with madness, 94; praise for Aquinas, 94–95; convalescence in American West, 95, 98; importance of intellectual tradition to, 95, 96, 110; as dependent master, 97; friendship with Harriet Monroe, 99; view of death as limit, 100, 101, 122–23; influence of Rimbaud on, 101; sexuality, connection to death, 105; adaptation of symbolist terminology, 107; importance of convention to, 107; on primitivism and decadence in poetry, 107–8; on "obscurantist" tradition in American poetry, 108; linkage of art and life by, 109; reason as protection for, 109; reason as faith to, 110; themes of mentorship in poetry of, 110; as classroom teacher, Philip Levine on, 112–13; on Robert Lowell, 113; contrasted to Louise Bogan, 114; qualities as mentor, 114; intellectual rigidity, 117; view of body compared to John Donne, 122–23; choice of reason over revelation, 131; limited praise of Lewis's work, 136–37, 146, 152; philosophy of mastery, 157–58; reviewed Roethke, 173; difficulty closing mentor relationships, 191. *See also* Lewis, Janet; *individual works by title*
Wolle, Helen (mother of H.D.): William Carlos Williams on, 55–56
Women of Trachis (Pound): H.D. praises, 42
"Wonder of the World" (Lewis): perception and relation in, 151
World War II: effects on H.D., 69–70

Yeats, William Butler, 104; Pound and, 25; autobiography of, 52; masks used by, 63; and moral climate of H.D.'s *Walls*, 81

Zabel, Morton Dawen: friend of Bogan, 190; mentioned, 193

THOMAS SIMMONS is associate professor of English and nonfiction writing at the University of Iowa. He has previously taught at Stanford, the University of California, Berkeley, and MIT, where he received the Everett Moore Baker Award for undergraduate teaching. His other books include *The Unseen Shore: Memories of a Christian Science Childhood* (1991) and *A Season in the Air: One Man's Adventures in Flying* (1993). A licensed pilot, he divides his time between Iowa City, the Pacific Northwest, and Alaska.